The Tanks of Operation Barbarossa

The Tanks of Operation Barbarossa

Soviet versus German Armour on the Eastern Front

Boris Kavalerchik

Translated by Stuart Britton

Pen & Sword
MILITARY

First published in Great Britain in 2018 and reprinted in this format
in 2021
by Pen & Sword Military
An imprint of Pen & Sword Books Limited
47 Church Street
Barnsley
South Yorkshire
S70 2AS

ISBN 978 1 39901 429 8

A CIP catalogue record for this book is
available from the British Library.

Illustrations by Yuri Kavalerchik.

Typeset in Ehrhardt
by Mac Style

Printed and bound in the UK
by CPI Group (UK) Ltd, Croydon, CR0 4YY

Pen & Sword Books Limited incorporates the imprints of Atlas,
Archaeology, Aviation, Discovery, Family History, Fiction, History,
Maritime, Military, Military Classics, Politics, Select, Transport,
True Crime, Air World, Frontline Publishing, Leo Cooper,
Remember When, Seaforth Publishing, The Praetorian Press,
Wharncliffe Local History, Wharncliffe Transport,
Wharncliffe True Crime and White Owl

For a complete list of Pen & Sword titles please contact
PEN & SWORD BOOKS LIMITED
47 Church Street, Barnsley, South Yorkshire, S70 2AS, England
E-mail: enquiries@pen-and-sword.co.uk
Website: www.pen-and-sword.co.uk

Contents

Introduction

Tanks brought about a revolution in military affairs and in a fundamental fashion changed the nature of conducting warfare. From the moment of their first appearance on the fields of battle, they attracted the interest of a multitude of people and continue to do so. However, to a great extent due to such elevated, general interest, numerous myths and legends have grown up around these combat vehicles, which often hinder a view of their genuine essence. In the mental image of some people, tanks have turned into a form of wonder-weapon, capable of independently deciding the outcome of any battle.

In this connection the answer to a long, painful question is interesting: what then caused the Red Army's catastrophe in the border battles of 1941? Alternative explanations have appeared in response to this question, and new ones continue to appear. In the list of its main reasons, Soviet official historiography cited the numerical superiority of the Wehrmacht in tanks. Stalin set the tone for this when he declared in a report to a session of the Moscow City Council on 6 November 1941: '… the reason for the temporary setbacks of our army consists in our lack of tanks and partially of aircraft.… Our tanks are superior to the German tanks in quality, and our glorious tankers and artillerymen have more than once put the much-vaunted German troops with their multitude of tanks to flight. Even so, we have several times fewer tanks. In this lies the secret of the German army's temporary successes.'[1] At the time the Leader was openly dissembling, trying to excuse his own miscalculations and blunders, but his argument was then picked up and broadly circulated by the numerous Soviet propagandists. During the war, which was also waged on the ideological front, this was to a certain degree justified. However, even after it ended, Stalin's point of view continued for a long time to be generally accepted in the USSR. For its proof a double ledger was shamelessly used, where all of Germany's available armoured fighting vehicles were totalled, while for the USSR only the new types of heavy and medium tanks, the KV tank and the T-34, were counted. At the same time, the latter tanks were called unequivocally the best tanks in the world, much superior to their German counterparts according to every criterion. In contrast, with one stroke of the pen all of the Red Army's other tanks were dismissed as light and outdated models that had extreme limitations due to the short operating lifetime of their engines, which were also prone to catch fire. On this basis they were usually not even included in the calculations, as if they had no sort of combat value.

Meanwhile, facts that directly contradicted such humiliating characteristics of the pre-war Soviet armour were deliberately hushed up. For example, the hundreds of medium T-28 tanks available in the war, the serial production of which ended only a year before the beginning of the Great Patriotic War (the war on the Eastern Front), were for that reason undeservedly forgotten. It wasn't mentioned that the majority of these supposedly 'outdated' tanks were not more than five years old. What then made them outdated and prevented them from being used to carry out basic combat assignments? This reasonable question, for understandable reasons, remained unanswered. The situation with the wearing-out of the tanks was also far from simple. Supporters of the official Soviet version were intentionally or unwittingly ignoring the system of conserving the service lives of combat vehicles that was adopted and implemented in the Workers' and Peasants' Red Army (RKKA) long before the war. In fact the main culprit in the frequent breakdowns of the Soviet tanks early in the war was not their short service life, but their low reliability from the outset, the main reasons for which were engineering flaws, the poor quality of production and the unsatisfactory technical service. Moreover this related to all of them, and not only to tanks of older types, but we'll discuss this in more detail later. We'll also discuss the tendency of the tanks to catch fire, but here we'll only note that all of the serially produced German tanks of the Second World War, without exception, were equipped with carburettor engines that operated on petrol. In this respect they were just as prone to fires as the older models of Soviet tanks.

History has repeatedly shown that even a substantial numerical superiority in force and means far from always guarantees a victory in armed struggle. A lot depends on the correlation of qualitative characteristics of the opposing forces. This is just as true in the case of tanks. Various, often directly contradictory, opinions exist as to whose tanks were better in the initial phase of the Great Patriotic War, German or Soviet. In order to answer this difficult question correctly, it is necessary to take proper consideration of what the tanks of the Wehrmacht and Red Army were really like; why they were made that way; how many there were; when the formations that were equipped with them appeared and how they evolved; the history of their use in wars and armed conflicts on the eve of the Great Patriotic War; how to compare them properly; and what factors had a decisive influence on the results of their combat use. This book is dedicated to answering these questions.

Chapter 1

The Main Factors that Determine the Design of Tanks

O ne of the most widespread mistakes is the tendency to look at tanks from former years from a contemporary standpoint and to evaluate them using modern criteria. Such an approach has its attractions: in the first place, it is simple, and secondly, it allows us to sense our superiority over the people of the past, who created and used those tanks, in which today we see so many imperfections and flaws. At the same time often the blaming of one or another detail of a tank for its shortcomings is in fact a result of the elementary misunderstanding of how, why and for what purpose each detail was made part of it from the beginning. It often isn't simple to determine the real plusses and minuses of one or another. Moreover, one and the same feature might in one case be a strong point, and in another case a shortcoming. The main point is that it must never be forgotten that every tank of all eras and nations without exception had both their positive and negative sides. Thus one mustn't issue snap judgements, only viewing the tanks from one side while putting some of them on a pedestal and tossing others into a waste bin entirely on the basis of some particular features that are taken out of context. It is much harder to look into the actual qualities and inadequacies of specific tank types, but also more interesting and useful for understanding them.

First of all it is necessary to conceptualize the role of tanks. They weren't some inherently abstract things, but represented working tools, used in order to resolve concrete problems. As a rule, teams of engineers design them according to the technical specifications formulated by armies, which use them to achieve objectives they've been given or future goals. That is why solitary geniuses, who worked in fits and starts according to their own comprehensions and insights, despite all their efforts and individual stellar accomplishments, rarely achieved substantive successes. This isn't surprising:

most of all they were hindered by an elementary misapprehension or even lack of desire to grasp what their potential customers really required. However, it mustn't be forgotten that the tasks of tanks vary in different countries and in different periods, and moreover they change with the passage of time. Thus it is necessary to shed light on what those tasks were at the time each tank was created, and which they were intended to meet. Without this understanding it is impossible to grasp why one particular tank was designed in one way and not another. In this connection it should be noted that the success or failure of various models of tanks is determined to a great extent by their capability to be adapted in a timely manner to the constantly changing tactical demands throughout their service life. In other words, the length of the career of many tanks depended directly on their ability to be updated; i.e., whether or not they had sufficient spare internal space and allowance for extra weight. This permitted, in the event of necessity, the enhancing of their combat qualities, principally in firepower and armour strength, while preserving adequate mobility and conditions for the crew.

There is one more important category that influenced the design of tanks – the level of modern technology, not only at the abstract worldwide level, but in the manufacturing capabilities of each specific factory that planned to produce them. This also includes the number and qualifications of its workers; the presence and capabilities of its manufacturing equipment; its financial resources; the availability of time, raw materials and component parts; the possibility of cooperating with other factories, etc. It was no less important to know the planned programme of tank production and the amount of time allowed for carrying it out.

Only a consideration of the influence of all these factors makes it possible to understand the real reasons for using one or another technical decision applied to the design of combat vehicles. At the same time it makes clear why one and the same decision might be optimal for one specific factory at one period of time, but impractical for the same factory at a different time. Moreover it might be unsuitable for different factories in the same country, and even more so for the industry of other countries. What is more, even the very best and leading design, if it proved impossible to manufacture in sufficient quantities within the necessary time using the available resources, would in essence be only a senseless waste of time, materials and funds.

Finally, the third group of characteristics that is directly reflected in the design of any tank is connected with its forthcoming use by troops. This relates to the average level of qualification and training of tank crews; problems with maintaining and repairing it; keeping it supplied with fuel, lubricants, ammunition and spare parts; its proposed period of service; the expected conditions in which the tank would be used and its reliability and durability influenced by them; the serviceability of the tank as well as its systems and components; the standardization of its parts, and so on. These features also frequently vary widely according to the country, the people and the period of time, and accordingly relate substantially to the understanding of 'what is good and what is bad' in the design of tanks for the concrete situation of their use.

It is easy to note that the deeper we delve into the study of the factors that influenced the design and manufacturing of tanks, the more quickly the number of factors grows and the more complicated it becomes. Therefore, let's take a look at the above cited factors and figure out how they operated in practice. We'll look first of all at the role of tanks.

Chapter 2

The Role of Tanks

Tanks first appeared at the height of the First World War. They were born out of the 'trench stalemate' in which the participants unexpectedly found themselves. Soon after the war started, no-man's land, entangled with dense rows of barbed wire swept by countless machine guns and field guns, became an impenetrable barrier in the path of the attacking troops. The front lines became essentially frozen in place for their entire extent over hundreds of kilometres. Back then, no one actually knew how to properly break through a defence that was saturated to the extreme with firing positions. According to the military theory that predominated at that time, a series of attacks should be conducted one after the other with powerful artillery support in order to resolve this problem. However, in practice, over the time it took to conduct repeated attacks, the enemy invariably managed to bring up fresh reserves to the battlefield and to seal off local penetrations. Further offensives, as a rule, led to the agonizing process of frontal attacks to force the enemy out of their next line of occupied trenches until the attacking side's strength was completely exhausted. In the best case it resulted in a limited success in the form of seizing an insignificant sector of ground, which had to be paid for with extremely heavy losses in men and materiel. Such a price was unacceptable for the combatants, and thus they began actively searching for a qualitatively new, effective instrument for breaking through a defence.

For the armies of the *Entente*, tanks became this instrument. They protected the attacking infantry from enemy bullets with their armour, laid down a path for them through the rolls of barbed wire, and destroyed with fire and their tracks those enemy weapons that survived the artillery preparation. Thus, the main role for tanks from the outset was the direct support of infantry when breaking through an enemy defence. For this reason they didn't need high speed, because the infantryman burdened with his gear and weapons could only advance at an average speed of 4–7 kilometres per hour.

Direct support of infantry for a long time remained the priority for tanks in the majority of armies that possessed them. In 1920 in France and the United States the armoured forces were deprived of an independent role and became subordinate to the infantry. It isn't a coincidence that the French 'Regulations for the use of tanks' that came out in the early 1920s give them the following definition:

> Armoured vehicles with mechanized propulsion are called tanks, the role of which is to facilitate the advance of infantry, crushing the stationary obstacles and the enemy's active resistance on the field of battle.
> [...]
> They are only a powerful support means in the infantry's possession. Tanks should coordinate their combat work of manoeuvre and fire with the actions of the infantry.[1]

A draft of the 1939 Field Manual of the Red Army (FM-39) postulated the very same: 'The primary task of tanks consists in directly supporting the infantry and in clearing a path for it during an offensive.' Only subsequently did it mention other tasks:

> Given the successful development of the offensive and in mobile combat tanks might be used for a deeper strike at the enemy's combat formations with the aim of destroying his artillery, reserves and headquarters. In this case they might play a decisive role in encircling and destroying the enemy. Tanks are an effective means for combating enemy tanks. On the defensive, tanks are a powerful means of counterattack.

Even after the beginning of the Second World War, a textbook for cadets in the Red Army's military academies still stated: 'The main role of the tank forces amounts to constant and comprehensive assistance to the infantry (or the cavalry) in the most rapid fulfilment of its combat assignments with the least losses.'[2]

In order to fulfil these main tasks, the first generation of tanks were equipped with armour that protected them from bullets and correspondingly armed with machine guns and cannons with a calibre from 37mm to 57mm. Guns of a larger calibre at that time were not often mounted on tanks. But when they were, short-barrelled cannons or howitzers were used, with a low initial muzzle velocity that was fully adequate for combating enemy infantry, its weapons and light field fortifications. In order to increase the density of the tanks' fire, sometimes they were made with multiple turrets, and the turrets were occasionally placed side by side. This arrangement allowed all of the tank's fire to be concentrated in front of it when on the attack, and while crossing an enemy trench to 'comb through' it with machine-gun fire simultaneously from both sides. Such tanks at that time were called 'trench sweepers'. Here is what the future Soviet Marshal M.N. Tukhachevsky, who at the time was occupying the post of Chief of Armaments of the Red Army, wrote about them:

> Concerning the British Vickers tank that was recently examined by me, I found it suitable like nothing else to the task of escort when attacking enemy trenches. ... The positioning of the turrets side by side allows the tank quite advantageously to develop strong flanking fire when crossing dug-in positions and trenches ... against which the breastwork offers no protection. ...
>
> At this critical moment, as can be seen, the tank lacks one more firing point in the form of a machine gun or light cannon, directed towards the front when moving in order to knock out targets (like a machine gun or cannon) of the second line of defence. ...
>
> It isn't difficult to grasp why the British then adopted the twin-turreted and triple-turreted scheme, which is very farsighted and more advantageous for overcoming an enemy defence when among their own infantry.[3]

Tukhachevsky was talking about the twin-turreted Vickers Mark E 6-ton tank, which was being produced in the USSR by licence under the designation T-26, and the triple-turreted Vickers Mk. III 16-ton tank, which became the prototype for the Soviet T-28 (*see* Chapter 7).

In our time many people, when comparing tanks of past times among themselves, evaluate them first of all from the point of view of their capability to combat enemy tanks. Such an approach is fundamentally incorrect, because before the Second World War, in the majority of the world's armies this assignment was given primarily to anti-tank artillery. Meanwhile tanks had their primary roles, as formulated in the Soviet textbook *Tactics of armoured forces*:

Armoured forces in the system of contemporary combined-arms battle are:
1) the best means for outflanking or enveloping an enemy defensive position detected or formed when penetrating flanks;
2) one of the most powerful means for breaking through an enemy line;
3) together with artillery and aviation are one of the means of simultaneously suppressing the tactical depth of the enemy's defence; and
4) an active part of the anti-tank defence of the infantry's (the cavalry's) attacking combat formation.[4]

Thus, tanks were authorized to engage enemy combat vehicles last and only in those cases when it was unavoidable. German tankers at the beginning of the war behaved in just that manner. Here is how Directive No. 0127 'On the shortcomings in the use and actions of tanks together with the combined-arms formations and measures to eliminate them' from the Commander of the Soviet Northwestern Front on 5 August 1941 characterized their actions: 'Enemy tanks, as a rule, refuse open combat with our mechanized formations, instead striving to bring our tanks under the fire of anti-tank artillery and large-calibre artillery.'[5] The 'Instructions on the use of a tank brigade in the main types of combat' issued to the troops of the Soviet Western Front on 27 September 1941 stated, 'The experience of combat operations demonstrates that German tanks, when our attacking tanks appear, fall back behind the combat positions of their infantry, which have organized an anti-tank defence.'[6]

At the same time the Soviet tankers, who had a high combat morale but insufficient tactical training, seized any opportunity to clash with the German tankers, forgetting in the process about carrying out their main assignments. This tendency, which jeopardized the success of the overall cause, was noted in People's Commissar of Defence Order No. 325 from 16 October 1942 'On the combat use of tank and mechanized units and formations', which was developed under Stalin's personal direction.[7] There, in particular, it indicated:

> Tanks, operating jointly with infantry, have as their primary mission the destruction of enemy infantry and should not be separated from their own infantry by more than 200–400 metres.
>
> In battle the tank commander organizes observation of the battle formations of the infantry. If the infantry has gone to ground and is not advancing behind the tanks, the commander of the tank unit allots some of the tanks to destroy the enemy firing positions which are preventing the advance of our infantry.
>
> […]
>
> If enemy tanks appear on the battlefield, the artillery conducts the primary fight against them. Tanks engage enemy tanks only in the case of a clear superiority of forces and an advantageous position.
>
> […]
>
> The [tank] corps should not engage in tank battles with enemy tanks if there is no clear superiority over the enemy. When encountering large enemy tank units, the corps designates anti-tank artillery and some of the tanks against the enemy tanks; the infantry for its part moves up its anti-tank artillery, and the corps, protected by all these means, with its main forces bypasses the enemy tanks and strikes at the enemy infantry with the aim of separating it from the enemy tanks and paralysing the actions of the enemy tanks. The main mission of the tank corps is the destruction of enemy infantry.[8]

Before the Second World War only the British considered the main task of their tanks was to combat enemy tanks, and therefore armed them chiefly with 40mm guns, while their ammunition consisted only of armour-piercing shells. At the same time some of the pre-war British tanks were equipped with 76mm howitzers. These were supposed to support the others, firing high-explosive fragmentation shells and smoke shells.

However, the war made its own laws, and in the course of it tactics often had to be changed. The growing numbers of armoured vehicles in the armies of all the fighting sides led increasingly to their direct combat contact, which was now difficult to avoid. Therefore tanks had to be adapted urgently for tank versus tank actions, primarily by increasing their firepower by equipping them with long-barrelled guns that fired shells with a high muzzle velocity. For the German tanks, starting in the middle of the war, the main task became finding ways to counter the quickly increasing number of constantly improving enemy tanks. Accordingly, their designs changed fundamentally. However, this happened after the period described in this book. At the beginning of the Great Patriotic War, there were different qualitative criteria for tanks.

Chapter 3

Germany's Panzer Forces

Determining the primary tasks of tanks and their tactics on the battlefield was important, but even more important was the correct strategy for the armoured forces. In Germany in the period between the world wars the question of how best to use tanks in future conflicts was given the most serious attention, and the panzer forces were granted an independent role. The German Field Manual *Truppenführung* (*Handling of Troop Formations*), which came out in 1933, postulated: 'Close support for the infantry deprives tanks of their advantage in speed and in some circumstances can doom them to be sacrificed on the enemy's defence.'[1] The 1933 Field Manual didn't renounce the need to support the infantry with tanks, but at the same time it unequivocally rejected the option of making tanks directly subordinate to the infantry. According to it, tanks could attack either together with the infantry, or from a different direction, without losing speed; however, they should break into the enemy positions simultaneously with the infantry.

The Reichswehr's first training panzer unit appeared in Zossen on 1 November 1933, nine months after Hitler assumed power. It numbered just eight tanks and six unarmed tracked carriages, and its size didn't exceed that of a company; in order to keep it secret it was initially called 'a motorized training command'. The 'command' rose like leavened bread and by 1 October of the following year it had become a tank regiment with a two-battalion composition. By the same time a second such regiment was formed. In order to equip the panzer units, the serial production of tanks began in Germany in July 1934. However, the tanks didn't go to reinforce the infantry, as happened in other countries. The bulk of them from the very beginning went to independent mobile formations – panzer and *leichte* (light) divisions. These formations were given the decisive role for achieving victory in the future blitzkriegs. The first German panzer division began to be formed immediately after the public disclosure of Germany's broad programme of militarization at the beginning of 1935. Its core became the panzer brigade that consisted of the two already existing panzer regiments. In August of the same year a newly minted experimental panzer division successfully held its first large-scale manoeuvres, in which 12,953 men, 4,025 wheeled vehicles and 481 tracked vehicles took part. The new and never-before-tested mobile formation convincingly demonstrated its right to exist, and on 15 October 1935 its presence was officially announced in the Wehrmacht, and two more panzer divisions began to be formed.[2]

In addition to the panzers, which provided the main shock force of these divisions, their roster of units included organic infantry, engineers and artillery, including anti-aircraft and anti-tank artillery. Their importance and the need for them were at times underappreciated, and all the attention was focused on the panzers. It was to their detriment, because alongside their doubtless merits, the tanks had many shortcomings that hampered their independent operational success. For example, the panzers ran into various natural obstacles – wide canals, ravines, hills, forests, deep snow and soft ground, not to mention rivers and lakes, swamps, and mountains – and man-made anti-tank obstacles that made the ground impassable for them. Tanks might be able to place accurate direct fire, but they were poorly adapted for combat against distant targets, especially beyond the field of vision; for destroying powerful fortifications; or for conducting plunging fire. Tanks were practically defenceless against enemy aircraft and were very vulnerable in close combat, especially in built-up areas and close terrain. They were capable of seizing ground, but were unable to mop up enemy from the gained territory completely and then hold it. From these considerations it is understandable why the effectiveness of tanks increased manifold when the panzer divisions began to include sappers who could lay down a path for them across natural obstructions and through enemy obstacles, artillerymen who could support them with fire, anti-aircraft gunners to give them air cover, and infantry that would unswervingly escort them into battle.

Anti-tank units were an inseparable part of the Wehrmacht's panzer divisions. It was they who were directly intended to counter enemy combat vehicles and allow their panzers the opportunity to pursue their main tasks, like launching paralysing strikes against vulnerable points in the enemy's dispositions, penetrating the defences and rampaging through the enemy's rear; or bypassing, enveloping and encircling enemy troops. It was very important for the infantry and supply columns of a panzer division to be transported in lorries, and for its artillery to have mechanized tow. Thereby all of the units and elements that were part of this mobile formation wouldn't become separated from their panzers when marching on roads. This allowed the panzer division to operate autonomously, to conduct swift and deep manoeuvres, and to enter combat immediately at full strength. All this happened very quickly; for example, according to the norms, a German panzer regiment should be able to deploy into combat formation from its march columns in less than 25 minutes.[3]

In order to improve the coordination of the panzer division's artillery with its panzers, the forward artillery observers received special combat vehicles like outdated command tanks or armoured halftracks. The protective armour allowed them to move right behind the attacking panzers and to spot targets and threats on the battlefield in a timely manner. The forward observers quickly called down the artillery's fire on the most important targets and corrected the resulting fire. At the same time in the Wehrmacht target indication and the correction of artillery fire were frequently conducted not only from the ground but also from the air. Soviet front-line veterans especially recalled the silhouette of the German twin-engine, twin-boom tactical reconnaissance and artillery spotter plane, the Focke-Wulf 189 *Uhu* ('Eagle Owl'), which they called the *Rama* ('Window Frame') due to its distinctive quadrangular shape in the sky. Its appearance overhead, as a rule, was the harbinger of deadly artillery barrages, which were not conducted as area fire, but, being corrected from above, were much more accurate and dangerous.

The cooperation of the Luftwaffe with the ground troops was not at all restricted to artillery spotting. In the Wehrmacht, there existed a widely used and repeatedly tested system of direct support of ground troops from the air. Aviation liaison officers as a rule took personal part in an offensive, located in the second echelon of the attackers in armoured combat vehicles that were equipped with radio sets, which allowed them to maintain contact with both ground and air force commanders, as well as with directly supporting aircraft. In case of necessity they called for air support, and before the mission had provided the pilots with detailed information about the location and nature of targets, orienting landmarks, weather conditions and possible enemy countermeasures. Immediately after take-off, the pilots established direct two-way contact with the forward air controllers and followed their guidance towards the targets. The German aircraft, as a rule, appeared above the battlefield within minutes of being summoned and operated with great effectiveness. This especially related to the Ju 87 Stuka dive-bombers, which were capable of pinpoint strikes. The forward air controllers were Luftwaffe officers and knew full well the capabilities of the aircraft and the specifics of employing it for air strikes. In essence, the Luftwaffe support given to the German panzer divisions served the role of long-range, self-propelled artillery.

Luftwaffe aircraft did not only destroy enemy troop concentrations and strongpoints that were blocking the ground force's advance. They also gave air cover to the German units and flew long-range reconnaissance missions, providing the army command with the most valuable information about the location, size and composition of enemy forces. No less important, especially for the forward units, was information about the condition of the terrain, roads and bridges over which they had to pass. In order to scout in tactical depth, the German panzer divisions and army corps were given reconnaissance squadrons that were directly subordinate to them. Before the start of Operation Barbarossa, these squadrons numbered 416 reconnaissance aircraft, of which 358 were operational.[4]

In addition to radio communications, a system of code signals was widely used in the Wehrmacht in order to accelerate the transmission of information, which pilots efficiently used from the air to signal the ground troops with the help of flares of different colours. For example, a red flare meant the detection of enemy anti-tank positions, while a violet flare warned of the appearance of enemy tanks. In order to signal the dropping of a written message, the pilots would fire a green flare. This might be simply notes, or maps on which the crews had just drawn the operational situation. They were placed into special cylindrical containers that emitted a yellow smoke when dropped, enabling the ground troops to find them quickly. By the same means, aerial reconnaissance photographs that had just been developed back at base were passed to the ground officers. These images were delivered en route by the same reconnaissance aircraft that were heading out on their next mission. In addition, pilots used smoke grenades to mark enemy positions they had just detected that might be difficult to spot from the ground. Forward German elements often received intelligence from their aircraft earlier and in fuller volume than the headquarters of their units and formations. Indeed, this was fully justified: the information went directly first to those who were in the most immediate need of it, with no delays by middlemen.

For their own part, German ground troops also had a system of code signals for the Luftwaffe. First of all, they had to designate their own positions in order not to be attacked by mistake by their own aircraft. For this purpose they used flags and large strips of white material that were easily distinguishable from the air. Special combinations of these strips signalled the need for the urgent delivery by air of weapons, ammunition, fuel, food, spare parts or equipment. As a rule, such requests were quickly carried out, although loads dropped by parachute didn't always reach the intended recipient because of the rapid shifting of lines and positions in the conditions of manoeuvre warfare.

Ground reconnaissance in the Wehrmacht's panzer divisions was implemented by an organic subunit – the panzer reconnaissance battalion. This usually moved in the division's vanguard, sending out combat patrols on motorcycles or in cars, armoured cars or armoured halftracks far in front or to the sides. The main tasks of the reconnaissance troops were to reveal the enemy; find vulnerable places in the enemy's defences; search for routes to bypass or envelop enemy positions; and seize bridges or important road hubs and hold them until the arrival of the main forces. Thus, the Germans actively and constantly conducted reconnaissance, both from the air and on the ground. The timely received and reliable information about the enemy and the terrain lying ahead allowed the German commanders to avoid venturing forward blindly, which their Soviet opponents often had to do, especially at the beginning of the war, and to make decisions that were based on real knowledge not only regarding their own troops but also regarding the enemy forces and the ground on which the combat actions would unfold. This enabled them to achieve maximal results with the fewest losses in a rapidly changing combat situation. At the same time, in order to ensure effective cooperation between combat vehicles, elements, units and formations, the Wehrmacht had an adequate amount of communication means, including radio sets.

The organization of the German panzer formations was constantly improved with respect to combat experience, and by the beginning of the Great Patriotic War was close to optimal for this period. It is interesting to trace the dynamics of its development. On the eve of the Second World War the five Wehrmacht panzer divisions each had on average 340 panzers. During the campaign in the West in the spring of 1940 the average number in the ten panzer divisions that took part fell by 24 per cent, to 258 combat vehicles. From August 1940 until January 1941 the Germans implemented a radical reform of their mobile forces. The number of panzer divisions was doubled up to twenty, but in the process the total number of tanks in them didn't increase significantly. Therefore, before the invasion of the USSR the average number of tanks in the seventeen German panzer divisions of the field army dropped by another 20 per cent, to 206.

One often comes across the opinion that the shock force of the Wehrmacht's panzer divisions thereby proved to be significantly undermined, and the only reason for this was the lack of tanks. Of course, the Germans were never supplied with enough updated panzer models. Therefore they had to use in the front line even the Pz.Kpfw.I and Pz.Kpfw.II light tanks that had become totally outdated by that time, as well as Czech-manufactured Pz.Kpfw.35(t) and Pz.Kpfw.38(t). As a result, at a conference with the OKH (*Oberkommando des Heeres*, or Army High Command) on 26 August 1940, Hitler agreed to leave one panzer regiment in the panzer division exclusively as a temporary measure. In the future he intended to increase the pace of tank production sharply, in order to bring the numbers in the Wehrmacht by the end of 1944 up to 26,700 combat vehicles and to restore the second panzer regiment in the panzer divisions.[5] This plan became the Führer's next utopian idea, but the temporary decision to decrease the number of combat vehicles in the panzer divisions was justified in practice. Moreover, as combat experience demonstrated, it was an extremely successful solution.

It mustn't be forgotten that this decision wasn't made out of thin air. The main argument for the possibility of such a reform was the results of a thorough and comprehensive analysis of the combat experience of the use of mobile forces in Poland and in France. This experience showed that the initial organization of a panzer division was overloaded with panzers and suffered from a lack of the infantry needed to support them in combat. In addition, the mass arrival in the forces of the latest medium Pz.Kpfw.III and Pz.Kpfw.IV tanks, which gradually replaced the light tanks with their weak armour and armament, allowed the possibility of substantially enhancing the shock force of a panzer division even if it had fewer tanks. Having reduced the authorized panzer strength in the panzer divisions, the Germans successfully stumbled upon the optimal correlation between the number of tanks and the amount of motorized infantry in these divisions. This allowed them to be used more effectively. It is significant that by the middle of the war, both the USSR and its Western allies had come to a similar correlation of tanks and infantry in their armoured formations and retained it until the end of the war, even though they had many more tanks available to them than the Germans.

One more positive result of the centralized use of tanks was a reduction in their irrecoverable combat losses. The point is that the tank is a heavy and complex combat vehicle that needs constant resupply with ammunition, fuel and lubricants, and spare parts; constant maintenance and mechanical service; and timely evacuation and repair in the event of mechanical breakdowns or combat damage. Where tanks were dispersed over a large area into small groups or solitary vehicles, then in the conditions of intense combat operations the repair teams and evacuation personnel often didn't have the time or opportunity to reach many knocked-out, broken-down or simply bogged vehicles. As a result, tanks that became immobilized for any reason and couldn't be repaired by the crews themselves were irrecoverably lost. Given the concentrated use of tanks as part of the panzer divisions, as a rule they didn't become widely separated from their mobile supply dumps and could quickly receive the help of repair teams.

The personnel of the German panzer forces underwent comprehensive training, and the majority of them by 1941 had fresh combat experience. It is important to note that the Germans ordered only as many panzers for the Wehrmacht as could be supplied with trained crews to operate them. All of their panzer elements, units and divisions had formed close collaboration in training manoeuvres and in combat, and had worked out tight cooperation both within their own units and in larger formations. In order to enhance the shock power of the panzer divisions, they were merged into motorized corps (*Armeekorps (mot)*), which included motorized divisions. These divisions at the time weren't equipped with tanks, but thanks to their full provisioning with motorized transport and prime movers, they weren't inferior to the panzer divisions in mobility and were capable of closely cooperating with them. Finally, in order to conduct Operation Barbarossa, four panzer groups were formed out of the motorized corps, at the head of which stood experienced, aggressive, decisive military commanders, who most importantly had been tested in recent fighting.

The flexibility of the organizational structure of Germany's panzer forces was also of no little significance. In the course of combat operations their composition changed according to the tasks they were carrying out. Various *kampfgruppen* (combat groups) that differed in complement and strength were smoothly formed within panzer units and formations. One or another sub-unit or unit was assigned to them according to need. At the same time the thorough training and the previously acquired practice of cooperation enabled them to function successfully together, on the fly.

Thus, the high level of organization, training, equipping and command and control made the Wehrmacht's panzer forces an extremely serious and dangerous adversary. They were essential for further German successes.

Chapter 4

The Wehrmacht's Panzers

The panzers that armed the Wehrmacht by the start of the fighting against the USSR fully corresponded to the German conception of their proper use at the time. When creating the first combat vehicles in Germany, their mobility and firepower were points of emphasis. It was considered that the thickness of the armour would be fully adequate if it made the tank invulnerable to armour-piercing bullets fired from machine guns that had a standard rifle calibre. It was just such machine guns that primarily made the front static in the First World War. In the opinion of military theoreticians at the time, protection against bullets should restore to the troops their lost mobility. Anti-tank guns didn't seem to be a special problem, because after all they were substantially inferior to machine guns in numbers and their rate of fire. Theoretical calculations demonstrated that a German battalion numbering 100 tanks, attacking on a front of 500 metres, was capable of breaking through the defence of a contemporary French infantry division armed with 72 anti-tank guns. This was the case even if it was allowed that each shot by the French anti-tank gun crews struck a target. The calculated loss of 50 per cent of the vehicles in such a scenario was believed to be fully acceptable. Plainly, the bloody experience of the First World War hung above the men who came to such a conclusion, when even a 90 per cent loss rate didn't seem excessive in order to achieve a strategic breakthrough of a front.[1]

The 171st Article of the Versailles Pact that had been signed by Germany after its defeat in the First World War forbade it from producing or importing armoured cars, tanks or similar combat equipment. However, as early as 1925 the Germans began secretly to violate this restriction, having initiated work on a project under the code name 'Großtraktor' (large tractor). Six tanks, which had been assembled by the summer of 1929, were the result. These were purely experimental vehicles, built out of soft steel plate at the Daimler-Benz, Rheinmetall and Krupp companies, two each. It was impossible to conduct their trials in Germany, so at the end of June of the same year the Germans sent them to the USSR, where on the basis of the Moscow Agreement signed on 2 October 1926 a secret 'Kama' tank school was organized near Kazan. Officers who were trained there later made up the basis of the teaching staff of the Wehrmacht's panzer courses created in 1935 in Zossen.[2] In addition to training Soviet and German cadets, comprehensive trials of the first German tanks of the interwar period were conducted in the school. In June 1930 four more tanks arrived there, built by the Krupp and Rheinmetall companies within the framework of the 'Leichttraktor' (light tractor) project. The Germans thoroughly analysed the results of these trials and came to very important conclusions that touched upon not only technical but also tactical aspects of their future combat vehicles. Their main conclusions were the following:

1. The tank commander should be fully freed from all functions other than command. In the 'Leichttraktor' the commander simultaneously carried out the duties of the loader. This led to a slower rate of fire and to difficulty in spotting targets and threats on the battlefield, as well as to loss of cooperation with other tanks.
2. For observation of the surrounding terrain, the tank commander should be provided with a cupola that offered a 360 degree field of vision. Furnishing him with an ordinary periscope was inadequate.
3. It was necessary to equip the turret with a floor on which the loader could stand, which would rotate together with the turret. This was especially necessary when using a power-assisted traversing mechanism, which significantly boosted the turret's rotation.
4. It was important to position the gunner's seat as close as possible to the tank's centre of gravity. This reduced the shaking of his body during the movement of the vehicle and gave him optimal conditions for observing the battlefield and taking aim at targets.
5. The tank's interior should be adequately roomy for its crew, significantly enhancing their effectiveness and reducing their fatigue.[3]

All of these conclusions lay at the basis of the designs of subsequent models of German medium and heavy panzers and contributed greatly to their future successes. Upon the termination of the work of the 'Kama' school in 1933, the tanks returned to Germany, but their story didn't end there. The four Grosstraktors produced by Krupp and Rheinmetall, as well as all of the Leichttraktors, were renovated and in the future used not only for training tankers, but also for working out new tactical and technical ideas. For example, after 1933 individual spring suspension for road wheels of a larger diameter was tested on one of the Rheinmetall Leichttraktors; it became the prototype for the suspension on the first Pz.Kpfw.III tanks.[4]

The first mass-produced German Pz.Kpfw.I light tanks were created above all to prepare the industry and country's armed forces to manufacture and use the future generations of more powerful tanks. The simplicity and inexpensiveness of their design allowed the Germans to get their serial production up and running quickly, although the path to it wasn't simple. The design of a new tank under the code name 'Kleintraktor' ('Small Tractor') began in 1930. The chassis were ordered from the Krupp company. In order to accelerate the work, it was decided to copy the advanced suspension system of that time, as found on the British Carden-Loyd tankettes. For this purpose, on 12 November 1931 three Carden-Loyd chassis were ordered in the United Kingdom from Vickers-Armstrongs through a middleman. The first of them arrived in Germany in January 1932, and the next two in October of the same year. However, Krupp's engineers didn't wait for their arrival, and began working out the design of the suspension on their own, using only photographs and sketches of the British tankette. The manufacturing of a prototype was delayed because of the raging global economic crisis, which hindered the Krupp factory from working rhythmically. The production of the prototypes of the chassis ended, finally, only on 29 July 1932, and they were shown to officers of the German Army Weapons Agency. At comparison trials conducted on the proving ground at Kummersdorf, the 'Kleintraktor' demonstrated superiority over the Carden-Loyd. The trials were held over a four-month period, during which the chassis travelled 1800 kilometres and were subject to numerous revisions. After the trials ended on 20 March 1933, Krupp received a contract for one chassis, and another contract for four more on 10 May 1933. They were all turned over to the purchaser in July-August of that same year. Only one of them was manufactured from hardened steel armour, and this one was subjected to test firing with 7.92mm armour-piercing bullets from a range of 30 metres. The rest, in order to economize and accelerate the manufacturing process, were made from soft steel plate and were intended only for troop trials. In the spring of 1933 the question of equipping the 'Kleintraktor' chassis with torsion bar suspension came up repeatedly, but the discussions came to nothing. In July 1933 the Weapons Agency ordered the first series of 150 chassis, which received the code name 'Landwirtschaftliche Schlepper' ('Agricultural tractor'), or La.S., and lacked turrets or weapons. Among the troops, however, it was called the Krupp Traktor after the name of its main producer. Germany at the time was still trying to conceal its violations of the Versailles Agreement, which had strictly forbidden the building of tanks. Interestingly, in addition to Krupp, five more companies (the Krupp branch business Grusonwerk, M.A.N., Rheinmetall, Henschel and Daimler-Benz) each received an order for three chassis. The Nazis, who had just assumed power, covertly began to prepare Germany's industry to produce the tanks that they needed for their future conquests. The production of the first series ended in October 1934. All these vehicles were sent to panzer schools and were used for a long time to train the future drivers of German panzers.[5] Skipping somewhat ahead, it should be noted that in addition to them, for the same purpose another 442 turretless training La.S. were built in 1937–1938.[6]

Alongside the development of chassis went the design of superstructures with weapons. Options were being developed with a 20mm anti-aircraft gun, a 37mm anti-tank gun, and a mortar, but none of these variants progressed beyond the stage of a preliminary design. In June 1932 the Krupp and Daimler-Benz companies began work on a competitive basis on a turret with a twin-barrelled machine gun of a standard calibre. The Weapons Agency was totally unable to come to a final decision regarding its design and constantly changed its requirements. Finally, in July 1933 Krupp received an order for 150 turrets and turret platforms for the first-series vehicles. This company had acquired vast experience in producing armour of both large and medium thickness for the German Navy and fortifications, but the manufacture of curved, welded armour plates of 13mm hardened steel turned out to be a difficult problem for it. Tests conducted on 22 January 1935 at the Kummersdorf proving grounds revealed that the armour didn't meet the military's requirements: it proved to be too brittle and cracks developed in it from the strike of bullets. Therefore in February 1935 the order was cancelled. Nevertheless, the Krupp company was instructed to produce out of soft steel plate 20 more turret assemblies and turret platforms for training tanks. As a result, the 'Krupp-Traktor' was never in fact armed. In addition, in contrast to all the other German tanks, these chassis were never equipped with radio sets.[7]

However, for the Wehrmacht's planned panzer divisions at least some sort of materiel was urgently required. In January 1934 it was proposed to order 200 La.S. of the second series from the Krupp company, which finally received its combat designation – the Panzerkampfwagen I (Pz.Kpfw.I), which means an armoured combat vehicle of the first model (*see* Plate 1). Then it was planned to switch to the production of the La.S 100 – the future Pz.Kpfw.II. However, its development experienced delays, and the German Army didn't want to wait any longer, so in July 1934 it simultaneously ordered 1,000 Pz.Kpfw.I tanks. The turrets for them, armed with twin machine guns of 7.92mm calibre, were being manufactured by the Daimler-Benz company. With such armament, the Pz.Kpfw.I was unsuitable for an anti-tank role, but it was fully satisfactory for taking on enemy personnel and soft vehicles. The 13mm of hardened, homogeneous armour reliably protected it from armour-piercing bullets fired by rifles and machine guns of standard calibre. The German Minister of War V. von Blomberg assigned the highest priority to this order over all others. In addition to Krupp, the M.A.N., Rheinmetall, Henschel and Daimler-Benz companies were building these tanks. The monthly output amounted to 60 tanks in 1935 and around 70 tanks in 1936, which can be considered a fairly good accomplishment, considering that not one of these companies had previously serially produced combat vehicles. By 1 August 1935, 318 Pz.Kpfw.I tanks were ready, and by the end of the year this figure stood at 720; by 1 October 1936 it was 1,160.[8] The brand new Pz.Kpfw.I tanks quickly began to arm the German panzer divisions, the open formation of which began on 15 October 1935. The first two panzer divisions were to reach the level of combat readiness by 1 April 1936, and just six months later a third panzer division joined them.[9]

Subsequently the Pz.Kpfw.I went through a significant modification. The need for this was prompted first of all by its inadequate power-to-weight ratio – just 11 horsepower per ton of weight. The Maybach company managed to create a 6-cylinder, 100 horsepower engine, which together with its radiator and exhaust fan was able to fit inside the Pz.Kpfw.I tank's existing engine compartment. This replaced the previous 4-cylinder, 60 horsepower engine. In addition, an idler wheel was added to the tank's suspension, the function of which was previously carried out by the last road wheel of a larger diameter. The new model received the designation Pz.Kpfw.I Ausf.B and went into production in the summer of 1936. The manufacture of the Pz.Kpfw.I was finally terminated in June 1937, after the assembly of 1,175 Pz.Kpfw.I Ausf.A and 399 Pz.Kpfw.I Ausf.B.[10]

By the end of 1933 it had become obvious to the German leadership that the planned arrival of medium tanks, which were to comprise the majority of the Wehrmacht's combat vehicles, was being hopelessly delayed. In these circumstances, there could be only one possible decision that would avoid any interruption in the schedule for the appearance of the new German panzer formations and their preparation for a future war. This was the next temporary measure – the creation of another light tank, the Pz.Kpfw.II. In the first half of 1934 the German Army Weapons Agency simultaneously instructed several companies to begin work on the development of the new tank. The next year Krupp and Henschel each presented two chassis to the Army, again built out of soft steel plate. The chassis built by the M.A.N. company competed with them. Daimler-Benz designed the turret with a weapon and turret platform for all of them. As a result of trials on the proving grounds in Kummersdorf, the military's choice fell on the chassis built by M.A.N. At the same time Daimler-Benz's design for the turret was approved, and in October 1935 the first test series of 75 tanks, which were produced by the M.A.N. company in three batches of 25 each, was ordered. In comparison with the Pz.Kpfw.I, the new light tank was larger and correspondingly heavier. The vehicles of the first series kept the 13mm armour of the Pz.Kpfw.I, but later it was increased to 14.5mm of armour, having somewhat reduced its hardness (which made the armour too brittle) and increased its malleability, while preserving its level of ballistic protection.[11] The main feature of the Pz.Kpfw.II was its automatic 20mm cannon, the Kw.K.30, which replaced the left-side machine gun as its main weapon and substantially increased its firepower. An attempt had been made to equip the Pz.Kpfw.I tank with these cannon back in June 1931, but it cramped the turret excessively. However, it fitted the larger turret of the Pz.Kpfw.II tank splendidly. Based on the high-powered anti-aircraft gun, the cannon was an efficient weapon for its calibre. Its effective range of fire reached 1,200 metres, while its rate of fire was 280 rounds per minute.[12] Such a weapon was chosen not just to give the Pz.Kpfw.II the ability to take on enemy tanks, although this was one of its roles. The shields of anti-tank artillery guns were defenceless against its shells. It was precisely these weapons, especially the light, rapid-firing anti-tank guns, that were justifiably considered to be the most numerous and dangerous adversary of the tanks of the period. In addition, the 20mm fragmentation shells were substantially superior to regular bullets in effectiveness when firing at infantry, lightly armoured equipment and residential buildings.

The first five vehicles were ready by 1 October 1936 after a delay of six months, but this didn't prevent the German Army Weapons Agency from placing an additional order for another 460 Pz.Kpfw.II tanks at the end of September. However, the fulfilment of these orders didn't go well. By 1 October 1937, in addition to the first 75 Pz.Kpfw.II, the army had received only 175 tanks of the second and third series. The average rate of output over this period didn't exceed 20–25 tanks a month. In essence, they were all pre-production prototypes, used for debugging the production machinery and eliminating the design shortcomings which appeared in the course of producing and testing these combat vehicles. The army's main complaints were prompted by the Pz.Kpfw.II's plainly outdated dependent suspension. Because of it, the tanks' speed suffered, especially in difficult terrain, since the suspension didn't allow them to make full use of their horsepower, which was 1.5 times greater than that of the Pz.Kpfw.I tank. In consequence, the last 75 tanks of the second and third series received an improved independent suspension using quarter-elliptic leaf springs. With this modification, the Pz.Kpfw.II entered serial production (*see* Plate 2). It began in the summer of 1937 and continued until April 1940. Over this time the M.A.N., Henschel, Alkett, M.I.A.G. and F.A.M.O. companies built 958 such tanks in four series, of which 210 were Ausf.A, 384 were Ausf.B, and 364 were Ausf.C.[13]

Between October 1938 and April 1939 the M.A.N. company produced 43 Pz.Kpfw.II of the next (Ausf.D) design, with a new hull, independent torsion-bar suspension and larger diameter road wheels, which increased the tank's top speed from 40 to 55 km/hr. However, immediately after their dispatch to the troops, these tanks were recalled to the factory and rebuilt into flame-throwing tanks, designated the Pz.Kpfw.II (Flamm) Ausf.A. To them were added 46 incomplete chassis of the 8th series, which were also modified for this project. Thus, from January 1940 to February 1941 the Wegmann company produced 89 such tanks. In March 1941 the final modification of the Pz.Kpfw.II, the Ausf.F, which was equipped with the earlier leaf spring suspension, entered the Wehrmacht's panzer forces. Until the end of June of the same year, the Ursus and F.A.M.O. factories managed to produce 49 of the Pz.Kpfw.II Ausf.F.[14]

The Pz.Kpfw.II wasn't distinguished by any original technical solutions that had influence on world-wide tank design, nor did it attract any particular attention or popularity. However, during Germany's campaigns against Poland and especially France in 1939 and 1940 it was the Pz.Kpfw.II that became the most numerous German panzer on the battlefields and served as the work horse for the Wehrmacht's tankers. So this rather mediocre tank nevertheless managed to play a leading role in theatre of combat operations and as far as it was capable compensated for the German lack of medium tanks. It then gradually departed from the stage …

In early 1934 the German Army Weapons Agency invited the Daimler-Benz, Krupp, M.A.N. and Rheinmetall companies to take part in a competition for the best design of a 10-ton tank, armed with a 37mm cannon. Initially this received the code name 'Z.W.', or in full 'Zugführerwagen', which translates as 'Platoon commander's vehicle'. After evaluating the preliminary designs, at the end of the year Daimler-Benz received an order for two tested chassis and subsequently another order for two more. The M.A.N. company also received an order for chassis, but for only one. Meanwhile Krupp and Rheinmetall were commissioned to build respectively one and two experimental turrets for them. In December 1935 Daimler-Benz won a contract for an initial series of ten tanks, equipped with Krupp turrets. On 3 April 1936 it received the designation 'Panzerkampfwagen III'. However, the large-series production of these panzers was held up by the need to correct serious design flaws. As a result almost three years was required for the production of four series of 60 panzers and their subsequent upgrades. The armament of the Pz.Kpfw.III had an interesting feature: two co-axial machine guns in the turret with the 37mm cannon, and a third machine gun positioned in the forward hull. Such an unusual combination was retained right up to the tank's re-arming with 50mm cannon, with only one co-axial machine gun. At the same time the first panzers had, as before, only 14.5mm of homogeneous armour that offered protection against bullets, and they lacked high mobility, primarily because of faulty suspension. With each modification of the Pz.Kpfw.III, the Germans continued to search for its optimal variant, suitable for large-scale production.[15]

Finally, in December 1938 the first vehicles of a successful modification, the Pz.Kpfw.III Ausf.E, passed military acceptance. They were assembled at the Daimler-Benz and M.A.N. factories, then subsequently at the Alkett, F.A.M.O., Henschel, M.I.A.G. and M.N.H. factories. The main features of the new model were a 300 horsepower engine, a 10-speed semi-automatic transmission and a new independent torsion bar suspension, which allowed the panzer's top speed to increase to 67 km/hr. The compact running gear provided the opportunity to free up space on the sides of the tank for additional hatches, through which the driver and radio operator could abandon the tank if it became necessary. An additional most important novelty of the Pz.Kpfw.III Ausf.E was the 30mm of face-hardened armour on the front and sides of the hull and on all sides of the turret. Its outer surface was extremely hard and, in combination with its strong and malleable core and inner surface, gave the tank a qualitative leap in its level of protection. It couldn't be penetrated by large-calibre bullets fired by machine guns and anti-tank rifles, nor by small-calibre shells, including those fired by France's most numerous 25mm anti-tank cannon. The thinner armour plates had through hardening. This modification became the basis for all further production series of this tank, but their output began with more than a year of delay because of the extensive difficulties with debugging a number of advanced technical decisions used in its design. The first 603 Pz.Kpfw.III, beginning with Ausf.E, kept the 37mm cannon as its main weapon, but in July 1940, in the course of producing the next model, the Ausf.G, a switch was made to the much more powerful 50mm L/42 gun. This was able to penetrate the 40mm armour of the French tanks at an angle of 30° at a normal range of 700 metres, at which the majority of fighting in central Europe took place, without protruding beyond the forward hull. Its ammunition included an effective high-explosive shell, which easily compensated for the absence of the second turret machine gun. Over the year that remained before the invasion of the USSR, 1,154 Pz.Kpfw.III were produced in Germany with this main gun (*see* Plate 3).

In October 1940 the 10-speed semi-automatic transmission was rejected, even though by this time it had been placed in almost 1,400 tanks, and the main problems with its reliability had been successfully resolved. The main reason for this decision was the human factor. The gear shifts in it were done in a rather original fashion. The driver initially moved a manual lever into the required position, and only then switched to the previously selected gear by pressing on a clutch foot pedal that was connected to a vacuum actuator. The process of switching gear happened noticeably faster than usual, and correspondingly reduced the loss of the tank's speed prompted by the interruption in the torque transfer to the drive sprockets. It was believed that such a system would accelerate the training and ease the tankers' work, but in reality it often confused them. The main problem was the need to retrain the men, who were used to the customary means of switching gear on regular training vehicles, where gear shifts were made by the corresponding lever after stepping on the clutch pedal. In addition, constant difficulty was observed with crews' transfer from the Pz.Kpfw.III to other panzer types and back again, because after all it isn't easy for a human to change acquired habits abruptly.

As a result, there were quite a few breakdowns and crashes, when the driver by habit pressed the clutch, expecting the engine to be disengaged from the transmission, but instead of this a gear was suddenly shifted. Moreover practice demonstrated that movement at high speed was leading to damage to the rubber rims of the road wheels as a result of their overheating, so the drivers were strictly prohibited from exceeding 40 km/hr when driving in higher gears. Indeed, combat experience by this time showed that in real fighting conditions a tank rarely had to accelerate to its top speed, and for a more satisfactory range of speeds a fewer number of gears was fully sufficient. Therefore, the Pz.Kpfw.III, beginning with the Ausf.H model, had a much simpler 6-speed transmission, adopted from the Pz.Kpfw.IV with a few changes. As a result the top speed fell to the same 42 km/hr at which the tank was used earlier, but on the other hand its manufacture became easier and less costly.[16]

Between May 1937 and July 1941 the Daimler-Benz, M.A.N., M.N.H., Henschel, Alkett, M.I.A.G. and F.A.M.O. companies managed to produce 1,822 Pz.Kpfw.III of the following modifications: 10 Ausf.A, 15 Ausf.B, 15 Ausf.C, 25 Ausf.D, 96 Ausf.E, 435 Ausf.F, 600 Ausf.G, 286 Ausf.H and 340 Ausf.J.[17]

In the USSR they became closely acquainted with the latest German tanks for the first time in September 1939. Back then, during the campaign in Poland, Red Army soldiers near Lvov managed to snatch from no-man's land two tanks that had been knocked out by the Poles: a Pz.Kpfw.II and a Pz.Kpfw.III. They were both transported back to the Soviet Union and were analysed at the armour research and test proving ground in Kubinka. The first of them, as might be expected, made no particular impression, although the analysts noted it had good armour and took a close look at the engine design, the transmission and the cooling system. However, the second acquisition proved much more useful. Judging by its description, this was a Pz.Kpfw.III Ausf.E, at the time the most up-to-date model. It was disassembled, painstakingly examined by proving ground experts, and earned their highest assessment. They especially liked its optical gear, particularly its commander's cupola, the compact engine with its efficient fuel and cooling systems, its transmission, and even its lifting jack. They were unable to test its performance because the engine had been badly damaged and part of the tracks had been lost.

In 1940 the Soviet military and tank designers were presented with an even better opportunity to study the Wehrmacht's materiel. According to an economic agreement between the two countries signed on 11 February 1940, the Soviet Union was able to purchase German industrial equipment and military items. Among other things a Pz.Kpfw.III tank was ordered. From the previously studied model it was distinguished only by a more powerful 50mm cannon and stronger frontal armour with a thickness of 60mm. From all the available evidence, this was one of the recently updated models, the Ausf.F or Ausf.G with appliqué armour plating in front. In the period from August to November 1940 it underwent joint testing together with Soviet tanks on the proving ground at Kubinka. On the measured kilometre, this combat vehicle exceeded, although not by much, its official top speed, having accelerated to 69.7 km/hr. The fastest Soviet tank was of course the BT-7, but even on wheels it managed to reach only 68.1 km/hr. The T-34 at the time was only able to achieve 48.2 km/hr. Even before the testing ended, on 13 September 1940 the head of the Red Army's Automotive-Armoured-Tank Directorate Fedorenko proposed to Voroshilov in a letter that the most successful engineering solutions of the Pz.Kpfw.III tank should be introduced into the design of new Soviet tanks, including a commander's cupola, evacuation hatches, the isolation of the fuel tanks and engine from the crew behind a sealed bulkhead, the arrangement of the engine cooling system, the transmission design, and the placement of a radio set in the hull.[18]

The further development of the Großtraktor line led to the appearance of the Pz.Kpfw.IV medium tank in Germany. However, before this, from 1934 to 1936 the Rheinmetall and Krupp companies produced a small series of tanks with three turrets, called the 'Neubau Fahrzeug' ('Vehicles of new construction'). As a result of the tests conducted on the Soviet proving ground near Kazan in October 1932 the Germans worked out the main requirements for a medium tank with a weight of 15 tons, which was initially called the 'Mittlere Traktor' (Medium tractor). Subsequently the weight of the vehicles rose to 18 tons. The Rheinmetall and Krupp companies were instructed to develop it. The former constructed a chassis and rounded turret with two guns – a 75mm main gun with a 37mm gun above it, while the latter built an angular turret with the same guns positioned side by side. As a result, between 1934 and 1936 five Neubau Fahrzeug tanks were built, with the hull and turret of the first two of them fabricated out of soft steel plate (*see* Plate 4).[19]

The other three, built out of genuine armour and with Krupp turrets, took part in the fighting against the British in Norway in April 1940 as a platoon attached to Separate Panzer Battalion z.b.V.40. In his report about their use, the commander of this panzer battalion, E. Folkheim, commented positively on their capability of firing at several different targets simultaneously thanks to the presence of the two additional machine-gun turrets, one in the front and one in the back. One of the Neubau Fahrzeug once bogged down in marshy ground and hopelessly broke down during the attempt to haul it out of the muck. The Germans hadn't found any sufficiently powerful prime movers in order to free the tank, and it had to be blown up. In order to replace it, one of the remaining Neubau Fahrzeug tanks, built out of soft steel plate, was shipped to Norway.[20] However, by this time the combat operations in Norway had come to an end, so the Neubau Fahrzeug tanks were used primarily for propaganda. Photographs of them systematically appeared in the German press, in order to create the illusion of numerous heavy tanks in the Wehrmacht. Photographs of their factory production were also published frequently. The deception worked: both Soviet and American intelligence agents in 1941, with no coordination between them, reported to their leadership about the serial production of heavy tanks in Germany: the 36-ton Pz.Kpfw.V and the 45-ton Pz.Kpfw.VI.[21] In reality nothing of the sort existed back then; they were simply using the Neubau Fahrzeug tanks with different turret arrangements – the Rheinmetall and Krupp variants – for them. The famous Pz.Kpfw.V Panther and Pz.Kpfw.VI Tiger appeared much later and didn't have anything in common with them, other than the code designations.

The results of the tests of the Neubau Fahrzeug didn't satisfy the German Army Weapons Agency, so the requirements for the next tank were radically reworked. First of all, it was decided to abandon the use of the low-speed aircraft engines which equipped the Grosstraktor and Neubau Fahrzeug, and instead to construct a special tank engine that would be light, compact, reliable and economical. The figure for its top RPMs was doubled in order to save transmission weight. The Maybach company received the contract for designing it. The final result of its work became a 12-cylinder carburettor engine with water cooling, the HL 100 TR, which had a maximum of 300 horsepower with 3,000 RPMs. It was this engine and its closest offshoots that became the most widely used engines of the German medium tanks and self-propelled guns of the Second World War.[22]

The second fundamental change in the design was the shifting of the drive sprocket to the front of the tank. Such a decision had its disadvantages, because it made the sprocket more vulnerable to enemy fire, while the transmission for it had to run through the entire tank, making it heavier and taking up useful space in the fighting compartment and driver's compartment. In addition, the operation of the transmission frequently created noise, vibration and fumes around it, thereby reducing the comfort of the tank crew. However, the German engineers that the following merits of such an arrangement more than offset its disadvantages:

1. The track, after separating from the ground and prior to its engagement to the drive sprocket, runs along the entire length of the tank, vibrating and shaking off loose small debris, mud and dirt. As a result, the drive sprocket suffers less wear and doesn't get jammed with mud and stones.
2. The upper track run, being under tension from the drive sprocket, flops around less while moving, and thus the tank is less likely to throw a track. Meanwhile the lower track running under no tension adapts itself better to uneven surfaces, although the rolling resistance at the same time rises insignificantly.
3. The task of shifting gears becomes substantially easier, since all the transmission's major components are in direct proximity to the driver. The lengthy actuating rods, linking him with the transmission's mechanism when it is placed in the rear of the tank, become unnecessary. The chafing between these rods and their guiding devices, as well as the unavoidable play in their joints, leads to the need for their regular adjustment, and increases the effort required to shift the transmission, thereby increasing the driver's fatigue.
4. The placement of the heavy components of the transmission in the nose of the tank shifts its centre of gravity forward and makes it possible to position the turret in the centre of the tank. This decreases the range of its sway when moving and improves the condition of the crew's work, as well as making it easier to place hatches for the driver and radio operator/gunner in the forward part of the hull's roof, without weakening its frontal armour with cutouts. Moreover, as a result of placing the turret further back, the main gun when pointed forward doesn't protrude as far beyond the tank, thereby improving its manoeuvrability in tight spaces.

Initially the new tank received the code designation 'B.W.', or Begleitwagen, which in translation means 'escort vehicle'. Already from this name it is obvious that it was created in order to support the light Pz.Kpfw.I and Pz.Kpfw.II tanks, as well as the medium Pz.Kpfw.III tanks in battle, and therefore it was accordingly equipped with the corresponding armament, consisting of a short-barrelled 75mm L/24 main gun and two machine guns. For those times the gun had a large calibre and could successfully handle firing missions that were beyond the scope of the machine guns and small-calibre cannons that armed the other German panzers: to suppress dug-in enemy infantry and their weapons; to destroy enemy artillery, especially anti-tank artillery; and to demolish light field fortifications. The low muzzle velocity of its shell in this case was not a shortcoming; on the contrary, it contributed to its effectiveness. The low loads on the shell in the process of firing made it possible to make it thin-walled and to increase its explosive charge. Thus, its high-explosive force and fragmentation effect increased significantly. An armour-piercing shell was also produced for this gun. Even though it had a relatively low armour penetration capability, it was sufficient to combat the tanks of those times successfully, the majority of which offered protection only against bullets. On 3 April 1936 the tank was officially designated the Panzerkampfwagen IV (*see* Plate 5).[23]

Initially it was intended for equipping a company of medium tanks, planned for forming the future panzer battalions. This combat vehicle remained in production throughout the entire Second World War and became the most numerous German panzer in history. The old rival companies Rheinmetall and Krupp once again competed for the contract. The engineers of Rheinmetall went down the path of least resistance and used a complicated and expensive suspension system taken from the Neubau Fahrzeug. Meanwhile Krupp designed a new, original chassis, but also didn't forget about standardization: it used the electric traversing mechanism for the turret from the same Neubau Fahrzeug, and borrowed the shape of the turret, commander's cupola and hatches from the Pz.Kpfw.III. Its initial design included an additional machine-gun turret on the right-hand side of the front of the tank, but this was quickly rejected in favour of a typical ball-mount machine gun, which was also copied from the Pz.Kpfw.III. Krupp won the contract, and on 30 April 1936 its first prototype was ready for trials.[24]

On 1 June 1937 the German Army Weapons Agency gave the Krupp company a directive to implement a deep standardization of their Pz.Kpfw.IV with the Pz.Kpfw.III built by the Daimler–Benz company. Both tanks were produced simultaneously, were in the same weight class, and were equipped with one and the same engine, so naturally the question arose about standardizing their chassis. Krupp received an order to cease all work on the further development of the hull, power plant and suspension of the Pz.Kpfw.IV and to wrap up the production of the second series of these tanks – the Pz.Kpfw.IV Ausf.B – which it had already started. For the next modification, the Ausf.C, it was intended to use the chassis of the fourth series Pz.Kpfw.III – its Ausf.E model. However, everything turned out to be more difficult, since the debugging of the numerous novelties embedded in these chassis didn't go as quickly as the Third Reich's leadership would have liked. In order to await results appropriate for practical use, the output of the Pz.Kpfw.IV would have to be interrupted by eight months. However, at this same time Germany was preparing for war at full speed, and such production losses of tanks that were so important for the future blitzkriegs were unacceptable. Therefore on 21 June 1937 the Weapons Agency instructed the Krupp company to begin production of the next series of Pz.Kpfw.IV immediately after wrapping up the current series.[25] The Second World War had already started, forcing the German engineers to work feverishly, first of all to strengthen the tanks' armour and armament, and to increase their production. As a result, the Germans never had a chance to improve the suspension system of the Pz.Kpfw. IV, and in fact it remained archaic for the entire extent of the war. This example plainly shows that it was not only objective factors that had a decisive influence on the design of tanks at times, but also subjective ones.

The Pz.Kpfw.IV splendidly recommended itself on the battlefields in Poland and France, but there were plainly not enough of them. Even after the Second World War started, the production of these tanks went too slowly; over the entire year of 1940 only 268 of them were built in Germany. This was far from sufficient for satisfying Hitler's growing appetite, so on 20 August 1940 he issued a special order to switch the production of Pz.Kpfw.III, Pz.Kpfw.IV and commanders' tanks to a special priority level of importance. Despite this measure, over the first half of 1941 only 188 Pz.Kpfw.IV were manufactured. The average monthly growth in production in comparison with 1940 amounted to 40 per cent, but all the same it didn't allow the Germans in the short term to bring the number of their panzer divisions to 36 according to Hitler's desire, which he expressed on 18 July 1941. Given a two–regiment composition, in order to equip so many divisions it would be necessary to have 2,160 Pz.Kpfw.IV tanks in formation; however, fortunately these plans were never realized. Between

November 1937 and the end of June 1941 the Krupp company produced 35 Pz.Kpfw.IV Ausf.A, 42 Ausf.B, 134 Ausf.C, 232 Ausf.D, 202 Ausf.E, and 67 Ausf.F, for a total of 712 tanks of this type.[26]

German panzer commanders had at their disposal special command tanks. The first 15 of them were built on the basis of the Pz.Kpfw.I Ausf.A back in the summer of 1935. In place of a pivoting machine-gun turret, they were equipped with a small stationary superstructure and radio transmitters, capable of working over a wider range of radio waves than those that were mounted in ordinary tanks. However, despite their lack of a weapon, these two-seat tanks proved to be cramped and uncomfortable, while the commanders who used them had to be constantly diverted from their duties in order to work at the radio set. Therefore between the summer of 1936 and the end of 1937, 184 new command tanks designated as the Kl.Pz.Bef.Wg were produced on the basis of the next model, the Pz.Kpfw.I Ausf.B (see Plate 6). In their spacious superstructure there was room for an additional crew member (a radio operator), and for a machine gun in a ball mount. The commanders of all German panzer battalions and panzer regiments, and their deputies, as well as the headquarters of the panzer brigades and panzer divisions, received such tanks.[27]

In the fourth quarter of 1938 the first Pz.Bef.Wg command tanks based on the Pz.Kpfw.III entered service. In contrast to the ordinary tanks, their turrets were tightly bolted to the hulls and couldn't turn, and in place of a gun and one of the turret machine guns they had dummy barrels. These served only concealment purposes, preventing the enemy from spotting the command tanks and targeting them first for destruction. At the same time these command tanks were given away by a sizeable antenna that was mounted behind the turret. The room freed up by the elimination of weapons and on-board ammunition was used for a powerful, supplementary radio set. Before the beginning of the Great Patriotic War, Germany managed to produce 205 Pz.Bef.Wg in various modifications: 30 Ausf. D1, 45 Ausf.E and 130 Ausf.H.[28] The majority of the Kl.Pz.Bef.Wg command tanks, in pace with their replacement by the Pz.Bef.Wg, were sent to the artillery regiments of the panzer divisions as combat vehicles for artillery spotters even before the victory over France.

The Wehrmacht didn't have any infantry support tanks at all, but in order to aid their soldiers on the attack, Germany created a totally new means of conducting battle – self-propelled 'assault guns'. Their originator was Colonel von Manstein, the future Feldmarschall, who advanced this idea of a new weapon back in 1935, and who conceived the name for them that was more suitable than all others – Sturmgeschütz, or assault gun (it officially acquired this name on 28 March 1940). Later, in a memorandum addressed to L. Beck, Chief of Staff of the OKH, on 8 June 1936, he proposed introducing a three-battery battalion of armoured assault guns in each infantry division, which would be responsible for offering direct support for the infantry, and at the same time formulated a fundamental difference in their tactics from the tactics of the panzers: '… the Sturmartillerie should not be utilized in the sphere of armour units, but rather in that of the normal Infantry Division. A clean separation of the two branches is necessary if the two do not want to operate according to the improper doctrine. The Sturmartillerie is to be trained as Artillery units and will have to learn their mission as escort batteries in the environment of the Infanterie.'[29]

Their low profile made the assault guns hard to spot on the battlefield, while their full armour – significantly thick for the time – made them difficult targets to knock out. Taken together, this enabled them to operate effectively at the spearhead of the attack, and, in the event of necessity, to perform in an anti-tank role. The main gun of their first modifications was the short-barrelled 75mm L/24 cannon, analogous in ballistics to the main gun that equipped the Pz.Kpfw.IV medium tank. Its shells were sufficiently effective to combat not only enemy infantry and their weapons but also contemporary tanks, the majority of which were lightly armoured. Von Manstein's sensible idea was welcomed, and within a week after the aforementioned memorandum, the fruits of his inspiration were officially ordered. The Krupp company was given the responsibility to develop the gun, while Daimler-Benz was to build chassis on the basis of its Pz.Kpfw. III tank with a new superstructure. A test batch of five vehicles was to come out in the following year. The first four of them (with wooden superstructures and without weapons) were supposed to appear in April and May, and the last, fully armoured and with a cannon, in July 1937. However, because of known problems with the base-type, the production and finishing of the new combat vehicles were repeatedly postponed for a long time. As a result, only in October 1939 did Daimler-Benz complete the assembly of the pilot batch that had been ordered, with superstructures made from soft steel plate on the basis of the Pz.Kpfw.III Ausf.B. None of these first five assault guns ever saw a battlefield, but all were used only for testing, as well as for instruction and training the crews. Finally, on 13 October 1939, Daimler-Benz received an order for a series of 30 vehicles, which were delivered between December 1939 and April 1940. The first four batteries, consisting of six assault guns each, participated in the French campaign of 1940. The last six assault guns of the first series went to the SS Regiment *Leibstandarte Adolf Hitler*, but they didn't have enough time to take part in the fighting before the campaign ended.[30]

The subsequent series of assault guns were ordered from the Alkett company, since Daimler-Benz was totally consumed with the production of tanks. Up to the end of June 1941 it managed to produce another 20 assault guns of modifications Ausf.A, 300 Ausf.B, 50 Ausf.C and 59 Ausf.D (*see* Plate 7).[31]

In essence, the German assault guns were turretless tanks, and not simply guns on self-propelled carriages. Because of the lack of a pivoting turret, they didn't of course possess such quick weapon manoeuvrability as the tanks had, but they weren't inferior to them in mobility and were superior to them in protection, having a compact silhouette and 50mm of frontal armour from the very outset of their production. In terms of the firepower of their main gun, the assault guns assuredly surpassed the Pz.Kpfw.III on which their production had been based, but were about 20 per cent cheaper to produce. During a prolonged war of attrition, their low cost was a very important advantage, so the output of assault guns in Germany continually grew and in 1945 even exceeded the production of tanks.

In the course of the victorious campaigns in 1939–1940, the Germans managed to capture an enormous amount of war booty, including thousands of combat vehicles. However, only a very insignificant portion of them went to arm the Wehrmacht. The legitimate question inevitably arises: Why did such efficient stewards as the Germans not make full use of these spoils of war? There were important reasons for this. We'll begin with the fact that the Wehrmacht had to acquire most of these vehicles through combat, so a significant number of them were damaged or had been completely destroyed.

For example, of all the British and French tanks that were activated for the campaign in the West in May–June 1940, only a little more than half acquired by the Germans were suitable for use.[32] Let's attempt to take a more detailed look into how many and where the captured Polish, French and British tanks were used in the Wehrmacht in reality.

In Poland the Germans obtained 111 tanks and tankettes that were suitable for repair. Eight Pz.Kpfw.(3.7cm)(p) – former Polish 7TP tanks – for a certain amount of time served in German panzer divisions: three in the 1st Panzer Division, three in the 4th Panzer Division, and two in the 6th Panzer Division. The 'Warsaw' Company that was equipped with these tanks and TKS tankettes on 12 June 1940, on 3 September of the same year was relabelled as the light Panzer Company 'Ost', and on 6 October it took part in a commemorative parade in the Polish capital that was occupied by the Germans. Another company consisting of 21 Pz.Kpfw.(3.7cm)(p) tanks was formed by an order dated 12 May 1941 and included in the Führer-Begleit-Bataillon (Führer Escort Battalion). However, just days before the start of Operation Barbarossa, all of its Polish tanks were sent to a military stockpile in Magdeburg, having been replaced by Czech Pz.Kpfw.38(t). Only the Polish tankettes throughout the war served in rear units and Luftwaffe security forces on Polish territory.[33]

In the West the Germans captured a total of 4,930 tracked combat vehicles of various types, including prime movers, that were suitable for use and got a programme up and running in order to restore them to operating condition and convert them to their needs. The lion's share of this equipment was of French manufacture. According to contemporary assessments, approximately 500 Renault FT-17/18, 800 Renault R-35/40, 600 Hotchkiss H-35/39, 50 FCM-36, 300 Samua S-35, and 160 Renault B1 and B1bis tanks fell into the German hands.[34] Of this total, by the beginning of 1942 approximately 500 FT-17/18, 125 R-35, 200 H-35/39 and 20 S-35 tanks had been repaired, and around another 400 H-35/39 and 120 S-35 tanks were equipped with German radio sets and split hatches for their commanders. In addition, a German commander's cupola was added to some of the S-35 tanks.[35] Between May and October 1941, 200 R-35 tanks were converted into anti-tank self-propelled guns by means of replacing their turrets with 47mm Czech cannons protected by front and side shields.[36]

Initially, the impressive piles of captured French weapons and combat vehicles gave rise to Hitler's brightest hopes. As early as 30 August 1940 General-Major Walther Buhle brought Hitler's demand to the attention of Germany's Chief of the OKH Staff Halder: 'Equip four panzer divisions with captured French tanks for carrying out occupation tasks.'[37] However, the matter never reached this level and the real scale of Germany's use of captured tanks in their designated role was far more restricted. This was in fact natural, because after all it isn't as simple to use foreign tanks as it might seem at first glance. For example, it is necessary to ensure their constant resupply with special ammunition, spare parts, tools, accessories, and the appropriate fuel and lubricants, which often differed from those used in Germany. At the same time it is necessary to create a system of service, maintenance and repair for the captured tanks; train their crews and mechanics in the proper manner; teach the troops to recognize them quickly from a distance without mistake; and so on. In addition to all these factors, the majority of combat vehicles of foreign manufacture didn't meet the German tactical requirements. Their modification to bring them up to the Wehrmacht's standards required a large expenditure of time and resources, so therefore they were used primarily as chassis for self-propelled guns and rocket launchers, prime movers, and ammunition carriers.

Captured tanks were used at times when building armoured trains. They were placed on railway platform cars, turning them in this manner into armoured gun mounts, which had the possibility of driving off the platform car onto the ground in order to support the actions of disembarking infantry. At the end of May 1941 Armoured Trains Nos.26, 27 and 28 each received three French S-35 tanks, while Armoured Trains Nos.29, 30 and 31 received two each. All took part in the fighting on the Eastern Front from the very beginning of the war.[38] Sometimes captured tanks were encountered in permanent fortifications as fixed firing positions. However, most of them were simply shot up on firing grounds as targets for the training of German artillery gunners, tankers and pilots.

The Germans turned over an insignificant number of these captured tanks to their allies. For example, Italy in 1940 received 109 French R-35 tanks, and the following year 32 S-35.[39] After Bulgaria joined the Tripartite Pact on 23 April 1941 the Germans gave it 40 R-35, and an additional 19

H–39 tanks in March 1944.[40] In 1943 Hungary acquired 2 S–35 and 15 H–39 in Germany. According to some evidence, several H–39 tanks reached Croatia.[41] That, respectively, was all.

Germany's Romanian allies in September 1939 interned 34 French-built R–35 tanks, which had crossed its border after the defeat of the Polish Army. Previously Romania had had time to import 41 such tanks from France of the 200 they had ordered, but after the war started these deliveries ceased.[42] The use of the French tanks by the Romanians during the Second World War did not go beyond these vehicles.

The Germans used only a limited number of captured tanks in their designated role, preferring to use them for auxiliary functions. For example, before November 1941, 250 former French FT-17/18, 30 R–35 and 60 H–35/39 tanks arrived to arm SS security units. In February 1941 I/Panzer Regiment 202 was equipped with 18 S–35 and 41 H–38, and, after the crews mastered the new equipment, in September of the same year they were sent to Yugoslavia in order to fight the partisans. Four months earlier 30 FT-17/18 had been sent to the same place for the same purpose. In May 1941 the training of 100 crews of these tanks began in order to guard important military factories in Germany and Czechoslovakia. Another 100 FT-17/18 at the same time were designated to defend the English Channel coastline against invasion forces, but their hulls and turrets were soon used to build stationary coastal fortifications. The next 100 FT-17/18 armed with machine guns in the same month of May 1941 were handed over to the Luftwaffe; in March 1943, 25 of them were serving in Holland, 30 in Belgium and northern France and 45 more in western France. They did not only guard airfields, but were also put to work as snowploughs in the winter to clear the runways. Initially 20 FT-17 and 10 H–35/39 were designated for occupation service in Crete, but in the autumn of 1941 the 212th Separate Panzer Battalion, which was equipped with 5 S–35 and 15 H–38, was shipped to the island instead of them.[43]

One can cite more examples of the use of captured French armour in the Wehrmacht, but even without them it is clear that it was of an extremely limited and primarily auxiliary nature. It is interesting that the Germans made the broadest use of the French FT-17/18 tanks, which had been produced during the First World War. However, even these hopelessly outdated veterans were suitable to carry out the simple and unimportant tasks they were given. In addition, the FT-17/18 tanks were extremely easy to repair and operate, and their small size and low weight allowed them to be transported in heavy lorries in order to prolong their service life.

Perhaps the best known example of the German use of captured tanks in Operation Barbarossa was the conversion of 60 French B1 and B1bis tanks into flame-throwing tanks. In the process of modifying them, the 75mm gun in the hull was replaced by a flamethrower, capable of spraying 80 bursts of flammable oil of 2–3 seconds' duration to a range of up to 30 metres. As part of 102nd Separate Flammpanzer Battalion, 24 of these flame-throwing tanks, together with six of their ordinary types, which received the designation Pz.Kpfw.B2 in the Wehrmacht, took part in the breakthrough of the Rava-Russky Fortified Sector 70 kilometres northwest of Lvov. However, they didn't serve in combat for very long. As early as 17 July an order came out about disbanding this battalion, and by 8 August this process was complete. Apparently the German command didn't consider the battalion's actions to be very successful. This should have been expected, because it had received its tanks only on 20 June and just three days later arrived at the front. The tankers, of course, didn't have enough time to master the unfamiliar vehicles and to acquire experience in servicing them. As a result, they frequently broke down due to mechanical problems. In addition, half of the tanks, which had been converted in great haste, didn't have radio communication. Moreover their flamethrowers, as it turned out, left much to be desired, so they were quickly replaced by other flamethrowers which had 1.5 times more range and a 2.5 times larger reserve of incendiary fuel.[44] For the record, the flame-throwing Pz.Kpfw.B2, as well as the German-produced Pz.Kpfw. II (Flamm), were considered by the Germans not as tanks but as specialized combat vehicles, and so they weren't part of their panzer divisions.

Only in the North did the Wehrmacht make an exception to the general rule: there German panzers fought not as divisions but as two separate panzer battalions, 40th and 211th. This was determined by the specific conditions of the northern theatre of operations, its remoteness and the hardship of using large masses of panzers because most of the terrain was impassable for tanks, and the unfavourable weather conditions. The 211th Panzer Battalion was armed with captured French tanks.[45] In the course of the war, in connection with the heavy losses in armour, the Germans resumed attempts to use French combat vehicles, but only in insignificant numbers and on secondary sectors of the front.

In May–June 1940 the Germans captured approximately 345 operational British tanks.[46] However, whereas the repair of the Polish and French combat vehicles and the production of spare parts for them could still somehow be resumed in the captured factories in these countries, this wasn't a possibility for the captured British tanks. Ammunition for them was particularly lacking. Therefore after testing to reveal their combat capabilities, they were used primarily as teaching aids in anti-tank gunners' schools or as targets on firing ranges. On the Eastern Front only a single company of British A13 Cruiser tanks, consisting of nine vehicles, fought as part of the 100th Separate Flammpanzer Battalion. They lasted for less than three weeks of fighting, after which they were written off as total losses.[47]

Other than panzers of German production, only Czech-manufactured tanks were widely used in the Wehrmacht, so it is therefore necessary to dwell on them. It is known that even before and during the First World War Czech factories were the main weapons manufacturers of the Austro-Hungarian Empire. Heavy siege guns, produced in the Czech Škoda factory, took part in shelling Belgian forts and the French fortress of Verdun. Before the Second World War Škoda was the second-leading producer of weapons in Europe. The Czechs had a lengthy and well deserved reputation as producers of high-quality armaments – rifles, artillery and armoured fighting vehicles – which they then sold to many countries, including the United Kingdom, Germany, Switzerland, Sweden and the USSR.

In 1931 Škoda built the first prototype of the MU-2 tankette, which was created under the obvious influence of the popular design of Vickers-Armstrongs' Carden-Loyd Mk. VI tankette. A year earlier the Czech ČKD company, which had the same British prototype, produced the P-1 tankette, and from 23 April 1934 to 17 August 1936 it delivered to the Czechoslovakian Army 50 light LT vz.34 (*Lehký Tank vzor 34*, or Light Tank Model 34) tanks. However, the first genuinely successful tank model was designed by the Škoda company by the summer of 1935. The Czechoslovakian Army accepted it under the designation 'LT vz.35' (Light Tank Model 35). As early as 30 October of the same year Czechoslovakia's

Ministry of Defence ordered 160 such tanks, and a total of 298 of them were built and purchased. They all went to equip the Czechoslovakian Army in the period between 21 December 1936 and 8 April 1938. Incidentally, according to an agreement, exactly half of them were produced by the ČKD company, Škoda's rival in the competition to create this tank. Advanced for its time, the LT vz.35 deservedly prompted large interest in it in several countries simultaneously, including the United Kingdom. In 1937–1939, 126 of these tanks were exported to Romania, and another 10 to Bulgaria in early 1941.[48]

At the time the USSR also conducted negotiations about purchasing it. Two examples of this tank successfully passed a broad and elaborate programme of testing on the Moscow-area proving ground in Kubinka between 14 September and 11 October 1938, covering over 1500 kilometres during this time without any substantial breakdowns. Nevertheless, an agreement couldn't be reached, even though the LT vz.35 made a most favourable impression on the Soviet experts. The point was that they only wanted to acquire one tank. The Czechs quite sensibly suspected that with this model, serial reproduction of it might be got up and running in the Soviet Union so they proposed to Moscow to purchase a licence for their production. As a result, the talks fell apart without an agreement, but the tank nevertheless served the cause of developing domestic tank design in the USSR. Soviet engineers sought by hook or by crook to find out more secrets of its design and the manufacturing procedures used to produce it. So one of them, N.F. Shashmurin, who later became one of the prominent designers of Soviet heavy tanks, received an assignment to get his hands on a sample of the Czech armour, in order to analyse its composition. It didn't seem possible to carve out a piece of the tank unnoticed, but the resourceful young engineer nevertheless contrived a way to solve the problem. According to his sketch, an accurate copy of the armoured cap of the fuel tank filler neck was crafted. They managed stealthily to replace the original with the copy, and sent it to a laboratory for analysis.[49]

However, the matter didn't end there. Examples of contemporary Western military equipment very rarely fell into the hands of the USSR, so in order to study them a special operation was conducted. Throughout the entire period of testing, in daylight hours the tanks were continuously accompanied by the representatives of the Škoda company who arrived with them, but during the night they were left in one of the hangers on the proving ground under the guard of Red Army soldiers. However, under the cover of darkness the sentries, at the order of the USSR People's Commissar of Defence K.E. Voroshilov, allowed a group of engineers from factories Nos 185 and 37 to enter the hangar and examine the LT vz.35 thoroughly. It was decided on the basis of the obtained information to use the tank's most successful features for future Soviet tank designs, including the suspension, transmission, steering drive, optical devices, gun sights and internal signalling device.[50] As will be shown below, some elements of the LT vz.35 design were used in the preliminary design of the heavy KV-1 tank.[51]

In the summer of 1939 the design bureau of the Leningrad Experimental Machine-building Factory No. 185, under the leadership of S.A. Ginzburg, worked out a design for the T-26M light tank. One of the designers' main goals was to reinforce the running gear of the mass-produced T-26, which because of its increasing weight over the years was working at the limit of its capabilities. At the same time the smoothness of the tank's motion was deteriorating, and its tracks were frequently thrown off when on the move, particularly during turns. The prototype T-26M, equipped with a suspension that was based on a slightly reworked design of the LT vz.35 tank's suspension, during trials covered 655 kilometres at an average speed of approximately 27 km/hr. The commission that conducted the testing came to the following conclusions: 'The running gear of the T-26M is strong, reliable and significantly improves the smoothness of movement, which also permits the use on the tank of a more powerful engine. The tracks are secured from being thrown, including during turns on slopes with an angle of up to 40 degrees, which is impossible on other tanks.'[52] All these remarks can be rightly addressed to the LT vz.35 as well.

A distinctive feature of the LT vz.35 was its pneumatic, power-assisted steering. The driver engaged the steering mechanism, clutch and brakes not directly but through valves that controlled the pneumatic actuators. As a result, significantly less effort was needed to drive the tank. For example, without the assistance of the compressed air, 65 kg of force had to be applied to the steering levers, but with it only 20 kg of force. The system of pneumatic boosters was rather complicated, but in normal conditions worked quite reliably. However, extremely cold temperatures knocked it out of action. The 37mm main gun of this tank was approximately equal to the armour-penetrating capability of the German 37mm tank gun, while its 25mm of frontal armour couldn't be penetrated by armour-piercing shells from the Oerlikon 20mm cannon from 250 metres and more.[53]

In March 1939 two LT vz.35 tanks were captured by the Hungarians, while another 52 wound up in Slovakia after Czechoslovakia broke apart. Thus, having occupied Bohemia and Moravia, the Germans acquired 244 LT vz.35 tanks, together with the other combat equipment of the Czechoslovakian Army. On 1 September 1939 202 of them were serviceable. They were given the name in the Wehrmacht of Pz.Kpfw.35(t) (*see* Plate 8).[54] The letter 't' in the designation was an abbreviation of the German word 'tschechisch', which in translation meant Czech, while the number '35' represented the year they were accepted to arm the Czechoslovakian Army. On the basis of this designation, some pseudo-experts declared it as a 35-ton tank, even though it weighed only 10.5 tons.

In order to bring the Czech tanks closer to their own standards, the Germans made several enhancements to the design. The most substantial were the addition of a fourth crew member – a loader; the replacement of the Czech-made radio set, which was capable of operating only in telegraph mode, with a German type that provided telephone-style communication; and the installation of an internal intercom system.

Ordinary tanks obtained just a Fu2 receiver while platoon commanders' tanks got a Fu5 radio set. The company and battalion commanders' tanks had both a Fu2 and a Fu5, which was installed in place of the forward machine guns. On the command panzers at the regimental level a Fu5 was complemented with a more powerful Fu8 radio set, but for this it was necessary to sacrifice the main gun, which was replaced by a dummy barrel. In addition, each of the command Pz.Kpfw.35(t) was equipped with a gyrocompass.[55] All of the Pz.Kpfw.35(t) tanks without exception went to the 1st Light Division, which was subsequently reformed into the 6th Panzer Division.

The utilization of the LT vz.35 in the Czechoslovakian Army revealed not only its merits, but also its shortcomings, such as its low speed in rough terrain because of its outdated Vickers-type bogie suspension, inadequate range, and cramped fighting compartment. It wasn't possible to correct these problems on the existing vehicles, so on 20 November 1937 a competition to create a new light tank was once again announced in Czechoslovakia. Its culmination was proving-ground tests, which began on 19 January 1938 and lasted over three months. The TNHPS' prototype produced by the ČKD company emerged as a convincing winner of the field trials by covering 5,584 kilometres (1,954 of them across rough terrain) without a single serious malfunction. After its service introduction, it received the official designation LT vz.38. The first 150 new tanks were ordered on 22 July 1938. The final tank of this series was accepted for military service on 23 November 1939. However, Germany occupied the Czech Republic on 15 March 1939, about two months before the first LT vz.38 tanks left the factory gates. They all entered service in the Wehrmacht and received the designation Pz.Kpfw.38(t) (*see* Plate 9).

Its chief designer was the Russian emigrant Aleksei Mikhailovich Surin. He took part in the Russian Civil War on the side of the Whites, and after their defeat he fled across the border and found work in the ČKD plant. He managed to create a model of a light tank that was outstanding for its time: compact, reliable and low-maintenance, with excellent cross-country performance and a harmonious combination of protection, armament and mobility. The best evidence of this is the fact that the tank itself (and combat vehicles that were created on its basis) remained in production for 12 years – an enviable record for those times. Surin used the most advanced components for the powertrain of his tank: a licence was purchased from the British Rolls-Royce company for a five-speed planetary transmission and a 6-cylinder 125 horsepower engine had Swedish origin, from the Scania company.[56] It is interesting that the Pz.Kpfw.38(t) was equipped with the so-called pre-selector gearbox, which shifted gear in the same way as the 10-speed transmission of the Pz.Kpfw.III. In the process of operation it also created the same problems for the driver as the German transmission.

By the end of the first half of 1941 the Czechs had manufactured a total of 860 of these tanks. The 260 tanks of the first two series – the Ausf.A and B – that were produced before May 1940 had 25mm of face-hardened frontal armour. In the course of producing the 110 tanks of the Ausf.C series, built until the end of August 1940, the frontal hull armour was increased to 40mm. This was kept for the Ausf.D vehicles, of which 105 were manufactured from September to November 1940. In the subsequent Ausf.E series of 275 tanks built until May 1941, the thickness of the front hull and turret armour was increased to 50mm with the installation of supplementary 25mm face-hardened plates. The same frontal armour equipped 250 tanks of the Ansf.F and 90 tanks of the Ausf.S series, which went into production in May 1941. The Germans made a number of adaptations to the Pz.Kpfw.38(t) to meet their requirements, analogous to those they had made to the Pz.Kpfw.35(t). This also concerned the command tanks created on its basis.[57]

In 1941 the Pz.Kpfw.38(t) armed five German panzer divisions: the 7th, 8th, 12th, 19th and 20th. The Czech combat vehicles played a prominent role in the 1941 fighting on the Eastern Front. Indeed this isn't surprising, since they comprised at the time more than a third of all the Wehrmacht's tanks on the Eastern Front, armed with a gun of at least 37mm calibre. Furthermore, the cannon mounted in the Pz.Kptw.38(t) at the same calibre was approximately 20 per cent superior to the German 37mm gun in armour-penetration capability due to the heavier armour-piercing shells it fired with slightly higher muzzle velocity. The distinctive feature of both Pz.Kpfw.35(t) and Pz.Kpfw.38(t) tanks was the machine-gun ball mount in the turret. It could be used either coupled with the cannon or pivoted independently from it in the range of 15° horizontally.[58]

The Czech light tanks were rightly considered some of the best combat vehicles of their class during the Second World War. This particularly relates to the Pz.Kpfw.38(t). However, despite all their doubtless qualities, they still didn't reach the level of German medium tanks, the role which they had to take because of the lack of the latter in the Wehrmacht. They also had substantial shortcomings, on which we will comment later. The chief one of these was that the Pz.Kpfw.35(t) and Pz.Kpfw.38(t) inherited organic flaws of light tanks such as limited size and weight. Because of this their commanders had to combine their main duties with the functions of the gun layers, while the available reserve for increasing its firepower and armour protection were plainly insufficient for keeping them long in production in the course of the war. That is why the last Pz.Kpfw.38(t) tanks left the factory assembly line within a year after Germany's invasion of the USSR. Nonetheless, a variety of combat vehicles on its chassis continued serial production until the very end of the war and even afterward.

Chapter 5

German Panzers in Combat

German panzers received their baptism of fire in the Spanish Civil War, in which 102 ordinary Pz.Kpfw.I and 4 command Kl.Pz.Beg.Wg. took part. There they encountered the T-26 and BT-5 tanks of Soviet production, which were armed with 45mm cannons. The machine guns of the German panzers were able to penetrate the armour of these adversaries with armour-piercing bullets only at close ranges of up to 120–150 metres. At a greater distance, the only thing left for the Pz.Kpfw.I to do was to dodge the shells fired by enemy tanks with vigorous manoeuvring, or to find cover quickly, or simply get away by fleeing. In order to give the Pz.Kpfw.I units the chance to fight on more even terms with the much better armed Republicans' tanks, each company of them had five anti-tank guns attached to it. In the autumn of 1938, in both of the tank battalions of three-company composition available to Franco's forces, one of the companies was armed with captured Soviet tanks that were equipped with cannons.[1]

On 20 April 1937 an article about the experience of the Spanish Civil War appeared in the French newspaper *L'Intransigeant*. In particular, it stated:

> The German tanks were a major disappointment (a two-man crew, 50 kilometres per hour, two machine guns, almost worthless armour). No defence against the fire of enemy anti-tank guns or against bullets from hand-held weapons. This experience gives the German high command a real case to reconsider.
>
> The German Panzer division has failed before it was even put into service.
>
> French tanks, slower but much better protected, remain 'King of the Battlefield'.[2]

Just three years later the Wehrmacht's virtually unstoppable panzer wedges convincingly demonstrated to the French the error of this point of view. Its authors simply didn't realize that the use of the Pz.Kpfw.I in Spain wasn't at all a test of the German principles of employing panzer divisions. In the first place, they were too few for this purpose and operated in groups of not more than company size, accompanying infantry on the battlefield as mobile armoured firing positions. Such a tactic had nothing at all to do with the full panoply of panzers in the panzer divisions, where they would closely cooperate with all types of forces.

The blitzkrieg tactic was demonstrated in practice for the first time during Germany's invasion of Poland in September 1939. On the eve of this event, the Wehrmacht was armed with 3,472 tanks, including 1,445 Pz.Kpfw.I, 1,223 Pz.Kpfw.II, 202 Pz.Kpfw.35(t), 78 Pz.Kpfw.38(t), 98 Pz.Kpfw.III, 211 Pz.Kpfw.IV and 215 command tanks. The Germans deployed against the Poles all of the combat-ready armoured formations and units available at the time: seven panzer divisions, two of which hadn't yet had time to fully form, as well as four light divisions, one separate panzer regiment and one separate panzer battalion.[3] The numbers and types of available panzers in their divisions, regiments and battalions is shown in Table 1.

The Polish forces opposing them possessed 2 armoured motorized brigades; 3 separate tank battalions of the High Command's reserve; 11 groups of tankettes that were attached to the cavalry brigades; 15 separate companies of tankettes, 14 of which were subordinate to infantry divisions and 1 to a cavalry brigade; and 3 more reserve companies armed with the hopelessly outdated FT-17 light tanks from the period of the First World War. Altogether they numbered 325 light tanks, including 102 FT-17, and 574 tankettes, but only 475 Polish combat vehicles were operational.[4]

A similar picture emerges with the other services and branches of the armed forces of the opposing sides. It isn't surprising, given such an imbalance of forces, that the fighting ended in Germany's rapid and convincing victory. Together with the Luftwaffe, it was secured primarily by the panzer and motorized divisions and units, which comprised just a quarter of all the German divisions that were activated for the campaign in Poland. The XVI and XIX Motorized Corps achieved the greatest success in the campaign; their panzer divisions weren't scattered in pieces in several directions, but were used instead as powerful shock fists. Guderian's XIX Motorized Corps particularly stood out; it was at this time that Guderian began to earn his

Table 1: Numbers and types of tanks in the German formations and units on 1 September 1939.

Division	Rgt. or battalion	Panzerkampfwagen							Total
		I	II	35(t)	38(t)	III	IV	Command	
1st Panzer	Pz. Rgts. 1 and 2	93	122			26	56	12	309
2nd Panzer	Pz. Rgts. 3 and 4	124	155			6	17	20	322
3rd Panzer	Pz. Rgts. 5 and 6, Training battalion	122	176			43	32	18	391
4th Panzer	Pz. Rgts. 35 and 36	183	130				12	16	341
5th Panzer	Pz. Rgts. 15 and 31	152	144			3	14	22	335
Kempf	Pz. Rgt. 7	61	81			3	9	10	164
10th Panzer	Pz. Rgt. 8	57	74			3	7	9	150
1st Light	Pz. Rgt. 11 and 65th Pz. Battalion		65	112			41	8	226
2nd Light	66th Pz. Battalion	41	42					2	85
3rd Light	67th Pz. Battalion		23	55				2	80
4th Light	33rd Pz. Battalion	34	23					5	62
–	Pz. Rgt. 25	78	58				6	9	151
–	1st Pz. Battalion of Pz. Rgt. 10	28	34			3	4	5	74
Total		973	1,127	112	55	87	198	138	2,690

Source: T.L. Jentz, *Panzertruppen: The Complete Guide to the Creation & Combat Employment of Germany's Tank Force, 1933–1942* (Atglen, PA: Schiffer Publishing Ltd, 1996), pp. 90–1.

reputation and the nickname 'Der schnelle Heinz' ('Fast Heinz'). His corps initially consisted of the 3rd Panzer and 2nd and 20th Motorized Divisions. After the successful destruction of the enemy forces in the 'Polish corridor', the 10th Panzer Division was also placed under his command. With these forces Guderian broke through to Brest and captured it on 14 September 1939. Over 10 days of active operations, the XIX Motorized Corps advanced 320 kilometres in combat, while losing only 2,236 men, including 650 killed, 1,345 wounded and 241 missing in action, which amounted to a casualty rate of less than 4 per cent of Guderian's men.[5] The Germans positively evaluated the impressive successes of their mobile formations. It isn't a coincidence that four motorized corps were activated for the campaign in the West in May–June 1940, and played a decisive role in the Wehrmacht's victory in France, thus becoming the prototype for the future panzer corps.

At the same time, however, in the course of the fighting serious shortcomings also emerged in the organization of the German panzer forces. Two different types of their formations were operating in Poland: panzer and light divisions. The latter from the beginning were conceived in order to replace the cavalry, which had lost their former significance under the pressure of inexorable technological progress. The cavalry had been considered a privileged type of force in Germany, in which German aristocrats had traditionally preferred to serve ever since the time of medieval knights. They didn't want the cavalry to disappear without a trace in the grey mass of army troops and attempted to preserve its place in the so-called light divisions. However, these artificial constructs didn't last long in the Wehrmacht, because their organic defects were apparent from the moment of their appearance. First of all, they didn't correspond to the basic German principle of concentrating combat vehicles, and because of this they were substantially inferior to the panzer divisions in shock power and combat resilience. Therefore, even before the start of the Polish campaign it had been decided to reform them into regular panzer divisions while simultaneously increasing their number of combat vehicles. However, this didn't happen until after the conclusion of the campaign. On 16 October 1939 the 3rd Light Division was reorganized into the 8th Panzer Division, and two days later the 1st and 2nd Light Divisions became the 6th and 7th Panzer Divisions respectively. The 4th Light Division was converted into the 9th Panzer Division on 3 January 1940. The 5th Light

Division, which had been hastily created on 18 February 1941 especially for the African campaign, was unique. From the beginning it had a full panzer regiment under its command, and less than half a year after its creation, on 1 August 1941, it was reformed into the 21st Panzer Division.[6]

The intensive combat operations in Poland revealed that the panzer divisions of the initial organization had too many panzers and not enough infantry, which were necessary to support them in battle. Taking recent experience into account, their tables of organization were adjusted, and the number of authorized panzers fell by almost a quarter. The German motorized divisions in Poland also showed themselves to be too cumbersome and difficult to control for mobile warfare, so one of their motorized regiments was stripped from them and went to newly forming divisions. In order to improve command and control of the mobile troops, Guderian recommended that the commanders and headquarters staff of the panzer battalions and regiments be kept closer to the combat formations of their forces. This gave them a better view of the battlefield and enabled them to react more efficiently to a rapidly changing situation. In order to increase mobility, headquarters was supposed to move in armoured vehicles and to have reliable radio communications.

The Wehrmacht's equipment in the course of the Polish campaign showed itself to be far less impressive than its tactics and operational skill. All of the German panzers from the beginning had only light armour that protected them from bullets. They had to rely on speed and manoeuvre as their main defence on the battlefield, but this proved plainly insufficient. As a result, over a month of fighting 819 German panzers – more than 30 per cent of their total number at the start of the campaign – were lost, 236 of them irrecoverably: 89 Pz.Kpfw.I, 83 Pz.Kpfw.II, 7 Pz.Kpfw.35(t), 7 Pz.Kpfw.38(t), 26 Pz.Kpfw.III, 19 Pz.Kpfw.IV and 5 command tanks.[7] The unexpectedly high panzer losses in the war and the high rate of mechanical breakdowns placed a heavy burden on the German system of service and repair, and it began to choke up. There was an acute deficit of spare parts and qualified mechanics, and in order to correct the situation the Third Reich's military industry had to be involved. As a result, after the victory in Poland Germany's tank factories were so burdened with repairing panzers that had been damaged in combat that in November the production of new tanks sharply fell, and this continued until the end of the year. For example, in September 1939 the German factories produced 83 new tanks, and in October 108, but in November only 67 left the assembly lines, followed in December by 63. The situation only turned around in January 1940, when 76 new tanks were produced, followed by 92 in February and 96 in March.[8]

The Polish anti-tank rifles proved to be a more dangerous adversary for the panzers than had seemed likely before the war, so the Germans undertook the production of an analogous weapon, while simultaneously strengthening the protection of their panzers. The Pz.Kpfw.I had no capacity for additional armour, so they gradually began to be converted into ammunition carriers and self-propelled guns. An additional 20mm of armour plating was installed on the front of the hull and turret of the Pz.Kpfw.II in February and March 1940.[9] The frontal armour of the Pz.Kpfw.III and Pz.Kpfw.IV tanks that were already in the process of being built had already been thickened to 30mm.

In the interval between the campaigns in Poland and the West, Germany wasted no time. In this period the quantity of the latest combat equipment substantially grew in the Wehrmacht. For example, the number of panzers armed with cannons of 37mm or greater calibre more than doubled. The sharp increase in the level of the troops' preparation, thanks to their ceaseless, intensive combat training, was of even greater significance. A clear example of this is the 6th Panzer Division. At the beginning of spring 1940 it rehearsed the intended crossing of the Maas (Meuse) River several times, using the Lahn River in the area of Limburg. At the end of April all of its tracked vehicles crossed the Rhine River in the Mayen area for training purposes.[10] Meanwhile the French Army, in contrast, because of a prolonged period of inactivity, gradually lost its former operating proficiency. In the course of the eight-month period of the 'Phony War', French soldiers spent most of the time in boredom, distracted only by building fortifications or assisting local farmers. Such 'exercises' did nothing to contribute to their combat spirit or military prowess.

On 1 May 1940 the Wehrmacht had 3,465 panzers. This number consisted of 1,077 Pz.Kpfw.I, 1,092 Pz.Kpfw.II, 143 Pz.Kpfw.35(t), 238 Pz.Kpfw.38(t), 381 Pz.Kpfw.III, 290 Pz.Kpfw.IV and 244 command tanks.[11] The lion's share of this total was activated for the campaign in the West, which started on 10 May 1940. Table 2 shows the distribution of combat

Table 2: Numbers and types of tanks in the German formations and units on 10 May 1940.

Division	Regiment	Panzerkampfwagen							Total
		I	II	35(t)	38(t)	III	IV	Command	
1st Panzer	Pz.Rgts.1 and 2	52	98			58	40	8	256
2nd Panzer	Pz.Rgts. 3 and 4	45	115			58	32	16	266
3rd Panzer	Pz.Rgts. 5 and 6	117	129			42	26	27	341
4th Panzer	Pz.Rgts. 35 and 36	135	105			40	24	10	314
5th Panzer	Pz.Rgts. 15 and 31	97	120			52	32	26	327
6th Panzer	Pz. Rgt. 11		60	118			31	14	223
7th Panzer	Pz.Rgt. 25	34	68		91		24	8	225
8th Panzer	Pz.Rgt. 10		58		116		23	15	212
9th Panzer	Pz.Rgt. 33	30	54			41	16	12	153
10th Panzer	Pz.Rgts. 7 and 8	44	113			58	32	18	265
Total:		554	920	118	207	349	280	154	2,582

Source: T.L. Jentz, *Panzertruppen: The Complete Guide to the Creation & Combat Employment of Germany's Tank Force, 1933–1942* (Atglen, PA: Schiffer Publishing Ltd, 1996), pp. 120–1.

vehicles by type across the Wehrmacht's panzer divisions on the Western Front on the eve of the German offensive.

The Allies opposed them with 3,254 French, 310 British and 270 Belgian tanks, which gave them one-and-a-half times numerical superiority in these combat vehicles.[12] In a comparison of the materiel of the armoured forces of both sides, it is apparent that the French tanks, as a rule, were noticeably superior to the German panzers in armour protection, but inferior to them in mobility and radio equipment. However, their main shortcoming was the unsatisfactory functional allocation of the crew members' duties. The commander of a French tank sat in a one-man turret, and he had to work simultaneously as a loader, gunner and radio operator. This had an adverse impact on his ability to carry out his main responsibilities of directing the crew and following the constantly changing situation on the battlefield. Meanwhile, the Germans, in addition to the commander, had a gunner and a loader in the turret of their medium tanks, while a radio operator handled communications. This provided them with substantial tactical advantages in combat, including significantly better cooperation, target indication and rate of fire. Thus the Wehrmacht's tankers more frequently had success in their armoured clashes with the enemy, despite the latter's superiority in armour protection. The German panzer cannons and anti-tank guns in the majority of cases were unable to penetrate the armour of the enemy's combat vehicles, while the light Pz.Kpfw.I and Pz.Kpfw.II proved to be useless in tank battles and were usually kept in the rear or on the flanks of the combat formations. The Germans usually prevailed thanks to their superiority in radio communications and the presence of tank commanders, who were freed from any other responsibility and thus able to operate in a much more coordinated fashion than were the French. They often managed to create a local superiority in force, to close to within short range of the enemy and fire at them from the flanks and rear, and ultimately to find a vulnerable spot in their defences. As a result, the field of battle was often left in the possession of the German tankers.

However, the most fatal weakness of France's armoured forces was not the design shortcomings of their combat vehicles but their ineffective organization. This country sent to the front a total of 3,347 tanks: 588 FT-17/18, 236 AMR-33/35, 990 R-35, 320 H-35, 543 H-39, 90 FCM-36, 58 D-2, 240 S-35, 275 B-1bis and 7 2C. The most important mobile formations of the French Army were three light mechanized divisions (DLM), which belonged to the cavalry and numbered 10,401 men and 223 tanks, and three reserve armoured divisions (DCR), which were subordinate to the infantry and numbered 6,444 men and 168 tanks each. Thus, only 35 per cent of the French tanks were concentrated in independent formations. Another 180 were part of five light cavalry divisions (DLC),[13] and the remaining 1,994 were in service with 41 separate tank battalions and 4 separate tank companies, which were tasked for direct infantry and cavalry support.[14] Meanwhile all Germans tanks in the field army were grouped in 10 panzer divisions, in complete accordance with Guderian's favourite maxim: 'Strike with a fist, not with outspread fingers!'

It is impossible not to note that the Germans were significantly inferior to the Allies in the level of motorization. German propaganda intentionally and ceaselessly created an image for the Wehrmacht of an army that was splendidly equipped with everything necessary, relentlessly carving its way forward in a multitude of panzers, halftracks, lorries and motorcycles. In reality, Germany's ground forces at the time had only around 120,000 lorries. The majority of German soldiers, just as in the old days, trudged along roads in clouds of dust kicked up by horse-drawn wagons and gun limbers. In order to compensate for the lack of motorized transport, the Germans sought to offset it with a more effective, centralized use. At the same time the French Army, with a smaller number of men, after the mobilization of civilian cars and lorries had approximately 300,000 vehicles in formation.[15] The British Expeditionary Forces had an even higher level of motorization. The British infantry division of that time had 13,863 men, 1,848 motor vehicles and prime movers, as well as 670 motorcycles. The British made no use at all of animal–drawn transport.[16]

However, there is another side to this coin. Troops with a high level of motorization and mechanization must be kept properly supplied with a corresponding amount of fuel. The complexity of this problem is often underappreciated, but the powerful engines of the hundreds of tanks and prime movers in a mobile formation, combined with the motors of thousands of lorries and other vehicles, are quite voracious. For example, in the period we are examining, the French 3rd DLM consumed 59,000 litres of petrol for each 100 kilometres of march along the roads. Approximately 62 per cent of this amount went to its tanks and armoured cars.[17] The Luftwaffe repeatedly destroyed columns of extremely vulnerable French petrol lorries on the march, paralysing the actions of units which the lorries were supposed to supply with fuel. Even if a few surviving fuel lorries managed to make it to their fosterlings, the refuelling took a long time, because they were driving up to tanks in succession and topping up each one with fuel, one after another. In the Wehrmacht this process was organized completely differently and much more effectively. Fuel was delivered to the intended recipients in ordinary lorries using standard 20-litre canisters, which were unloaded onto the ground at distribution points. The tankers quickly took what they needed, refuelled all the tanks simultaneously on their own and then returned the empty canisters to the stockpile. There they were loaded onto the same lorries and put back into circulation again. The German panzers carried a few full canisters for topping up in case of necessity.

In general and on the whole, to judge formally, none of the adversaries had a decisive superiority in force and means. At first glance, their overall potential was approximately equal. However, this impression is deceptive, because the main weakness of Germany's foes lay in their lack of unity and integration. The Belgian and Dutch armies were not only not subordinate to the Allied command, they didn't even have any common operational plans, yet they comprised approximately a quarter of the anti-Nazi coalition's total ground forces. The absence of any coordination regarding a key point in the coming battles – the Ardennes – was particularly telling. As it turned out, the French didn't consider it to be their zone of responsibility, and neither did the Belgians. Both were planning, in the event of necessity, to conduct only holding actions and a slow retreat, leaving their neighbour to conduct the defence of this area. As a result, no one was planning to defend the Ardennes seriously, and this circumstance became a splendid gift to the Wehrmacht. It was precisely there that the Germans planned to deliver a knock-out blow to their enemies, and by weakening secondary sectors of the front, they concentrated seven of their ten available panzer divisions there. In addition, at the beginning of March 1940 Panzer Group von Kleist, the first of its type, was formed up, given the name of its commander. It included half of all the Wehrmacht's mobile formations and units: five panzer and three motorized divisions, as well as a motorized regiment. They were organized into three motorized corps. One more motorized corps was covering von Kleist's right flank against attacks from the north.

A German panzer group represented a large and powerful army, the likes of which had never been seen before in military history. It numbered 134,370 men and 41,140 various vehicles, including 1,222 panzers, 545 tracked vehicles and 39,373 wheeled vehicles. Using the regulation intervals between vehicles when on the march as one column, this military formation would have stretched for 1,540 kilometres – enough to cross the entire Third Reich from Luxembourg to Königsberg (today's Kaliningrad) in East Prussia![18] Simply organizing the coordinated movement over short distances of all the units of such a juggernaut while keeping it supplied with everything necessary even under the simplest conditions was a monumental task. Moreover, it would have to make a fighting advance of some 600 kilometres to reach the English Channel, and the most difficult and decisive stage on its route would be the 170-kilometre sector of the Ardennes with its hilly and forested terrain and only a few narrow, often twisting roads.

The German staff officers wracked their brains over planning the panzer group march in an area with a limited network of roads. Only four routes were set aside for it, which meant that von Kleist's transport columns, given simultaneous movement, would each stretch for almost 400 kilometres. At the moment when the forward elements of the panzer group reached the Maas River, more than half of its forces hadn't even yet crossed the border with Luxembourg. However, the camel nonetheless managed to pass swiftly through the needle's eye, forced a crossing of the Maas River at Sedan and broke through towards the English Channel. As a result, 1,700,000 crack soldiers of the Allied armies were trapped and forced to capitulate. Only around 370,000 of them were evacuated from Dunkirk, having abandoned on the coastline virtually all their heavy weapons. These events determined the fate of the battle, and indeed that of the entire campaign. In its second phase the Wehrmacht, in essence, only finished off mortally wounded foe ...

Skilfully handling such a powerful instrument as the tactical and strategic panzer formations, the Germans were confidently forcing their will on all their adversaries on the fields of battle. Their effective, quick and agile methods of conducting combat operations left the Allies no chance for success; from the outset, they were embracing old linear tactics with an orderly, methodical and slow development of the situation. Having collided with a turn of events that was completely unexpected, they were stunned, staggered and unable to regain their balance quickly. The widespread 'tank fright' in their troops also made an undoubted contribution to their defeat, as did their sensitivity to outflanking manoeuvres and envelopment. The idea of the offensive through the Ardennes proposed by von Manstein, and then worked out and implemented by the Wehrmacht command, was fruitful, but the crude operational blunders made by General Maurice Gamelin, the commander of the Allied forces during the Battle of France, multiplied the scale and rapidity of the Allies' catastrophe.

The shortcomings in the plainly outdated system of training of the Allied forces, and primarily of their command cadres, particularly stood out. In contrast to the German system, it left no room for showing initiative and independence. Trained to fight strictly according to regulations and commands from above, the French and British soldiers and officers became lost, having fallen into conditions to which they weren't accustomed, when any delay in front of the enemy, in expectation of the next orders from above, was equivalent to defeat. Their habits of slow action according to the First World War model were hopelessly inferior to the Wehrmacht's tactics, which were based on speed and constant pressure. Therefore the Allied forces were constantly late in occupying important objectives and key terrain points. As a rule, the Germans were showing up there first, and time and again were convincingly winning head-on battles with the enemy engaging them on their own terms. It was very important that the Germans not only worked out the new tactics and new operational principles of combat operations well in advance, but had also completely mastered them in peace-time training exercises, including those for the command staff as well. Thanks to the special attention that the German Army paid to this most important type of combat preparations, the typical German army captain or major in 1940 already had more experience in participating in multi-divisional manoeuvres than the average British or French general.[19] Moreover, they had already tested their tactics in practice during the Polish campaign, and had made the necessary corrections to them according to its results. Thus they felt quite at home in the turbulent maelstrom of manoeuvring warfare. The Allies, in contrast, had to grasp, analyse and master this new form of warfare in the process of it. However, for this they didn't have the time, space or resources.

The French campaign lasted for just six weeks, but the German victory didn't come cheap. They lost 839 panzers irrecoverably (182 Pz.Kpfw.I, 240 Pz.Kpfw.II, 62 Pz.Kpfw.35(t), 54 Pz.Kpfw.38(t), 135 Pz.Kpfw.III, 97 Pz.Kpfw.IV and 69 command tanks), almost a third of all the panzers that were committed to the fighting. Another 11 (8 Pz.Kpfw.I, 2 Pz.Kpfw.II and 1 Neubau-Pz.Kpfw.IV) had to be written off after the campaign in Norway. There, 54 German panzers had fought as part of the 40th Separate Panzer Battalion, which included 29 Pz.Kpfw.I, 18 Pz.Kpfw.II, 3 Neubau Fahrzeug and 4 command tanks. In addition, another five panzers were lost at sea while they were being shipped to Norway.[20]

Such heavy losses forced the Germans to take urgent steps to reinforce the armour protection on their combat vehicles. The final major series of the Pz.Kpfw.II – the Ausf.F model – received frontal armour with a thickness of 30–35mm.[21] Starting from December 1940 until the end of 1942, the updating of the previously produced Pz.Kpfw.III Ausf.E, F and G was in progress. They were re-equipped with the 50mm L/42 long-barrelled gun, while the front hull armour and turret platform were strengthened with additional 30mm face-hardened armour plating. As a result, the total armour thickness in these places was brought up to 60mm, and they became impenetrable to the most widely used 37mm and 45mm anti-tank guns of that time. By the end of

June 1941, 172 panzers had passed through this programme.[22] The Pz.Kpfw. III Ausf.H was updated in a similar manner at the factory while in the process of being built. From the very start recent combat experience was utilized in full measure in the design of the next series of this tank, the Ausf.J. The front of the turret, turret platforms and hull of this model were protected by 50mm of face-hardened armour, which was approximately equivalent to the strength of 60mm of the previous appliqué armour.[23] The Pz.Kpfw.IV was also not forgotten; beginning in February 1941, 30mm of face-hardened armour plating was welded onto the frontal hull of its Ausf.A, B and C models. Similar updating began even earlier on the Pz.Kpfw.IV Ausf.D, from July 1940, and the last 68 of these panzers received 50mm of homogeneous frontal armour at the factory. The same armour, which couldn't be penetrated by 37mm or 45mm armour-piercing shells, from the very beginning of their production was applied to the Pz.Kpfw.IV Ausf.E and F.[24] In May 1941 they began to face-harden the frontal armour, which also had a thickness of 50mm, on the German assault guns as well.[25]

In April 1941 the Wehrmacht was able to conduct its last successful blitzkrieg, smashing the armies of Yugoslavia and Greece, together with the British expeditionary corps that had landed on the Peloponnesian peninsula. Six panzer divisions and three motorized divisions of the German mobile forces were committed to the Balkan campaign. They listed a total of 839 tanks: 18 Pz.Kpfw.I, 260 Pz.Kpfw.II, 125 Pz.Kpfw.38(t), 275 Pz.Kpfw.III (166 of them with a 50mm gun), 118 Pz.Kpfw.IV and 43 command tanks. The irrecoverable losses in this action turned out to be small: 56 panzers (7 Pz. Kpfw.I, 13 Pz.Kpfw.II, 7 Pz.Kpfw.38(t), 21 Pz.Kpfw.III and 8 command tanks), of which only 17 were the result of combat. The rest sank when attempting to ford raging rivers or fell off the edge of narrow, twisting mountain roads. The 2nd and 5th Panzer Divisions had to fight longer than the others. They pursued the retreating British troops to the southern tip of Greece, and ended the operation only at the end of April. The intensive actions in difficult, mountainous terrain led to a great deal of wear and tear on the combat vehicles. As a result, almost two months after the end of the Balkan campaign, on 21 June 1941 the 5th Panzer Division's 31st Panzer Regiment had only 23 tanks; all the remaining tanks were under repair. The 2nd Panzer Division suffered even more heavily. The majority of its men, in wheeled vehicles, conducted a march from Greece to Yugoslavia, and from there travelled to Germany by railway. Meanwhile the tracked vehicles, including the panzers, were sent to Italy by sea aboard two transport ships, *Marburg* and *Kubfels*. On 21 May 1941 they blundered into an underwater minefield that had just been deployed by the British in the Ionic Sea; both hit mines and sank to the bottom with all of their valuable cargo.[26] As a result of all these problems, the 2nd and 5th Panzer Divisions were not able to restore their combat capabilities and take their place on the Eastern Front until September 1941.

However, in the final analysis this victory proved to be a pyrrhic one, because as a result of it Hitler had to delay the timetable for the invasion of the Soviet Union. However, he could hardly have been able to maintain it, even if the aforementioned events in Greece and Yugoslavia hadn't hindered it. The initial start date – 15 May – hadn't been chosen at all by coincidence. Prior to this date, it wasn't possible even to hope that the spring thaw would end and the ground would dry out sufficiently to allow the passage of heavy vehicles. However, the unusually wet weather in the spring of 1941 would force Hitler to reschedule the start date to 1 June anyway because of the saturated ground and high rivers.[27] But because of the Balkan campaign, it didn't start then either. The Germans had to postpone the invasion of the USSR until 22 June 1941. Thus, had they not engaged in the Balkan campaign, they would have received three additional weeks for conducting Operation Barbarossa. Today it can be said with certainty that the delay to its start was fatal both for its course and, especially, its finish. Because of this critical delay, Moscow couldn't be taken before the onset of the autumn muddy season.

On 1 June 1941 the Wehrmacht had 5,162 tanks, including 877 Pz.Kpfw.I, 1,074 Pz.Kpfw.II, 170 Pz.Kpfw.35(t), 754 Pz.Kpfw.38(t), 350 Pz.Kpfw.III with a 37mm gun, 1,090 Pz.Kpfw.III with a 50mm gun, 517 Pz.Kpfw.IV and 330 command tanks.[28] Their distribution in the panzer divisions of the invading German Army is shown in Table 3.

It is significant that by this time the extremely outdated Pz.Kpfw.I, which had no capacity for updating, was for the most part withdrawn from the front lines. Because of the lack of better tanks, only the recently formed 12th, 19th and 20th Panzer Divisions had a total of 126 Pz.Kpfw.I in their panzer regiments. Another 26 of these light tanks were included in the panzer regiments of the 9th, 17th and 18th Panzer Divisions. The remaining 185 Pz.Kpfw.I tanks which took part in the invasion of the Soviet Union equipped one company in the pioneer battalions in each of the German

Table 3: Numbers and types of tanks in the Wehrmacht's panzer divisions on the Eastern Front on 22 June 1941.

Division	Regiment	Panzerkampfwagen									Tot.
		I		II	35(t)	38(t)	III		IV	Command	
		Sapper	Ordinary				37mm	50mm			
1st Panzer	Pz.Rgt. 1	11		43				71	20	11	1!
3rd Panzer	Pz.Rgt. 6	13		59			29	81	32	15	2:
4th Panzer	Pz.Rgt. 35	10		51			31	74	20	26	2?
6th Panzer	Pz.Rgt. 11	11		47	155				30	13	2!
7th Panzer	Pz.Rgt. 25	11		55		167			30	15	2?
8th Panzer	Pz.Rgt. 10	11		49		118			30	15	2:
9th Panzer	Pz.Rgt. 33	11	8	32			11	60	20	12	1!
10th Panzer	Pz.Rgt. 7	11		47				105	20	17	2(
11th Panzer	Pz.Rgt. 15	11		44			24	47	20	20	1(
12th Panzer	Pz.Rgt. 29	11	40	34		109			30	8	2:
13th Panzer	Pz.Rgt. 4	8		45			27	44	20	13	1!
14th Panzer	Pz.Rgt. 36	11		45			15	56	20	11	1!
16th Panzer	Pz.Rgt. 2	12		44			23	48	20	10	1!
17th Panzer	Pz.Rgt. 39	10	12	45				106	30	13	2?
18th Panzer	Pz.Rgt. 18	11	6	50			99	15	36	12	2?
19th Panzer	Pz.Rgt. 27	11	42	35		110			30	11	2:
20th Panzer	Pz.Rgt. 21	11	44	31		121			31	2	2⁴
Total:		185	152	756	155	625	259	707	439	224	3,5(

Source: T.L. Jentz, *Panzertruppen: The Complete Guide to the Creation & Combat Employment of Germany's Tank Force, 1933–1942:* (Atglen, PA: Schiffer Publishing Ltd, 1996), pp. 190–3, 206.

panzer divisions. At the same time, all such tanks, except the vehicles of the company commanders, were fitted with *Abwurfvorrichtungen*, an apparatus on the rear deck of the tanks for carrying and dropping an explosive weighing up to 50 kilograms in order to destroy fortifications and obstacles. From inside a closed-up Pz.Kpfw.I that was equipped with this apparatus, it was possible to drop this explosive charge on the needed spot.[29]

It is necessary to note that it is these combat engineer Pz.Kpfw.I tanks that are chiefly responsible for the discrepancies in the numbers of German panzers that were assembled for Operation Barbarossa which one often encounters in historical literature. Some authors don't include them in the number of combat tanks because they weren't part of panzer regiments, and instead consider them as specialized combat engineer vehicles. However, in our opinion this is inaccurate, because the mounting of the device on the Pz.Kpfw.I had little effect on its combat capabilities, and these light tanks unquestionably played an important role in the course of combat operations.

The disagreement over the number of tanks in the German panzer divisions is eye-catching and surprising for the pedantic Germans, who have long been known for their love of order. The main reason for the discrepancy in the number of tanks was the varied organization of their panzer divisions. Some of them had panzer regiments that consisted of two panzer battalions, while others had a three-battalion composition. Mostly this is explained by the desire to equalize the strength of divisions that were equipped with panzers of different models. The Czech light tanks were inferior to the power of the German medium panzers, so all of the panzer divisions that were armed with them (the 6th, 7th, 8th, 12th, 19th and 20th Panzer Divisions) each had three panzer battalions. The 17th and 18th Panzer Divisions received a third panzer battalion, possibly because their panzer regiments had the outdated Pz.Kpfw.I. At the same time the 9th Panzer Division had to be satisfied with Pz.Kpfw.I tanks, even though it had only a two-battalion composition. On the other hand the 3rd Panzer Division was given a third panzer battalion for some unknown reason. However, this still doesn't include all the variations: in the 4th, 7th and 10th Panzer Divisions the panzer battalions for some reason consisted of four panzer companies, while at the same time all the other panzer divisions had panzer battalions that consisted of only three panzer companies. Meanwhile the Wehrmacht, of course, had established tables of organization and equipment for elements, units and formations. The authorized number of tanks in the units of a German panzer regiment according to the Table of Organization and Equipment (TO&E) from 1 February 1941 is shown in Table 4.

If the 11 authorized Pz.Kpfw.I in the pioneer battalion are taken into account, then the divisions with a two-battalion panzer regiment were supposed to have 173 tanks, while those with a three-battalion panzer regiment were to have 250 tanks. However, not a single German panzer division at the time was equipped according to the acting TO&E. Undoubtedly, the history of each specific division and its traditions had an impact on the real situation. However, the main reason was the lack of up-to-date tanks, especially the Pz.Kpfw.IV. Because of this, in the majority of

Table 4: Number of tanks in a German panzer regiment according to the TO&E, 1 February 1941.

Submit			Panzerkampfwagen				
			II	III	IV	Command	Total
Regiment headquarters				1		2	3
Light panzer platoon			5				5
Panzer Battalion	Battalion headquarters			1		2	3
	Light panzer platoon		5				5
	HQ tank subunit		2	3	1		6
	Light panzer company (two in the battalion)	Company HQ		2			2
		Light panzer platoon	5				5
		Panzer platoon (three in company)		5			5
		Total in company	5	17			22
	Medium panzer company	Company HQ			2		2
		Light panzer platoon	5				5
		Panzer platoon (three in company)			4		4
		Total in company	5		14		19
	Total in battalion		22	38	15	2	77
Total	In a two-battalion regiment.		49	77	30	6	162
	In a three-battalion regiment.		71	115	45	8	239

Source: T.L. Jentz, Panzertruppen: The Complete Guide to the Creation & Combat Employment of Germany's Tank Force, 1933–1942 (Atglen, PA: Schiffer Publishing Ltd, 1996), pp. 147–9.

German panzer battalions of that time, a third panzer platoon was absent in the medium panzer companies. Usually, there was also no Pz.Kpfw.IV in the headquarters company. Thus, each battalion as a rule had 10 Pz.Kpfw.IV tanks instead of the authorized 15.

However, not all of the German panzers that were assembled for the invasion of the USSR belonged to panzer divisions. Two separate panzer battalions were designated for actions in the far north. For the full picture, it is also necessary to mention the three separate Flammpanzer battalions, which were attached to the troops responsible for breaching powerful fortified works. Their tank park can be seen in more detail in Table 5.

Table 5: Number of tanks in the Wehrmacht's separate panzer battalions on the Eastern Front on 22 June 1941.

Separate Battalion	Panzerkampfwagen										Total
	I	II	II Flamm	B2 Flamm	B2	35S	38H	A13	III	Command	
40th Panzer	48	9							15	8	80
211th Panzer						10	24				34
100th Flammpanzer		25	42					9	5	1	82
101st Flammpanzer		25	42						5	1	73
102nd Flammpanzer				24	6						30
Total:	48	59	84	24	6	10	24	9	25	10	299

Source: T.L. Jentz, *Panzertruppen: The Complete Guide to the Creation & Combat Employment of Germany's Tank Force, 1933–1942* (Atglen, PA: Schiffer Publishing Ltd, 1996), p. 193. T. Jentz, *Flammpanzer. German Flamethrowers 1941–1945* (London: Osprey Publishing Ltd, 1997), pp. 13–14. N. Askey, *Operation Barbarossa. Volume IIA. The German Forces, Mobilisation and War Economy from June to December 1941* (Raleigh, NC: Lulu Publishing, 2013), p. 451.

In total the Germans committed 3,801 tanks against the USSR as part of 17 panzer divisions, 2 separate panzer battalions, and 3 separate Flammpanzer battalions.

On 20 June 1941 the Wehrmacht had 377 assault guns.[30] They were all located in separate battalions and batteries that were part of the division's establishment, or were attached to the troops on the main axes of attack. Of this total, for the invasion of the Soviet Union 272 assault guns were formed into 11 battalions (the 184th, 185th, 190th, 191st, 192nd, 197th, 201st, 203rd, 210th, 226th and 243rd) and 7 separate batteries (the 659th, 660th, 665th, 666th and 667th, plus one each in the Lehr Brigade 900 and *Grossdeutschland* Motorized Regiment). Another 12 equipped two separate batteries that belonged to SS troops (in the SS Motorized Division *Das Reich* and in the SS Motorized Brigade *Leibstandarte Adolf Hitler*). In addition, from June 1941 one battery of six assault guns was included in the SS Motorized Division *Totenkopf*. However, it initially went through a period of combat training in Germany, and wound up on the Eastern Front only at the end of August 1941. Thus, 284 assault guns took part in Operation Barbarossa from the beginning.[31]

Chapter 6

Soviet Armoured Forces

In 1927 the Red Army's tank park consisted of 15 combat vehicles of domestic production and another 77 British and French tanks that were captured in the course of the recent Russian Civil War.[1] Given such a miserly number of tanks, it isn't possible to say they had any significant influence on the practical activity of the troops. Nevertheless, Soviet military theory was in full blossom back then. The young but educated and energetic practitioner and theoretician of military matters K.V. Triandafillov made a particularly large contribution to it. In 1924 the People's Commissar of the Army and Navy M.V. Frunze promoted the 30-year-old military academy graduate to the most important post of Chief of the Operations Department of the Red Army's Headquarters, and he fully justified the trust that was placed in him. In addition to carrying out numerous current tasks and responsibilities, over his short career Triandafillov managed to write a series of articles and books on military history and military theory. In them he not only analysed the experiences of the First World War and the Russian Civil War, but on the basis of his analysis he developed practical recommendations for military planning, building up and organizing the Soviet armed forces for the future. The theory of the 'deep operation', which was ahead of its time, became Triandafillov's main intellectual brainchild. It found its full reflection in his well-known work 'Kharakter operatsii sovremennykh armii' ('Nature of the operations of contemporary armies'), which was published in 1929. It contained all of his thoughts and findings, presented new perspectives for the development of operational art, and provided a theoretical foundation for the further path of modernizing and developing the Red Army.

The basic idea of the 'deep operation' was a breakthrough of the enemy's defence to its entire depth with one fast and overwhelming strike. In order to exploit the success, mobile forces – tanks, motorized infantry and mounted troops – would be quickly introduced into the created gap before breaking out into operational space. Using air support, they would ceaselessly advance, destroying the enemy's artillery, communications centres, headquarters and reserves. At the same time numerous airborne landings would be made in the enemy rear with the aim of seizing vital road hubs and bridges, as well as disrupting enemy command and control. Thereby the rapid pace of the offensive and a deep penetration would be secured, which would not permit the enemy to regain his senses and organize effective resistance. In the process, several simultaneous breakthroughs should be made at the same sector of the front, which would lead to the complete collapse of the enemy's entire defensive system. Thereby a tactical success achieved by overcoming the enemy's defences would develop into an operational success over the entire battle. The depth of a *front*'s offensive operation, conducted with the forces of two or three shock armies on the axis of the main attack and one or two armies on a secondary axis, was planned to reach 150–200 kilometres at a pace of up to 15 kilometres per day.[2]

K.B. Kalinovsky became a dedicated adherent of Triandafillov's teachings. He also received a higher military education and moreover became familiar in detail with German theoretical thought at the 'Kama' tank school. Using his acquired knowledge and own experience, Kalinovsky developed the theory of the 'deep operation', adding to it the idea of using groups of medium and heavy tanks in order to resolve independent tasks when developing a successful breakthrough of the enemy's defence.[3] Being an expert and ardent supporter of armoured forces, he successfully commanded the first of them to be formed in the Red Army – first an experimental mechanized regiment, and then the mechanized brigade that grew from it.

Triandafillov and Kalinovsky were close colleagues and like-minded men. Young, energetic and talented, they might have been able to achieve a lot in life. However, early on the morning of 12 July 1931 an absurd tragedy cut short their lives: not far from Moscow the airplane in which they were flying at low altitude to Kiev for a field exercise struck a tree in thick fog and crashed without survivors.

The ideas that were embedded in the theory of a 'deep operation' demonstrated their fruitfulness and vitality on the battlefields of the Second World War; however, in the Red Army they were still very far from being successfully applied. The actual level of training of the soldiers and commanders at every level of the Red Army, as well as the organizational structure of the forces and their equipment, plainly didn't meet the requirements of this advanced theory. Moreover, a number of its well-known progenitors, advocates and followers for a variety of reasons didn't survive until the Second World War and didn't have time to develop and elaborate the theory. Many of them, like the two authors of serious publications on the theory and practice of mechanized forces, V.P. Kryzhanovsky and V.V. Favitsky, became victims of the arbitrary actions in those infamous and tragic years of 1937 and 1938. Plainly, the theory of the 'deep operation' appeared well ahead of its time in the pre-war USSR.

It had greater influence on the development of the Red Army's armoured forces. Their establishment followed a twisting and turning path. Initially the main task of the Soviet tanks was to provide direct support to the infantry and cavalry in battle. Tank elements and units were supposed to become part of rifle and cavalry formations, or to be held in the reserve of the Supreme Command for use on decisive sectors of the front. The theory of the 'deep operation' prompted a genuine need for the organization of independent formations of mobile forces, capable of quickly converting a successful breakthrough of the tactical zone of a defence into an operational success. The mechanized brigade became the first of them. It was created in May 1930 at the initiative of Kalinovsky, who subsequently led it himself. Initially 60 tanks and 32 tankettes arrived to arm the brigade, but in the following year it had 119 tanks. After the tragic death of its commander in 1931, the brigade acquired his name as an honourific title.[4]

In March 1932 the first two mechanized corps began to form up in the Leningrad and Ukrainian Military Districts, each of which included two mechanized brigades and one rifle/machine gun brigade. They also had reconnaissance, chemical, combat engineer, signals, and anti-aircraft battalions, a traffic control company and a maintenance depot. In 1934 two more corps were added, one of which was formed on the basis of the *Kalinovsky* Mechanized Brigade. According to their TO&E, each of these mechanized corps was armed with 490 tanks, 215 armoured cars and 60 guns.[5] Based on the experience of two years of exercises and manoeuvres, in 1935 their TO&E was simplified at the expense of their rear services, leaving them with only reconnaissance and signals battalions. Now there remained 463 light tanks; in order to increase mobility, all of the brigades of the mechanized corps switched to fast BT tanks. However, they retained 52 chemical tanks based on the T-26 and 63 amphibion T-37As.[6]

What immediately catches the eye is the excessive abundance of tanks in the mechanized corps, as well as the lack of infantry and artillery. Such substantial shortcomings undoubtedly hindered them from effectively operating in an independent role. However, it would be naïve to expect from them a perfect and balanced structure; after all, the Soviet mechanized corps became the first major armoured formations in the world, and their main significance lay in this. The further improvement of their TO&E was something that would come with time and experience.

Another five mechanized brigades were formed up in addition to the mechanized corps in 1932, and by 1935 there were 16. They consisted of four tank battalions, an artillery battalion, a rifle/machine gun battalion and a combat engineer battalion, plus reconnaissance and chemical companies, and they were equipped with 220 light tanks, 56 armoured cars, and 27 artillery pieces.[7] Thus the organization of the mechanized brigade had essentially the same drawbacks that were observed in the mechanized corps. In 1933 a single moto-mechanized brigade, equipped with T-27 tankettes and armoured cars, appeared in the Red Army. By 1938 the USSR, alongside the four mechanized corps, now had 17 mechanized brigades, one armoured brigade (consisting of five separate tank battalions and located in the Trans-Baikal Military District) and one moto-armoured brigade (formed from out of the moto-mechanized brigade), as well as 4 tank brigades (equipped with medium T-28 and heavy T-35 tanks in addition to the light BT and T-26) and 3 reserve tank brigades.

In 1938–1939 the Red Army's armoured forces went through their next major reorganization. The number of tanks in a tank platoon increased from 3 to 5, so the total number of BT tanks in the brigades grew from 157 to 278 (not including 49 training tanks). The brigades equipped with T-26 tanks now had 267 of them, supplemented with 36 training tanks. Correspondingly, the number of tanks in the mechanized corps rose to 560 combat tanks and 98 training tanks.[8] At the same time the mechanized corps were renamed tank corps, while the formation of another three such corps was rejected because of their unwieldiness, the difficulty in controlling them, and the complexity of their logistics.[9] The first practical experience of using two of the Soviet tank corps during the campaign in Poland in September 1939 fully confirmed these problems. So on 15 November 1939 Voroshilov reported to the Red Army's Main Military Council:

> In the existing tank brigades, the auxiliary subunits are to be reduced, and the rifle/machine gun brigades and rifle/machine gun battalions of the tank corps and brigades are to be abolished.
>
> The mechanized corps, as a cumbersome formation for command and control, will be converted into separate brigades, and the existing four headquarters of the mechanized corps will be disbanded.[10]

The Main Military Council did the bidding of the People's Commissar of Defence and with a decision on 21 November 1939 scratched out the first-generation mechanized corps of the Red Army.[11] Instead of improvements being made to their organizational and command structure, they were all disbanded in January–February 1940.[12] Once again, the brigades, which were renamed from mechanized brigades into tank brigades, became the highest organizational formation of the Soviet armoured forces. In the process, the 16 tank brigades that were armed with 258 light BT tanks, and another 12 that were equipped with the same number of T-26 tanks, were now called light tank brigades. Meanwhile, the three brigades that were equipped with 117 medium T-28 tanks and 39 light BT tanks, and the one brigade that was equipped with 32 heavy T-35 tanks and 85 medium T-28 tanks, became known as heavy tank brigades. In addition, the Soviet armoured forces at the time included 10 tank regiments, 3 moto-armoured brigades, 4 motorcycle battalions, a training battalion of the Trans-Baikal Military District, a regiment of the Military Academy of Mechanization and Motorization, as well as armoured trains. The total authorized manpower of the tank units amounted to 97,568 men.[13] It was with just these armoured forces that the Soviet Union approached the Second World War.

Tanks also went to arm the Soviet infantry. Each rifle division by its wartime TO&E was supposed to have a battalion equipped with 54 tanks. In addition, it was planned to convert 15 rifle divisions into motorized divisions, having included in them two motorized regiments, one artillery regiment and one tank regiment with 257 tanks. Eight such divisions were supposed to appear in 1940, and the rest in the first six months of 1941.[14]

The rapid accumulation of tanks in the Red Army was accompanied by unavoidable growing pains. Unfortunately, the immensely complex problem of training an adequate number of men capable of mastering the new technology completely was plainly underestimated. In contrast to the mass production of tanks, for which no money was spared, only miserly resources were devoted to the combat training of their crews. For example, each tank was allowed to expend only 25 service hours per year, of which just 15 hours went to tactical exercises, while the remaining 10 went to participation in parades.[15] Thus, the combat equipment in the Red Army was traditionally given much more care and attention than the men. However, the armoured vehicles were conserved at the expense of the deteriorating combat readiness of the crews, who were plainly given an insufficient amount of time for practical training for war. Yet after all, the thorough, individual training of many thousands of tankers was just a start. The need to give their commanders the chance to grasp the art of leading their elements, units and formations in both theory and practice, to learn how to organize close collaboration and mutual support between elements, units and formations on the battlefield, as well as with other services and branches of the armed forces, mustn't be forgotten. No less important were questions of organizing the combat, technical, and rear service and support functions for the combat operations of tank units and formations. All of these many essential tasks were plainly under-evaluated, and the resolution of them was put off until later. However, 'later' never came ...

The next wave of fundamental changes swept through the Soviet armoured forces soon after the conclusion of the inglorious war with Finland. A commission created by the Red Army's Main Military Council in order to assimilate the experience of the war observed on 20 April 1940:

On the basis of the use in combat conditions of the existing formations and those that were newly created: the commission considers the separate tank battalions of the rifle divisions and motorized rifle divisions, the separate tank companies in the rifle regiments, and the tank regiments of the rifle divisions, as completely impractical organizational units.

Such organizational forms lead only to the dispersal of the combat vehicles, their improper use (right down to guarding headquarters and rear areas), the impossibility of timely repairing them, and at times even the impossibility of using them.

The commission proposed: 'Disband all of the separate tank battalions of the rifle and motorized rifle divisions, the separate light tank regiments and battalions, with the exception of the 1st and 2nd Separate Red Banner Armies and of the regular cavalry divisions, and create tank brigades.'[16] Its recommendations were implemented, though as we will soon see, the aforementioned units and elements became necessary for completely different formations.

The impressive results of the 1940 campaign in the West prompted further changes in the organizational structure of the Red Army. The Wehrmacht's main shock force in the campaign was the motorized corps, which consisted of panzer and motorized divisions. It isn't surprising that at the very height of the fighting in France, on 21 May 1940 Stalin summoned the Chief of the Red Army General Staff B.M. Shaposhnikov, his deputy I.V. Smorodinov, and the Head of the Automotive-Armoured-Tank Directorate D.G. Pavlov and gave them the directive to form several tank corps quickly on the model and likeness of the German motorized corps. In his opinion, they should include two tank and one motorized rifle division. He wanted to have not less than 200 tanks in the tank regiments, and a total of 1,000–1,200 tanks in the corps.[17] It was a big ask: just a half year previously the Soviet tank corps consisted of two tank brigades and one rifle/machine gun brigade, with a total of only 560 tanks. Even with such a relatively modest structure, according to the results of the campaign in Poland they were regarded as too cumbersome and difficult to control. Actually, this was the main reason for disbanding them, but now the Red Army was given the task to create tank corps that were twice as large as the previous ones. However, in the army orders aren't discussed but carried out, especially orders from the top, so Smorodinov and Pavlov immediately got busy with putting together the TO&E of the future corps. Not even a week had passed when on 27 May 1940 the People's Commissar of Defence S.K. Timoshenko and Shaposhnikov visited Stalin with a detailed proposal to form six tank corps. Each of them was to be equipped with 1,030 tanks. In addition to the two tank divisions and one motorized division, they were to include a motorcycle regiment, a roadwork battalion, a signals battalion, and an aerial reconnaissance squadron.[18]

To Stalin, the number of proposed tank corps seemed inadequate, so at his directive over the next five days the project was substantially revised. The new variant made provision for eight tank corps of the same composition. It was planned to allocate them in the following manner: the Belorussian and Kiev Military Districts would receive two tank corps each, while the Leningrad, Odessa, Moscow and Trans-Baikal Districts would each receive one tank corps. In addition to the tank corps, two separate tank divisions were to be created for the Trans-Caucasus and Central Asian Military Districts. In order to form all of these new tank corps, they converted 5 headquarters of rifle corps and 2 headquarters of cavalry corps, 6 rifle and 5 cavalry divisions, 17 tank brigades, the 4 motorized divisions that existed by that time, and the majority of the tank battalions that were stripped from the composition of rifle divisions. In addition to them, the 26 tank brigades, 3 moto-armoured brigades, the training regiment and battalion, as well as the 18 tank battalions (each with 54 T-26 tanks) of the rifle divisions that were located in the Far East were retained in the armoured forces. This time Stalin gave the go-ahead, and on 9 June 1940 Timoshenko approved the plan of forming the new corps, having renamed them mechanized corps, and sent the corresponding orders to the military districts.[19]

This unquestionably timely and viable measure was founded on a strong material base. The USSR at the time possessed plenty of tanks, munitions and transport for fully equipping the new formations. There were also enough trained personnel and command staff. By the beginning of October 1940 all of the mechanized corps were fully staffed with men, though the situation with equipment was worse. Half had received 83–102 per cent of their authorized number of tanks, while another three mechanized corps had 61–78 per cent of them, and the last one had available just 47 per cent.[20] In the circumstances, the idea suggested itself not only to complete the equipping of the first eight mechanized corps, but also to form more of them on the basis of the available resources. Indeed, it followed without delay: on 14 October 1940 Timoshenko, together with the Red Army's new Chief of the General Staff K.A. Meretskov, sent a report regarding the creation of new units and formations to the Politburo and the USSR Council of People's Commissars. The largest of them was another mechanized corps, the ninth, designated for the Kiev Special Military District. In order to counter enemy tanks, it was also proposed to form 20 machine gun/artillery motorized brigades. In addition 20 newly re-created separate tank brigades equipped with the T-26 were designated for reinforcing and assisting infantry in combat. Their addition to the already existing formations enabled the provisioning of each rifle corps with a brigade of infantry support tanks. They weren't provided only for the Far Eastern rifle corps, since their divisions still retained authorized tank battalions.[21] On 16 October 1940 all of these proposals were approved by the Politburo of the Central Committee of the All-Union Communist Party of Bolsheviks.[22]

However, on 14 January 1941 G.K. Zhukov replaced Meretskov, and less than a month later, on 12 February, the General Staff led by him proposed a new mobilization plan, MP-41, to the Soviet leadership. Its most important section, which had the most far-reaching consequences, suggested the creation of 60 tank divisions (with 375 tanks in each) and 30 motorized divisions (with 275 tanks in each), which would bring up the total number of mechanized corps to 30.[23] Each of them would have an authorized number of 1,031 tanks. Stalin approved this plan virtually without any changes.[24] However, on 23 April 1941, by Decree No. 1112–459ss of the Central Committee and the USSR Council of People's Commissars, the headquarters of the newly created and fully staffed and equipped 29th Mechanized Corps of the Trans-Baikal Military District was disbanded together with the corps' units, and all of its divisions became separate.[25] Accordingly, by the time of Operation Barbarossa, the Red Army had 29 mechanized corps. Taken all together, there were 61 tank and 31 motorized divisions. The figures are more than impressive, if you don't know the real situation behind them.

The true history of the origination of the idea of forming the second wave of pre-war mechanized corps still isn't known fully. In his memoirs, Zhukov described it as follows:

> In February 1941 the General Staff worked out a wider plan of creating armoured formations than was provided for by the government's decisions in 1940.

Considering the amount of armoured forces in the German Army, the People's Commissar and I requested the use of the existing tank brigades and even the cavalry divisions when forming the mechanized corps, since they were closer to the armoured forces in their 'spirit of manoeuvre'.

I.V. Stalin apparently didn't have a definite opinion on this question back at that time and was in a state of uncertainty. Time passed, and only in March 1941 was the decision made about forming the 20 mechanized corps that we had requested.[26]

Relying on the fragmented evidence in our possession today, one can only conjecture about the real reasons for such a sharp increase in the number of newly formed mechanized corps, for which the necessary equipment wasn't available. It is known, for example, that at a meeting of the Main Military Council in the Kremlin on 13 January 1941, Stalin asked the commanders of the military districts that were present about the number of mechanized corps that they would need. According to the account of one of the attendees, the future General of the Army M.I. Kazakov, 'Kirponos (Leningrad Military District) requested one or two corps; Kuznetsov (Baltic District) – two or three corps; Pavlov (Belorussian District) – three or four corps; Zhukov (Kiev Special Military District) – four or five corps; Cherevichenko (Odessa District) – one or two corps; Efremov (Trans-Caucasus District) – one or two corps; Apanasenko (Central Asian Military District) – one corps.'[27] Thus, talk was only about 13–19 mechanized corps, of which 9 were already available. At the meeting, Marshal Kulik reasonably proposed to connect the forming of the new divisions to the actual capabilities of Soviet industry to meet their materiel needs. However, he was called to order and accused of not understanding the essence of the Red Army's mechanization and motorization. The political leadership literally imposed on the military top brass a number of tank and motorized formations that was impossible for the country to meet, so Zhukov, once he became Chief of the General Staff, quickly forgot about his own recent request.

The information from the GRU (Main Intelligence Directorate) played far from the last role in this matter; according to it, the Germans had brought up the number of their motorized corps to 8 or 10, and the total number of their tanks up to 10,000.[28] In reality, the Wehrmacht had only around half of this number of combat vehicles at the time. Such a large exaggeration of their real number didn't come about by coincidence: in the USSR it was assumed that the Germans would put all of their captured French tanks to combat use. As we've already shown, this didn't happen. However, back then, when planning for the future war, as a basis the planners used the figures obtained by the intelligence service – 10 German motorized corps, armed with 10,000 tanks. Subsequently, apparently by simply multiplying their number by 3, the planners derived their own force strength necessary to counter them. From this they came to the conclusion that the Red Army would have to have 30 mechanized corps, with approximately 1,000 tanks in each. After all, it is well known that for the success of an offensive, it is necessary to have a three-fold superiority in strength and means.

However, this was only simple arithmetic; the reality required much deeper knowledge from Zhukov, which back then, alas, he didn't have. To be fair, we'll note that the lack of an adequate education and work experience corresponding to his high post weren't Zhukov's fault – more his misfortune. Indeed, this wasn't uncommon. Unfortunately, at the time there were many such men among the Soviet commanders on every step of the career ladder, and the higher up the ladder an incorrect decision was made, the heavier the consequences. This rule is confirmed in full measure by the example of the second wave of pre-war mechanized corps. The decision about their massive, simultaneous establishment without a corresponding material base and trained cadres became an enormous mistake, which brought about the heaviest consequences. In the senseless chase for quantity, quality was ignored. What is worse, in order to create the new formations, already more or less tightly knit units and formations were used, which at least had practical experience of joint actions in exercises and manoeuvres, even if they lacked combat experience. The freshly baked mechanized corps simply didn't have time to acquire this experience and cohesion and were fighting entities in name only.

The structure even of those formations in which the number of tanks had been brought up to the authorized level was also far from optimal. For example, the motorized rifle regiment of the new tank division, which consisted of three rifle battalions, had just one regimental 6-gun battery. To justify this, it was stated, 'in comparison with an ordinary rifle regiment, anti-tank guns have been excluded in the regiment of the proposed organization, considering that for this purpose tanks will be used which will be attached to this regiment'.[29] As a result of this decision, the ability of the motorized rifle regiment to repulse an enemy tank attack was seriously weakened. Simultaneously, the shock power of the tank regiments was also reduced; their subunits would be diverted to carrying out anti-tank tasks on behalf of their motorized riflemen.

In order to work out a rational organization for the Soviet armoured forces, the lengthy and bloody experience of a major war was required. The Red Army leadership at the time didn't have this, so once again the TO&E of the mechanized corps proved to be badly overloaded with tanks. At the same time they were greatly understrength in infantry, artillery, transport, means of communication and repair services, and – most importantly – in qualified cadres. Plainly, from the very beginning a precise schedule should have been put together for creating the mechanized corps and this should have been done in sequence. It was possible and necessary to undertake the formation of the new corps only as the preceding corps became ready. Indeed, in no case should all of the tank brigades have been hastily disbanded simultaneously. However, in the Soviet Union the political and military leadership followed a different course, and as a result by the beginning of the war many tank and motorized divisions were not combat-capable because of an acute lack of tanks and other equipment.

Worst of all, the appearance of the enormous quantity of new formations took place practically simultaneously. This adversely affected even some of the already formed mechanized corps of the first wave. In order to accelerate the creation of the brand new corps, they included in them divisions taken from the existing ones. For example, the 10th Tank Division was taken from the 4th Mechanized Corps and transferred to the 15th Mechanized Corps, the 15th Tank Division was taken from the 8th Mechanized Corps and given to the 16th Mechanized Corps, and the 19th Tank Division was transferred from the 9th Mechanized Corps to the 22nd Mechanized Corps. In order to replace them, respectively, the 32nd, 34th and 35th Tank Divisions began to form. All of the available tank brigades and separate tank regiments, 2 motor-armoured brigades, 2 rifle divisions, 5 cavalry divisions and the separate cavalry brigade, the motorized divisions and machine gun/artillery motorized brigades that had recently appeared in the Red Army and other units were drawn upon to organize the new formations. In order somehow to equip the numerous mechanized corps, operational tanks were scrounged from everywhere they could be found. The authorized tank battalions of the rifle divisions that still existed at this time were removed from them. At the same time the acute lack of human and material resources nevertheless forced the Soviet command to establish priorities. The 19 mechanized corps that had been chosen to reach their combat readiness first received priority for getting men and equipment. Fourteen of these mechanized corps were designated for the western military districts. One more was prepared for the Trans-Caucasus Military District, one for the Moscow Military District, and three – together with two separate divisions (a tank division and a motorized division) – went to the Far East. In addition to them, the seven mechanized corps of reduced composition were assigned to priority formation: six for the western districts and one more for the Moscow Military District. The last four mechanized corps of reduced composition were put on the back burner. They were to be located in the Soviet Union's interior military districts.[30]

The USSR lacked the time, equipment and trained cadres in order to complete the staffing and equipping of all the mechanized corps before the war. This would have required an enormous quantity of tanks – almost 31,000. Alone, more than 16,000 heavy and medium tanks of the new types were necessary. With the rate of tank production as it stood in 1941 (5,220 tanks a year), all of the mechanized corps would have been fully equipped only by the end of 1943.[31] Even by the beginning of 1942, it was planned that only 4 of the 19 top priority mechanized corps would be provided with the authorized number of tanks: the 1st Mechanized Corps of the Leningrad Military District and all three mechanized corps and two separate divisions (tank and motorized) in the Far East. Among the rest of the top priority mechanized corps, three were to receive by that time 92–94 per cent of their tanks, four 81–89 per cent, another four 72–77 per cent, two 65–69 per cent, and the final two only 52–57 per cent. Of the number of priority mechanized corps of reduced composition, six would be equipped by then with 10–35 per cent of their authorized number of tanks, and the other one with just 1.6 per cent of its authorized number of tanks. The 20th Mechanized Corps of the Western

Special Military District, which was covering the Moscow axis, ended up as this most short-changed formation. It was planned to give the lower-priority mechanized corps of reduced composition between 12 per cent and 30 per cent of their authorized number of tanks by 1 January 1942.[32]

Putting it briefly, there was no way that it would have been possible to ensure the complete provisioning of the numerous mechanized corps with their materiel within the accepted period of time. All of the available resources of Soviet industry at the time were already burdened to the limit with the mass production of tanks. However, even this wasn't sufficient to meet the need, so the Head of the Red Army's Automotive-Armoured-Tank Directorate General Lieutenant Ia.N. Fedorenko in June 1941, just on the eve of the war, proposed to construct two new factories to produce tanks, and another factory to build the engines for them. In addition, he was demanding the expansion of the capacity of the existing tank-building factories and for other factories to be drawn into the process of building tanks.[33] At the same time the importance of, and need for, producing lorries (especially with good off-road capabilities and large cargo capacity), armoured personnel carriers, prime movers, and self-propelled anti-tank and anti-aircraft carriages, as well as other types of special equipment, was plainly neglected. They were being produced in extremely small quantities or not at all. Indeed, essentially there weren't the resources for their production, because everything was being put towards the relentless manufacture of tanks. Moreover, the mechanized corps weren't equipped with auxiliary equipment, transport or means of communication, and the problems of keeping them supplied with fuel and ammunition weren't resolved. All of these matters were set aside for later. As a result, many of them remained formed only in a formal sense. Meanwhile, with the beginning of the war, they were given combat tasks as fully-fledged powerful and mobile formations.

Zhukov himself recognized the mistake that was made, writing in his post-war memoirs: 'However, we didn't consider the objective possibilities of our tank industry. In order to equip fully the new mechanized corps, 16,600 tanks alone of the new types were required, and a total of around 32,000 tanks. It was virtually impossible to get this number of vehicles in the course of one year out of thin air, and there were also not enough technical personnel and command cadres.'[34] In an expunged excerpt of his memoirs, striving to play down the scale of his miscalculation with respect to the newly formed mechanized corps, he writes somewhat differently:

> As a result of the incorrect conclusions from the experience of the war in Spain, and also the war in Finland, at the suggestion of participants of the wars, Stalin proposed disbanding the mechanized corps and to have in place of the corps a tank brigade of three-battalion composition as the highest armour unit. In this matter, the Head of the Armoured Forces D. Pavlov, S.K. Timoshenko, K.A. Meretskov and other participants in these wars, who occupied top command positions over the troops, played a most negative role. On the basis of opinions shared at a conference of the Red Army's top command staff (in December 1940), a proposal was made by me to correct the mistake made and without delay to set about forming fifteen tank and mechanized corps, which in case of need could be brought together into tank armies without particular difficulties. Unfortunately, the discussions on this matter with the Politburo and with Stalin personally stretched for two full months, and only at the beginning of March 1941 was the decision reached to form fifteen corps, but this decision was made just three and a half months before the beginning of the war.[35]

In his words Zhukov proposed forming just 15 mechanized corps, which 'could be brought together into tank armies without particular difficulties'. Here the former Chief of the General Staff was plainly dissembling – both about the number of new mechanized corps, and regarding the ease in creating tank armies. In fact he didn't see the need for creating larger tank formations at the time. The irrefutable facts say that the usage of the mechanized corps as the Red Army's main shock force wasn't sufficiently considered before the war, let alone thought through.

Here is another curious fragment from the Marshal's same unpublished manuscript:

> The largest omission in our military-political strategy was the fact that we didn't draw proper conclusions from the experience of the initial stage of the Second World War, yet the experience was already plain

to see. As is known, the German armed forces unexpectedly invaded Austria, Czechoslovakia, Belgium, Holland, France and Poland, and with a ramming strike of major armoured forces overran the resistance of opposing forces and quickly achieved the assigned objectives. Our General Staff and People's Commissar of Defence didn't study the new methods of conducting the initial stage of the war, didn't instruct the troops on the corresponding recommendations regarding their operational and tactical retraining or rework the outdated operational-mobilization plans or others, connected with the initial period of the war.[36]

If the People's Commissar of Defence didn't study, and the General Staff didn't consider, how then did the Chief of the General Staff himself regard the study of the Wehrmacht's operations in the initial stage of the war? The former temporarily acting head of the GRU's Information Department, V.A. Novobranets, in his *Zapiski voennogo razvechika* (*Notes of a military intelligence officer*) presents an interesting fact in this respect. He describes Zhukov's reaction to a report, prepared on the basis of an analysis of the 'Official account of the French General Staff on the French-German War 1939–1940', that was given by the Commander-in-Chief of the French Army, Gamelin, to the Soviet military attache in Paris. Handing over this document, the French general had said, 'Take it, study it and look to see that such a fate doesn't befall you.' An entire group of officers of the Information Department worked over the analysis of the experience of this war, and soon the report 'O franko-nemetskoi voine 1939–1940' (On the French-German War of 1939–1940) was completed and presented to Zhukov. In it, in addition to an analysis of the reasons for the rapid defeat of the French Army and the British Expeditionary Force, the report contained proposals to improve the organizational structure of the Soviet armed forces. However, this wasn't to be: 'The answer received was such that it is embarrassing to write about it. A decision had been written out clumsily and ignorantly on our report above the signature of Zhukov: "I don't need this. Let me know how many refills of fuel were expended per one wheeled vehicle." Having read this statement, the officers of the Information Department shrugged their shoulders and quietly looked at each other and at me.'[37]

Meanwhile, in addition to everything else, the report contained an analysis of the use of the German panzer corps and the panzer groups (in fact, panzer armies) that had just been created by the Germans for the first time, the attacks of which just a half year later threw all of the Soviet plans into disarray. Obviously, Zhukov hadn't yet grasped the essence of the fluid structure of the German panzer groups, which united two or sometimes three motorized corps under a single command, and which, depending on the situation, were often reinforced with infantry. This was a qualitatively different means of resolving operational and strategic tasks than the Soviets' separate mechanized corps with their inflexible and far from perfected TO&E. No one had given any thought to at least making a rough estimate of the proper composition of the mechanized groups, which had been foreseen by the theory of the 'deep operation', as a means for resolving strategic tasks in the interests of the high command, or of creating headquarters in a timely manner in order to command them. As it happened, many of the mechanized corps, especially the ones that were better equipped, in accordance with the cover plans were made subordinate to the commanders of the first-echelon armies of the border districts. For example, in the Baltic Special Military District both mechanized corps were subordinated to the border armies: the 12th Mechanized Corps to the 8th Army, and the 3rd Mechanized Corps to the 11th Army. In the Western Special Military District, the most powerful 6th Mechanized Corps was assigned to a border covering area, which was in the zone of responsibility of the 10th Army's command; the 11th Mechanized Corps was subordinate to the 3rd Army, and the 14th Mechanized Corps to the 4th Army. Meanwhile the 13th Mechanized Corps had been designated for strengthening the troops in the sector of the 13th Army, which was still in the process of forming up. The commander of the Western Special Military District, Pavlov, had under his control only the two most weakly staffed and equipped mechanized corps, the 17th and 20th, which respectively had just 63 and 94 tanks.[38] There was an analogous picture in the Kiev Special Military District. Its mechanized corps were distributed among the forces that were directly covering the border: 22nd Mechanized Corps to the 5th Army, 4th Mechanized Corps to the 6th Army, 8th Mechanized Corps to the 26th Army, and 16th Mechanized Corps to the 12th Army. There remained in the reserve of the Kiev Special Military

District command the 9th, 19th, 24th and 15th Mechanized Corps. Only the last of these had been relatively well equipped with tanks – 73 per cent of the authorized strength, while the remaining reserve mechanized corps had only 22 per cent to 44 per cent of their authorized number of tanks. Thus, the mechanized corps that had a plainly insufficient number of tanks wound up (with rare exceptions) in the reserves of the military districts (the future *fronts*). This undoubtedly limited substantially the ability of the *front* commanders to have any real influence on the course of combat operations given an unfavourable development of the situation.

The staffing and equipping with tanks of the mechanized corps of the border military districts by the beginning of the war is shown in Table 6. This plainly shows that many of the mechanized corps at the beginning of the war were far below nominal strength in men and tanks. In some of them, their available tanks were really only sufficient to support the training process. However, the low manpower and inadequate equipping of the mechanized corps as shown in Table 6 were far from their only weaknesses. Their subordinate formations and units were frequently positioned in various areas at a distance of up to 100 kilometres from one another. In the event of necessity, it was not at all simple to gather them quickly into a fist. Moreover, according to an order from higher command, the mechanized corps sometimes were literally pulled apart into separate pieces right on the eve of the war. For example, the 1st Mechanized Corps was under the command of the Leningrad Military District, but its 1st Tank Division on 17 June was made officially subordinate to the 14th Army and departed from the Pskov area to Murmansk Oblast's Alakurtti (about 1,500 kilometres to the north). In the Baltic Special Military District the 5th Tank Division was transferred out of the 3rd Mechanized Corps and made directly subordinate to the 11th Army. The 28th Motorized Regiment of the 12th Mechanized Corps' 28th Tank Division remained in Riga, while its 55th and 56th Tank Regiments on the night of 18/19 June moved out towards the border, to the Šiauliai area. Because of this, the division's tanks wound up 120 kilometres away from their motorized infantry, and were compelled to enter combat without their support.[39]

Meanwhile, the concentration of the German forces on the country's western border was continuing. Soberly thinking military men, despite

Table 6: The staffing and equipping of the western military border districts' mechanized corps at the war's outset.

Military District	Mechanized Corps	Personnel		Tanks			
		Number	% of TO&E	Number	% of TO&E	Of which, KV and T-34 tanks	% of TO&E
According to TO&E		36,080	100.0	1,031	100.0	552	100.0
Leningrad	1st	31,348	86.9	1,039	100.8	15	2.7
	10th	26,065	72.2	469	45.5	–	0.0
Baltic Special	3rd	32,101	89.0	648	62.9	107	19.4
	12th	30,597	84.8	806	78.2	–	0.0
Western Special	6th	32,382	89.8	999	96.9	378	68.5
	11th	21,605	59.9	360	34.9	7	1.3
	13th	17,809	49.4	282	27.4	–	0.0
	14th	19,332	53.6	518	50.2	–	0.0
	17th	16,578	45.9	63	6.1	–	0.0
	20th	20,391	56.5	94	9.1	–	0.0
Kiev Special	4th	33,734	93.5	892	86.5	414	75.0
	8th	31,927	88.5	956	92.7	171	31.0
	9th	31,524	87.4	286	27.7	–	0.0
	15th	33,935	94.1	733	71.1	136	24.9
	16th	26,383	73.1	680	66.0	–	0.0
	19th	21,687	60.1	279	27.1	14	2.5
	22nd	30,320	84.0	652	63.2	31	5.6
	24th	21,556	59.7	185	17.9	–	0.0
Odessa	2nd	32,396	89.8	527	51.1	60	10.9
	18th	26,879	74.5	282	27.4	–	0.0
Total:		538,549	74.6	10,750	52.1	1,333	12.1

Source: 1941 god – uroki i vyvody [Year 1941 – lessons and conclusions], (Moscow: Voenizdat, 1992), p. 29; M. Kolomiets, 1941: Boi v Pribaltike 22 iunia–10 iulia 1941 goda [1941: Fighting in the Baltics 22 June-10 July 1941], Frontovaia illiustratsiia, No. 5 (2002), pp. 10, 13; M.V. Kolomiets, Sovetsky tiazhelyi tank KV-1 [Soviet heavy tank KV-1] (Moscow: Iauza/EKSMO, 2017), p. 218. E. Drig, Mekhanizirovannye korpusa RKKA v boiu [RKKA's mechanized corps in battle], pp. 423, 551; Na zemle Belarusi: Kanun i nachalo voiny [On Belorussian soil: Eve and start of the war] (Moscow: Kuchkovo pole, 2006), pp. 81–2; TsAMO RF, f. 229, op. 161, d. 89, l. 90; f. 38, op. 11360, d. 2, ll. 2–16; as cited by Glavnoe avtobronetankovoe upravlenie: Liudi, sobytiia, fakty v dokumentakh, 1940–1942 [Main Automotive-Armoured-Tank Directorate: Men, events, facts in documents, 1940–1942], p. 91.

Stalin's assurances that there was no way Hitler would choose to fight a war on two fronts, were sensing the growing danger of a Nazi invasion. In such a situation, to leave the tank formations of the western districts unfit for combat verged on being a crime; after all, 27 of the tank regiments there had no tanks at all.[40] The head of the Red Army's Automotive-Armoured-Tank Directorate Ia.N. Fedorenko, as was said, had a gut feeling that a major war was fast approaching and he didn't want the Soviet tankers to face it unarmed. Therefore on 14 May 1941 he reported to the People's Commissar of Defence that because of the incomplete provisioning of the mechanized corps with tanks, they 'were not completely combat-ready. In order to increase their combat capabilities before the arrival of their tanks, I consider it necessary to arm the tank regiments of the mechanized corps with 76mm and 45mm anti-tank guns and machine guns, so in the event of necessity, they would be able to fight as anti-tank regiments and battalions.'[41]

The Red Army had available 1,200 76mm divisional guns and 1,000 45mm anti-tank guns, as well as 4,000 light DP machine guns, which were enough to equip 50 tank regiments each with 24 76mm divisional guns and 18 45mm anti-tank guns, and 80 machine guns. In order to tow these guns and to transport the men and ammunition, it was also planned to assign to the regiments 1,200 ZIS-5 3-ton cargo lorries and 1,500 GAZ-AA 1.5-ton cargo lorries. Fedorenko's proposal concerned the tank regiments of 16 mechanized corps, 11 of which were stationed in the border districts. On 15 May the People's Commissar of Defence approved the allocation of armaments and lorries to the following mechanized corps: in the Leningrad Military District to the 10th Mechanized Corps; in the Baltic Special Military District to the 3rd and 12th Mechanized Corps; in the Western Special Military District to the 13th, 17th and 20th Mechanized Corps; in the Kiev Special Military District to the 16th, 19th and 24th Mechanized Corps; in the Odessa Military District to the 2nd and 18th Mechanized Corps; in the Moscow Military District to the 21st Mechanized Corps; in the Orel Military District to the 23rd Mechanized Corps; in the Kharkov Military District to the 25th Mechanized Corps; in the North Caucasus Military District to the 26th Mechanized Corps; and in the Central Asian Military District to the 27th Mechanized Corps.[42] On the following day the Chief of the General Staff sent to the corresponding districts directives about implementing this decision by 1 July 1941. The measure should 'be conducted in a manner so as not to disrupt the regiment's organizational principle as a tank unit, having in view that in the future, tanks will be arriving to arm them.'[43] Of course, this decision was a palliative, but it allowed the units that had not yet obtained their tanks to be used at least somehow, until receiving the combat vehicles from factories.

We'll examine this question in more detail on the basis of the Western Special Military District, where it was planned to supplement the military equipment with not fewer than 11 tank regiments. The district was given 480 guns and 590 vehicles to tow them, including 102 guns (48 76mm and 54 45mm), 160 light machine guns, 48 ZIS-5 lorries and 74 GAZ-AA lorries for the 13th Mechanized Corps. The mechanized corps that were less equipped had to receive as follows: 17th Mechanized Corps – 168 guns (96 76mm and 72 45mm), 320 light machine guns, 96 ZIS-5 lorries and 112 GAZ-AA lorries; 20th Mechanized Corps – 210 guns (120 76mm and 90 45mm), 400 light machine guns, 120 ZIS-5 lorries and 140 GAZ-AA lorries. After reaching the decision about supplementing the weapons, the delivery of guns of 45mm and 76mm calibre began arriving in the district in an increasing flow. For example, over the month of June alone, the Western Special Military District received 117 45mm anti-tank guns and 110 76mm Model 1902/30 divisional guns, used as anti-tank weapons. The total number of 45mm anti-tank guns and 76mm divisional guns in the district increased by 513 in the second half of the year.[44]

The temporary equipping of the tank units with anti-tank artillery only partially resolved the problem with arming them; moreover, by 14 June the regiments of the Western Special Military District's mechanized corps that had been designated for this still hadn't received the anti-tank guns.[45] It was already impossible to master the unfamiliar materiel over the eight days that remained until the German invasion. In addition, the mechanized corps were not only experiencing a lack of tanks, but also a lack of small arms. For example, according to data for the beginning of June 1941, in the western districts for mobilization and deployment they were still short of 20,500 light machine guns and 2,000 machine guns to replace the missing tanks.[46]

The acute lack of qualified personnel, especially in the higher ranks, played an even larger role. On the eve of the war the mechanized corps only had 22–40 per cent of their necessary command staff, and many key posts were left vacant. In commanding officers of armoured forces alone, they were still short of approximately 20,000.[47] Indeed, the available personnel, as a rule, had a low level of education and plainly inadequate combat training. No wonder, because after all the 1941 mobilization plan required bringing up the personnel of the Red Army's mechanized forces to 1,065,230 men after deployment, a figure almost six times greater in comparison with the preceding plan, which required only 181,461 men for this purpose.[48] To retrain the enormous number of former cavalrymen and infantrymen into competent tankers in a short period of time wasn't possible. Moreover, a significant portion of the Red Army troops had only recently begun their military service. Approximately two-thirds of the rank and file of the 11th Mechanized Corps had been called up in May 1941.[49] The discussion here is not only about the soldiers' lack of individual skills. In the brand new formations, the cohesion and teamwork of the elements and units was totally lacking. The majority of the tank crews hadn't gone through shakedowns even as part of a platoon or company, not to mention any larger unit. According to the approved programme of training, the recruits of the spring call-up in the Kiev Special Military District's mechanized corps were to complete their training as follows: of individual soldiers and tanks crews by 1 July; of platoons by 1 August; of companies by 1 September; and of battalions by 1 October 1941.[50] The war that began on 22 June unceremoniously forced a rescheduling of these plans…

In a nut shell, one can say that the actual combat readiness that had been attained by the mechanized corps by the beginning of the war only remotely corresponded to the importance and volume of the missions they were given. The very first encounters with the Germans revealed this in full measure. The under-equipped, under-trained and under-armed Soviet tank units and formations had to enter the heaviest fighting hastily and ill prepared. As a result, the seemingly numerous and formidable (on paper) mechanized corps of the Red Army quickly melted away in the fire of the border battles, without being able to inflict painful damage on the Wehrmacht. As early as 15 July 1941 the *Stavka* of the Supreme High Command ordered what was left of them after three weeks of fighting to be disbanded.[51]

Far from all of the pre-war Soviet tanks were assembled in the mechanized corps. On 1 June 1941 they had 16,555 tanks, or approximately 72 per cent of the Red Army's available 23,078 tanks.[52] The rest were located in the Far Eastern rifle formations; motorized rifle and cavalry divisions; the airborne corps; fortified regions; military schools and academies; naval units; and NKVD units. However, these were widely dispersed in small groups and were accordingly unable to exert any noticeable influence on the course of the war.

Tank duels

Tank duels took place infrequently and, of course, they alone did not determine the war's outcome. Even on those rare occasions when they did happen, the winners were as a rule the more experienced and better trained crews, who could more effectively exploit both their own strengths and the enemy's weaknesses. The decisive advantage was obtained by those who managed to spot the enemy first, to attack its flank or rear, to use the folds and features of the terrain better, and to shoot more accurately. However, purely technical factors also significantly influenced the outcome of tank duels. In the case of a frontal encounter on open and flat terrain, the penetrating power of the armour-piercing shell of the tank gun and the thickness of its own frontal armour gained a special importance. It was these factors that determined the distances over which tankmen could successfully knock out an enemy tank. The difference between these distances created a safe zone within which one of the participants in the tank duel could destroy his opponent with impunity. The distances at which the most common Soviet tanks at the beginning of the Great Patriotic War could penetrate the frontal armour of their German opponents at 30° angle of impact and vice versa are shown in the following series of drawings.

Figure 1.

Figure 2.

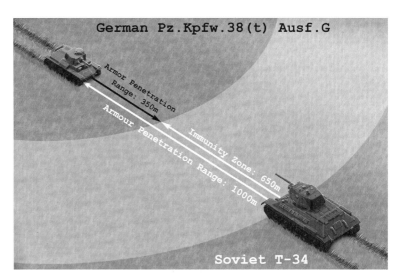

Figure 3.

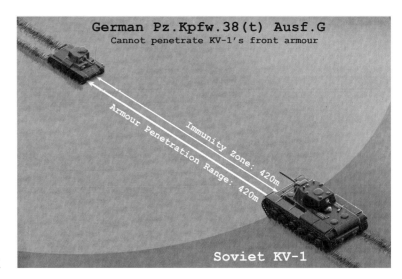

Figure 4.

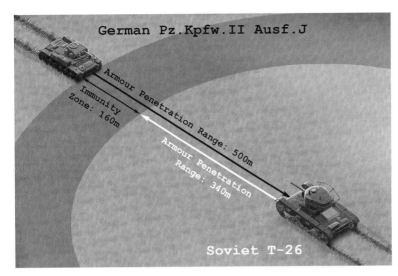

Figure 5.

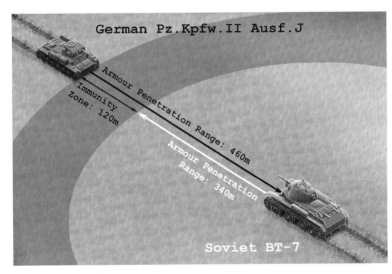

Figure 6.

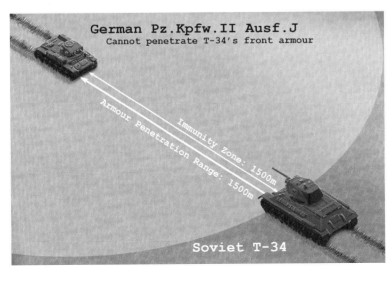

Figure 7.

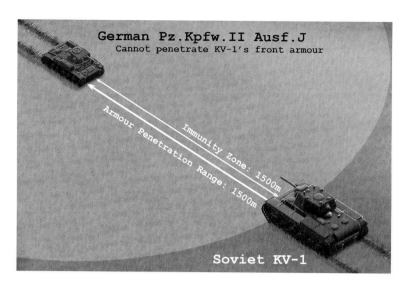

Figure 8.

Figure 9.

Figure 10.

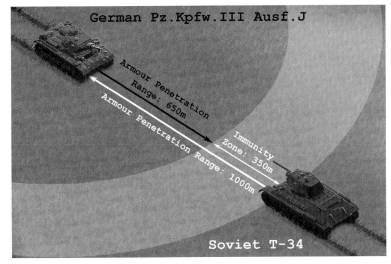

Figure 11.

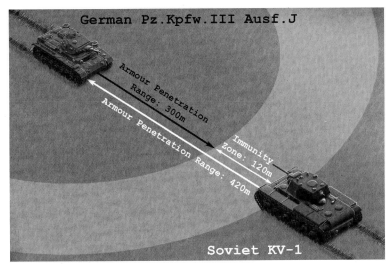

Figure 12.

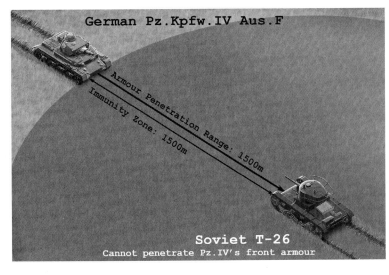

Figure 13.

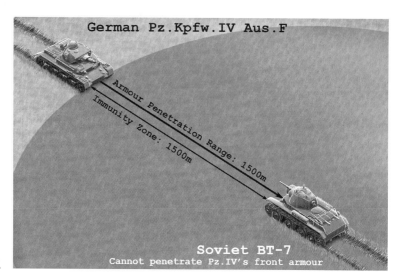

Figure 14.

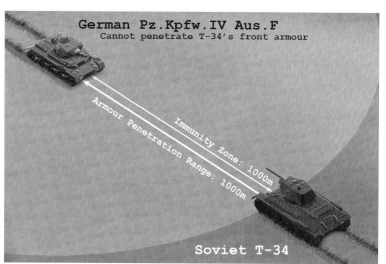

Figure 15.

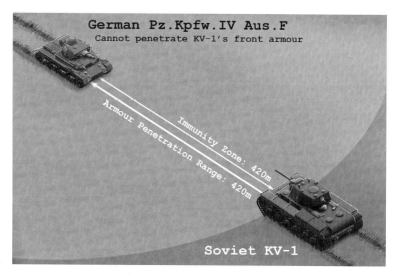

Figure 16.

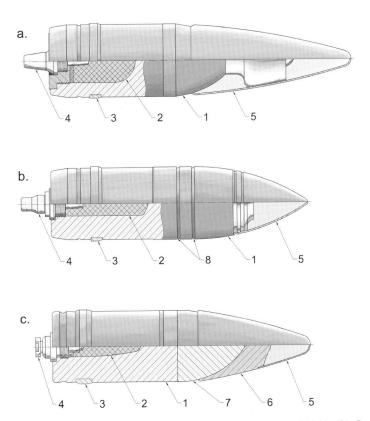

Figure 17: Types of shell: (a) Soviet 76mm armour-piercing shell (BR–350A); (b) Soviet 76mm armour-piercing shell (BR–350B); (c) German 75mm armour-piercing shell (Pzgr 39).

Key: (1) shell's body; (2) bursting charge; (3) driving band; (4) fuse with tracer; (5) ballistic cap; (6) penetrative cap; (7) weld-on head; (8) undercut localisers.

Figure 18: Location of the T–34's forward fuel tanks.

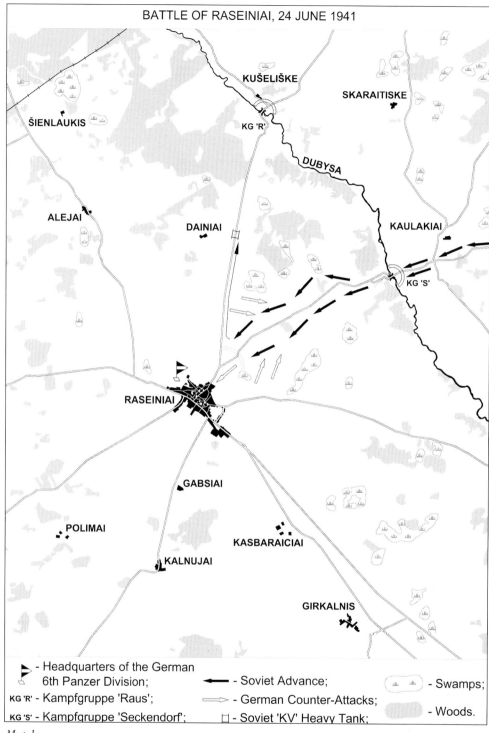

BATTLE OF RASEINIAI, 24 JUNE 1941

Legend:

- Headquarters of the German 6th Panzer Division;
- KG 'R' - Kampfgruppe 'Raus';
- KG 'S' - Kampfgruppe 'Seckendorf';
- Soviet Advance;
- German Counter-Attacks;
- Soviet 'KV' Heavy Tank;
- Swamps;
- Woods.

Map 1.

Chapter 7

The History of Tanks in the Red Army

The development of the design and production of tanks in the Soviet state had to start virtually from scratch. There were not any tanks in Czarist Russia. The projects that appeared from time to time, with varying degrees of feasibility, as well as Porokhovshchikov's and Lebedenko's prototypes of tanks that had been fabricated in metal but showed a complete lack of viability, can in no way be considered a foundation of a tank building industry. The situation was worsened by the chaos that reigned in the country and the collapse of its industry as a result of the long years of the First World War, two revolutions, and the fratricidal Russian Civil War that followed them. The loss of qualified cadres, and first of all engineers and technicians, was particularly heavy. Many of them perished in the course of those turbulent events, died from starvation or disease, or emigrated abroad. In these conditions, the only real path towards establishing a new, innovative and extremely complicated industrial branch was the copying of foreign models.

The light FT-17 tank produced by the French Renault company, which was very successful for its time, was selected as the prototype for the first Soviet combat vehicles. It became the origin of the classic layout that still dominates in our time: in front, a driver's compartment, behind it, a fighting compartment, where – for the first time in the history of tanks – the main gun was positioned in a pivoting turret, and in the rear, the engine compartment. The simplicity in production and the low cost of the design allowed the French in 1918 to produce 3,094 FT-17 tanks before the Armistice. Thereby the FT-17 of French production alone became the most widely produced tank in the First World War; they were also being built in the US and Italy.

On 18 March 1919, during the Russian Civil War, in the fighting near Berezovka railway station 80 kilometres outside Odessa, Red Army troops of N.A. Grigor'ev's brigade, which at the time was part of the 2nd

Ukrainian Soviet Army, seized rich war spoils from the French and Greek interventionists, including four FT-17 tanks. On 1 May of the same year one of the tanks took part in a holiday parade on Red Square in Moscow. The RSFSR's Council of People's Commissars on 10 August 1919 reached the decision to organize the production of tanks according to the FT-17 model at the Krasnoe Sormovo Factory in Nizhny Novgorod. The task wasn't as simple as it seemed at first glance. Certain components of the tank were lost while it was being transported by rail to the factory; among them were such important assemblies as the transmission. It required almost two years of work and colossal efforts on the part of both Nizhny Novgorod's workers and subcontractors to build 15 tanks. The Izhorsky Factory in Petrograd produced the armour for them, and the AMO Factory in Moscow built the engines. They differed from the prototype primarily in the use of Fiat engines instead of Renault engines, and Hotchkiss 37mm guns in place of the Puteaux 37mm guns. Each combat vehicle received its own name, yet there were only enough weapons for 12 of them. After this, the production of the tanks with the official designation 'Renault-Russky' came to an end; it proved to be unsustainable for a country facing much more urgent concerns (*see* Plate 10). The contrast between the capabilities of the French and Soviet industries of those years was more than evident. These tanks never managed to serve in the Russian Civil War, and a more peaceful fate befell them. In 1922 five of them were sent to the famine-stricken Volga region to plough fields in the place of tractors. In the spring of 1930 they were taken out of service and sent to a stockpile.[1]

Then began a multi-year break in Soviet tank building. The country was licking its wounds from the Civil War and was husbanding everything. By the end of 1923 the 5,000,000-strong Red Army had fallen to 610,000 men, but despite this, there still wasn't the means to maintain it at that level. For example, the artillery was supplied with only 60 per cent of what it needed, the cavalry only 75 per cent, and the decision was made to abandon the development of armoured forces for a time.[2]

Only on 2 June 1926 was the first programme for tank building. planned for a three-year period, approved in the USSR.[3] Within its framework a tank was designed and built; it received two designations: the T-18 and the MS-1 (*see* Plate 11). The letters 'MS' (the abbreviation of the words *malyi soprovozhdeniia*, 'small escort') reflected this tank's main task – to accompany infantry into combat. In appearance, the tank resembled the Renault-Russky, but with smaller dimensions and lower weight. The armour and main gun were analogous, although the top speed and operating range of the MS-1 almost doubled that of its predecessor. Having successfully passed through intensive trials between 11 and 17 June 1927, the tank was approved for the Red Army and was kept in production until the end of 1931. Over this period of time 959 MS-1 were built, primarily at the Bolshevik Factory in Leningrad. They saw combat when, in November 1929, nine of them took an active part in the fighting with the Chinese during the conflict over the Chinese-Far Eastern railway. However, the first production series of Soviet tanks didn't last long. Because of the absence of a system of repair in the Red Army at the time and the acute lack of spare parts, as early as the end of 1932 60 per cent of the MS-1 tanks were inoperable.[4] By the beginning of 1938 approximately 100 of the MS-1 were beyond repair and went to the scrapyard to be disassembled and their hulks were melted down. In 1936, 160 of these tanks that had totally exhausted their engine lifetimes were handed over to the fortified regions of the Leningrad Military District for use in building fixed fortifications. Within two years the majority of the 700 surviving MS-1 had also ended their short service lives, becoming part of the fortifications of military districts and coastal defences, while their chassis, engines and transmissions were converted into metal.[5] Meanwhile the turrets of these tanks were re-equipped with twin machine guns or 45mm cannons, both to increase their firepower and to bring their ammunition in line with the calibre of guns that were already being widely used in the Red Army of that time. Only around 70 MS-1 still retained their mobility; these joined tank companies of garrisons of fortified regions to serve as mobile firing positions. Their 37mm guns were also replaced by 45mm guns.[6]

In 1928 the implementation of the large-scale plans for the industrialization of the Soviet Union began. In the first Five-Year period the emphasis was on the construction of heavy industrial plants. With their opening, the mass production of tanks became possible, so now the question of the correct choice of their types and models for arming the Red Army became particularly acute. The Soviet leadership approached this matter with all seriousness. At a meeting of the USSR Revolutionary Military Council that took place on 17–18 July 1929 the 'System of arming the RKKA with tanks, tractors, lorries and armoured vehicles' was adopted. It was developed under the leadership of Triandafillov and included the following tank types: wheeled-tracked tankettes with a weight up to 3.3 tons; light tanks (like the MS-1) with a weight up to 7–7.5 tons; medium tanks weighing up to 15–16 tons; and heavy tanks, the requirements of which still had to be worked out.[7] The task now was to build these combat vehicles, which corresponded to the stipulations of the 'System …' and were suitable for production in both the factories that already existed at that time and the newly constructed ones.

However, this wasn't at all simple. First of all, the inadequate knowledge and lack of sufficient experience with tank building among the Soviet engineers and designers of that time hampered the process. There was also an acute need for highly educated professionals, so the projects and prototypes of the combat vehicles that appeared at the time suffered from too much complexity and excess weight. They lacked both reliability and manufacturability, and their costs exceeded all sensible limits. The country could not afford such tanks, so it is understandable that the Soviets turned to the best foreign experience in order to accelerate their own tank building. History demonstrated the correctness of this path, because of the approximately 80 designs for tanks and tankettes that were worked out in the USSR between 1931 and 1939, not a single one was put into service. Tanks of foreign origin were serving in the Red Army at the time. Soviet tank builders acquired their own particularly style only towards the end of the Great Patriotic War.

Just as the 'System …' was being approved, domestic experts were becoming familiar with the latest Western technology of the time in the aforementioned secret 'Kama' tank school. The study of the experimental models of German tanks and experience with their use on the proving grounds was undoubtedly enormously beneficial to Soviet tank building. Their best features were noted in the proper manner, evaluated, and then adopted. For example, the design of future Soviet tanks began to employ the co-axial machine gun in the turret, and welding began to be used for the manufacturing of turrets and hulls. The first Soviet optical sights for tanks and radio sets were also developed on the basis of German prototypes.

On 5 December 1929 the Central Committee Politburo adopted the decree 'On the fulfilment of the programme of tank building'. In particular, it stated:

Send an authoritative delegation consisting of representatives from VSNKh [Supreme Council of National Economy] and People's Commissariat of the Army and Navy on an official trip abroad, and give them the assignment:

a) to select and purchase types and models of tanks;
b) to explore the possibility of receiving technical assistance and design engineers.[8]

In order to implement this decision, on 30 December 1929 a delegation under the leadership of I.A. Khalepsky, the head of the Red Army's recently created Directorate of Mechanization and Motorization (which up until 22 November 1934 was called the Automotive-Armoured-Tank Directorate), was sent abroad. The delegation was authorized to purchase models of all the tank types that were included in the adopted 'System ...'. First they visited Germany, Czechoslovakia and France, but tank models suitable for the Red Army weren't found in Germany, the Czechs decided not to show anything, and the French refused to sell their tanks. Thus the delegation acquired only models of artillery prime movers and tow lorries, fast tractors, as well as half-track vehicles in Germany and France.[9]

Great Britain, the creator of the first tanks, was regarded as the leading producer of tanks in the world at the time, and the leading British company in the design and production of armoured equipment was Vickers-Armstrongs. So Khalepsky's delegation went to the United Kingdom as well. The business talks went well, and the delegation was able to order all the necessary examples, except for a heavy tank, which the British refused to sell. This refusal was not a company whim; it was experiencing a difficult period at the time. After the end of the First World War, it was no longer receiving lavish orders for hundreds and thousands of pieces of military equipment. In the 1920s there was only talk of test examples, or in the best case, a few dozen tanks sold to the British Army. In order to keep its tank production going, the company had to make no small efforts in order to develop the export of its output. However, its hands were tied by the government, which allowed the sale of the latest tanks only to Great Britain's trusted allies. Others were only allowed to purchase combat vehicles that were inferior to the tanks that were arming or were being planned to equip the British Army. In addition, the tanks proposed for export by the Vickers-Armstrongs company could not have any features that had been designed by government employees. Thus, the heavy five-turreted Independent tank that was being tested at the time was not allowed to be sold to the USSR.[10]

However, the British willingly sold 20 small and inexpensive Vickers Carden-Loyd Mk.VI tankettes. On their basis, the Soviets developed their own T-27 tankettes, which went into service on 13 February 1931 (*see* Plate 20). The main difference from the British prototype was a new engine and transmission system designed on the basis of the GAZ-AA lorry's motor and transmission. By fortunate coincidence, both the Soviet and the original British engines and transmissions stemmed from the very same source: the American Ford company. This circumstance, of course, facilitated the replacement of the engine and transmission. In order not to ruin an already successful design, the military agreed to do without the wheeled-tracked running gear that was required by the 'System ...'. Serial manufacture of the T-27 continued between 1931 and 1934, initially at the Leningrad Bolshevik Factory, then at Moscow Factory No. 37 and the Gorky automobile factory. In total over this time, 3,295 such tankettes were built.[11]

In the small or light tank category, the delegation purchased the Mk. E, or 6-ton tank. The Vickers-Armstrongs company initially designed and built this tank in 1928 as a venture exclusively for export. It strove to make it as universal and inexpensive as possible, hoping to satisfy the maximum number of potential customers. The tank turned out splendidly. It proved to be compact and mobile; with decent armour and adequately armed for its time; and simple to produce, maintain, repair and operate. Thanks to these qualities and its inexpensive cost, it deservedly became a large commercial success for its creators. Between 1930 and 1938 Bolivia, Bulgaria, China, Finland, Greece, Poland and Thailand all bought it.[12]

However, this tank design proved to be most successful in the Soviet Union. The contract for the purchase of 15 of these twin-turreted tanks was signed on 28 May 1930, and at the end of the same year the first four Mk.E tanks arrived in the USSR. Three of them went through extensive testing in the Moscow area between 24 December 1930 and 5 January 1931. At a demonstration in front of representatives of the high army command between 8 and 11 January 1931, the Mk.E made a deep impression on all those attending with its agility and cross-country performance. Engineer S.A. Ginzburg, who led the commission at its trials, emphasized in his report that the tank '… despite the reviewed shortcomings, is capable of developing high speed and manoeuvrability, and is without a doubt the best model of all the foreign tank models that are known at this time'.[13]

After such a glowing review, on 13 February 1931 the tank was officially accepted by the Red Army under the designation T-26 as 'the main tank for escorting the combined-arms units and formations, as well as for the tank units of the High Command Reserve' (see Plate 15) Its mass manufacture began in 1931 at the Bolshevik Factory, the tank production part of which in February of the following year was separated into an independent plant – the Voroshilov Factory No. 174. The tank continued to be produced until the end of 1940, and over this time it went through substantial changes. Initially it was a typical twin-turreted 'trench sweeper', armed with only two machine guns. Starting from the spring of 1932 a 37mm cannon replaced the machine gun in the right-hand turret. In the summer of 1933, one large turret, equipped with a 45mm gun, appeared in place of the two small turrets. This substitution didn't present any particular difficulty, since Vickers-Armstrongs had proposed such a variant of arming the tanks from the very beginning, and so the design of the hull had been prepared for it. In 1938 the tank's turret was converted to a conical shape in order to improve its resistance to penetration. As a result of the numerous modifications, the combat weight of the last produced T-26 had grown by more than 70 per cent in comparison with its prototype and exceeded 10 tons.

During the Winter War with Finland in February–March 1940, 89 T-26 tanks received supplementary armour plates with a thickness of 30–40mm, which made them invulnerable to 45mm shells fired from a range of not less than 400–500 metres. The armour protection of these tanks rose substantially, but in the process the weight of them reached 12 tons. Bringing up the weight to twice that of the initial variant far exceeded its initial design capacity. The tanks were now badly overloaded, so it was recommended to drive them only in lower gears.

Altogether, over the ten years of production in Leningrad, 11,503 T-26 in 23 serial modifications were produced. Of these, 2,038 were twin-turreted tanks (of which approximately 450 had the 37mm cannon in the right-hand turret), 4,192 had a single turret, 3,887 had been equipped with radios (of which 471 had an additional anti-aircraft machine gun mounted on the turret), 162 were remote-controlled, and 1,224 were flame-throwing or chemical warfare tanks. In addition, the Stalingrad Tractor Factory between 1933 and 1940 built no fewer than 183 T-26 tanks, and in 1941, after the war had begun, Factory No. 174 put together another 47 out of the stock of components and parts it had there. With such numbers, on the eve of the Great Patriotic War the T-26 became the most mass-produced tank in the world.[14]

As the prototype for the future Soviet medium tank, 15 Vickers Mk.II, or 12-ton tanks, were purchased. However, after signing the contract, the Soviet delegation's members spotted an unusual three-turreted combat vehicle on a British proving ground. It was one of the three prototypes of the medium Vickers Mk.III, or as it was also called, the 16-ton tank, that had been built by this time. This tank was perhaps the most advanced for its time. The Vickers Mk.II was inferior to it in every category (which is why they sold it to the USSR). However the British Army, in addition to the prototypes, ordered only three more Vickers Mk.III tanks that were built in 1933–1934. The main shortcoming of the Vickers Mk.III was its high cost, which in fact decided its fate. However, contemporary British tank experts consider this tank to be the pinnacle of British tank manufacture of those times. In the future, because of the excessive pursuit of low costs, it underwent a continuous decline until the appearance of the Centurion tank in 1945.[15]

The members of Khalepsky's delegation back then, of course, couldn't know all this, but at first glance they sensed it was a promising design, and they were right. In June 1930 Khalepsky's deputy on the delegation, Ginzburg, travelled to the United Kingdom on a second official trip and by hook or by crook collected pieces of information about this secret tank. The British curtly refused to discuss its sale and proposed instead to design something similar for Soviet needs. However, the price of their proposal proved unacceptable, and the Soviets decided instead to design and develop their own tank, using the information that Ginzburg had gleaned about the Mk.III in the United Kingdom. Engineers of a special Tank-Tractor Design Bureau of the All-Union Gun-Arsenal Consortium under the leadership of the same Ginzburg successfully resolved this difficult task. Their design represented a unique hodge-podge. For example, the overall layout, transmission schematic and running gear, together with a few other design decisions, were adopted from the Vickers Mk.III. The position of the engine, the configuration of the cooling system and the design of its components, as well as the steering clutches, were taken from Christie's tank. The Vickers Mk.E became the prototype for the drive sprockets, tracks, support rollers, and the control linkages of steering clutches and brakes. The design of the lower suspension was taken from the German Grosstraktor built by Krupp, and the small turrets from the T-26 tank. However, the 400 horsepower engine was more than twice as powerful as the British prototype and offset the tank's weight, which exceeded 25 tons by the end of production. On 29 May 1932 the tank, designated the T-28, completed its first run across the factory yard (*see* Plate 19). Based on the results of trials conducted with the tank that had been built by the Bolshevik Factory, a team from its Design and Engineering Department headed by O.M. Ivanov introduced substantive revisions to the prototype. After a review of the updated drawings, at the end of September 1932 the decision was made to organize the serial production of the T-28 at the Leningrad Krasnyi Putilovets Factory, which was subsequently renamed the Leningrad Kirov Factory.[16] This factory, which had enormous experience producing various types of complicated machinery, received additional manufacturing equipment in order to produce such complex tanks as the T-28, and its work force was reinforced with qualified workers. Production cooperation with other factories was also established. The Leningrad Kirov Factory didn't let the Red Army down: between 1933 and 1940, 503 T-28 tanks were accepted by the army.[17]

The T-28 successfully passed its final test in the war with Finland between 30 November 1939 and 13 March 1940. There, the 20th *Kirov* Heavy Tank Brigade, which was equipped primarily with the T-28, was operating on the main axis. On 19 December 1939 its tanks broke through the famous Mannerheim Line to its entire depth, but without supporting infantry, they were forced to return to their jumping-off positions, having lost 29 T-28 tanks in the process. Altogether, 172 tanks of this type took part in the fighting with the Finns, and a total of 482 were knocked out of action for various reasons, including non-combat reasons. This apparent discrepancy is explainable by the fact that many of the tanks were repeatedly repaired and put back into service after breakdowns and battle damage; in some cases tanks went through this process up to five times! Only 32 T-28 tanks had to be written off: 30 of them were left burned out on the battlefield, and two fell into the hands of the Finnish Army.[18]

After the experience of the Winter War, the T-28 began to be shielded with add-on armour, bringing up the thickness of the frontal armour to 60mm. In the process its weight reached 32 tons. Some 111 T-28 tanks had been updated in this way before the Great Patriotic War. Its firepower was also increased by equipping it with a 76mm L-10 cannon with a 26-calibre long barrel, in place of the 16.5 calibres of the former KT-28 cannon. By the beginning of the Great Patriotic War, approximately 300 T-28 had received the new gun.[19] This tank was distinguished by its ease of handling, comfort for its crew, excellent cross-country performance and high cruising speed. It also had great potential for further improvements, but unfortunately, it was never fully exploited.

As mentioned above, the Red Army wasn't able to acquire a prototype for the heavy tank as required by the 'System of arming the RKKA with tanks, tractors, lorries and armoured vehicles'. This tank was intended as a qualitative reinforcement of the rifle and tank formations when breaking through particularly powerful and well-fortified enemy defensive belts. At the time, it was considered necessary for such a vehicle to have the ability to place heavy fire simultaneously in every direction, so it was decided to arrange the layout of the weapons according to the model of that very same British five-turreted Independent heavy tank that the Soviet delegation had been unsuccessful in purchasing. (Incidentally, the Independent never in fact went beyond the stage of a prototype, but in the USSR at the time they didn't know this and believed it was a serially produced tank, which was arming the British Army.)

The design and development of the first heavy Soviet tank didn't begin from scratch. It was based on the design of the 'positional', as it was called back then, TG (Tank Grotte, or sometimes seen as Grote) tank, created by the German engineer Edward Grotte. Since the end of 1929 he had been working in the USSR with a group of engineers from Germany under strict secrecy according to a contract and heading the AVO-5 design bureau at the Leningrad Bolshevik Factory. Soviet engineers had been included on his team with the task to acquire foreign experience. Two of them – N.V. Barykov and L.S. Troianov – subsequently rose to become prominent creators of tanks and self-propelled guns for the Red Army. The TG tank was far ahead of its time: it had a fully welded design, independent suspension, anti-projectile armour and a powerful long-barrel 76mm cannon as its main gun. The tank was built and tested, but it turned out to be too expensive to produce (one TG was more expensive to build than 25 BT-2 tanks) and difficult to build, so it never entered serial production.[20]

After the departure of Grotte and the other Germans back to Germany, in August 1931 the director's position at AVO-5 was taken over by Barykov, who had previously worked there as Grotte's deputy. The design bureau received an assignment 'by 1 August 1932 to develop and build a new 35-ton breakthrough tank of the TG type'. Unsurprisingly, the new design used the TG engine and its transmission system with herringbone gears and pneumatic servo-steering. The suspension, as in the case of the T-28, was devised along the lines of the Grosstraktor tank built by the Krupp company, but substantially improved. The assembly of the first tank, designated the T-35, was completed on 20 August 1932 (*see* Plate 20). After tests in the autumn of that year, many changes had to be made in its design. For example, the M-17 engine, which was also an aeroplane engine, replaced the M-16 engine. The transmission's pneumatic control, which was easy to handle but difficult to manufacture and unreliable in operation, was replaced by a traditional mechanical control. The engineers made both the main and small machine-gun turrets uniform with the corresponding turrets of the T-28 tank, while the medium gun turrets were made uniform with the BT-5 turrets but without a rear bustle. The Leningrad Factory No. 174, which built two T-35 prototypes, was burdened to the limit with the manufacture of the T-26, so according to a decree from the USSR government in May 1933 serial production of the T-35 shifted to the Kharkov Locomotive Factory.[21] In order to support the production of the T-35 and further improve its design, a special KB-35 (Design Bureau-35) was organized there, headed by I.S. Ber.[22] The skills of the Kharkov workers and the technical level of their factory were far inferior to the Leningrad workers and their equipment, so the production of the enormous and complex T-35 tanks was problematic, and the factory constantly failed to meet the targets. Virtually all of the tanks were being assembled one by one, and numerous revisions were constantly being introduced into the design, so the majority of them noticeably differed from each other. Between 1932 and 1939 the Kharkov Locomotive Factory managed to produce only 59 serial T-35s. Without exception, they were all overloaded, and this problem grew in step with their production. If the first vehicles weighed 38 tons, then the last to be built weighed up to 54 tons, which gave rise to many problems. In particular, the engines often overheated, the transmission failed and the tracks broke, especially in soft soil or when moving over fallen trees.[23]

According to commanders' reports, at the start of its operations with the troops, 'the tank could overcome a slope of only 17°, and was unable to get out of a large puddle'.[24] Yet according to its official TTKh (Tactical-technical Characteristics), the T-35 could handle a 20° gradient, but, as it turned out, only on paper. It was very hard to manoeuvre, especially on uneven or saturated soil, because of its heavy resistance to turning as a result of the excessively high ratio between the lengths of the track and the distance between them. On the T-35 this amounted to 2.5, while the optimal figure is 1.5 and certainly below 1.8.[25] The reliability of these tanks, especially in the first years of their production, left a lot to be desired. Prior to the beginning of the Great Patriotic War, the T-35 didn't take part in any combat operations. However, on parades in Moscow and Kiev the five-turreted armoured behemoths, bristling with the barrels of guns and machine guns in every direction, looked massively impressive.

Khalepsky's delegation made one more important acquisition in the USA, where John Walter Christie lived and worked. He was a brilliant representative of that vanishing species of natural inventors, who had never completed higher education and had no love for following the instructions of others regarding how and why something needed to be designed. As a result, not a single one of his combat vehicles was officially accepted by the American Army. However, the talented engineer still managed to leave behind a notable trace in the history of global tank building. He loudly announced it himself at a demonstration of the M1928 tank in 1928. This vehicle, which weighed 7.7 tons, was able to develop an unheard-of speed, especially for those times: 68km per hour on tracks, and 113km per hour on wheels.[26]

A difficult dilemma faced Khalepsky in America. On one hand, he had the opportunity to acquire the fastest tank in the world, in which many promising engineering decisions had been used. Moreover, its Liberty engine at the time was being serially produced in the USSR under the M-5 brand. On the other hand, this tank had no place in the recently approved 'System of arming the RKKA with tanks, tractors, lorries and armoured vehicles'. However, all doubts were tossed aside when information suggested that the Poles were planning to purchase the M1928. At that time Poland was considered one of the most likely opponents of the USSR in a future war. Moscow had no desire to yield to it an advantage in wheeled-tracked tanks, especially considering their capability of rapidly covering a large distance, which was very important for the Soviet Union with its endless expanses and limited road network.

Christie also wanted very much to sell his tank at last. He had spent five years developing the tank and had gone way over budget, having spent almost $382,000 on the project at his own expense, and was in desperate need of cash. A deal with the Russians not only promised him a long-awaited way out of his predicament, but also alluring prospects for the future. In order to fulfil the Russian order more quickly, he even held up the delivery of one of his tanks to the American Army for four and a half months; it had ordered one to familiarize itself with the new tank and to conduct tests.[27] As a result, on 28 April 1930 Christie signed a contract with the Soviet delegation for the sale of two tanks and spare parts for them, a complete set of design documents, and the rights to produce the tank, for a total sum of $164,000. It is curious that the USA at the time didn't even recognize the Soviet Union, but the arrangement, nevertheless, was completed officially through Amtorg – a procuring agency that had been created by Soviet representatives in New York on 1 May 1924 especially for conducting trade with the Americans.

The contract had to be carried out within four months, which is to say, no later than the end of August. However, Christie somewhat overestimated his production capabilities. He also showed more concern about the quality of his product than observing the contract deadline, and continued to make improvements to his tanks while building them. In the end, he gave them a new name, the M1931, but he was four months late in shipping the tanks and moreover sent them without turrets, weapons and complete documentation. For this Amtorg paid him $25,000 less than the agreed sum. In response, Christie took offence and refused to travel to the USSR for two months in order to offer his technical expertise in the production of the tanks, as he had previously offered to do.[28]

The new combat vehicle acquired the unusual designation BT, an abbreviation of the words *bystrokhodnyi tank*, or 'fast-moving tank'. On 23 May 1931 the Defence Committee with the USSR Council of People's Commissars made the decision to organize the production of the tanks at the Kharkov Locomotive Factory, without any design changes whatsoever. It would seem that this might be simpler, but the factory ran into unforeseen problems, and here is why: on the one hand, by themselves these combat vehicles weren't overcomplicated; after all, Christie's factory in the state of New Jersey, where they had been built, was in essence a rather small workshop. On the other hand, however, Christie had used the imperial system of measurement, while the Soviet Union used the metric system. But the main point was that these were still raw prototypes, which were far short of the requirements of large-scale production and not tailored to the existing technology of the Kharkov Locomotive Factory and the average skill level of its workers. The American models required serious adaptations, a task that was given to the T2K tank design bureau headed by I.N. Alekseenko that was especially organized at the factory. However, such a task was plainly beyond the bureau's capabilities, because there was an acute lack of experienced and knowledgeable tank-building professionals in provincial Kharkov. The bureau had only 22 members, of whom only seven had an engineering degree. The rest were self-taught, lacking both sufficient fundamental knowledge and adequate work experience. The Red Army's Directorate of Mechanization and Motorization knew about these problems and at the end of May 1931 sent their top experts on an official trip to the Kharkov Locomotive Factory: Professor V.I. Zaslavsky, who a year later would become the head of the Department of Tanks and Tractors at the Military Academy of Mechanization and Motorization; S.A. Ginzburg, the head of the Main Design Bureau for developing tanks; and N.M. Toskin, a qualified military engineer and chairman of the tank section of the Directorate of Mechanization and Motorization's Technical Committee. The latter had spent almost a year in the United States, taking part in the negotiations with Christie, accepting the order from him, and shipping it on to the USSR. It was Toskin who headed the work connected with setting up the serial production of the new tanks, and led it until his return to Moscow in January 1932.[29]

Unexpected obstacles constantly arose in the path of the 'overseas guest', which in February 1933 received the official designation BT-2 (*see* Plate 16). Its M-5 motor had been taken out of production in the aviation industry for being outdated, so the Soviets had to purchase Liberty engines, a large number of which had been built back in the years of the First World War for the BT in the United States. There were also not enough armaments for it, as a result of which only 190 tanks received the 37mm cannon, while the rest were equipped with twin machine guns. Altogether, between 1931 and 1933, 623 BT-2 tanks were built. In March 1933 the Kharkov Locomotive Factory switched to the serial production of a new tank model, the BT-5, which continued until the end of the next year (*see* Plate 17). Over this time they produced 1,884 such tanks, of which 263 were command tanks equipped with radios. The main difference between the BT-5 tank and the preceding model was the new turret, which was designed based on the T-26 turret and was armed with a 45mm cannon. All of the imported Liberty engines had already been used for the BT-2 tanks, so in order to equip the BT-5, the Soviets overhauled M-5 aeroplane engines that had already served out their expected flight life. Such a solution to the problem could only be temporary, because the number of M-5 engines was constantly declining after it had been removed from production.

In the autumn of 1935 the BT-7 with the M-17T engine began to roll off the assembly line (*see* Plate 18). This engine was a variant of an aviation motor that was produced in the Soviet Union under licence from the German BMW company. In addition, this tank differed from the previous models in its new welded hull in place of the former riveted hull, and in its smaller-link tracks. In September 1937 conical welded turrets began to be mounted on the BT-7. Before the end of 1939, 2,596 ordinary BT-7 and 2,017 command BT-7, equipped with a radio set, were built.

In addition to them, in 1937 155 BT-7A artillery tanks were built, intended to provide fire support to the troops. Just 11 of them had radio sets. They were armed with the 76mm KT-28 cannon in a special turret, which had originally been designed in Leningrad for the T-26 tank. Incidentally, by the end of 1938 21 of these tanks – because of a lack of 76mm guns – had to be armed with the 45mm gun in standard conical turrets. Between December 1939 and September 1940, 787 BT-7M tanks were produced – the final series of this large family of combat vehicles. Their main feature was their new V-2 diesel engine, although 72 of them, designated for the NKVD troops, still had the petrol M-17T engine.[30] In the process, the tank's weight rose to 14.65 tons and when it was moving on wheels the overloaded solid rubber rims on them began to disintegrate after just 50–100 kilometres. In contrast, using tracked movement, they were good for about 2,000 kilometres.[31] Therefore it was recommended for the BT-7M to use only tracked movement, and the section about running on wheels was removed from its service manual.[32]

The ordering of tanks from the British Vickers–Armstrongs company continued after 1930. On 5 February 1932 eight amphibious tanks were purchased from it. They tried to copy them in the USSR even earlier, as soon as information about them appeared in the open press, but these attempts failed. Using the experience of this work and models acquired from the United Kingdom, the amphibious T-37A tank was developed at the Moscow Factory No. 37 under the leadership of N.N. Kozyrev (*see* Plate 12). Its running gear once again was designed in accordance with the German Grosstraktor built by Krupp, and its ability to swim was ensured by two floats mounted on the sides. It was put into Red Army service on 11 August 1932, even before the assembly of the first prototype was completed. Production began in 1933, and over the next four years Factory No. 37 built 1,909 ordinary tanks, 643 radio-equipped tanks and 75 chemical tanks.[33]

Thus, the work to put into practice the 'System of arming the RKKA with tanks, transports, tractors and lorries' was successfully implemented. In connection with this, Decree No. 71 from 13 August 1933 from the Council of Labour and Defence in particular had the following to say about the arming of the Red Army with tanks: 'Approve ... to keep in production the following types of combat vehicles for the first half of the Five-Year period: a) T-37 – as a reconnaissance tank; b) T-26 – as a multi-service tank; c) BT – as an operational tank; d) T-28 – as a tank of qualitative reinforcement of the TRGK [Tank Reserve of the High Command]; e) T-35 – as a powerful, special purpose tank.'[34]

However, it was impossible to say the task had been achieved, because all the tanks listed in the decree were in need of improvement. The T-37A, for example, from the beginning had been planned to make long journeys on heavy flatbed lorries, which at the time still weren't available in the USSR. Lengthy marches under its own power, which these tanks hadn't been designed for, led to widespread breakdowns of the running gear and the overheating of engines, so at the end of 1934 work began on a new amphibious tank. The original intention to make it operational on both wheels and tracks proved unrealistic, and on 29 February 1936 the Red Army put into service the purely tracked amphibious T-38 tank, which had been designed in the Design Bureau of Factory No. 37 headed by N.A. Astrov (*see* Plate 13). They decided to reject the floats, which were vulnerable to combat damage, and the T-38's ability to swim was secured only by increasing its water displacement. However, these tanks' buoyancy reserve was insufficient, so when overloaded by just 120–150kg they would flood with water and sink. They also sank even without being overloaded when attempting to make sharp turns on the water; when quickly changing speed on the water; when entering or exiting the water to or from a steep bank; and even in a moderate swell. Their reliability and off-road capabilities were also totally inadequate, but the Red Army had nothing better, so between 1936 and 1939, 1,347 T-38 tanks were built, of which 165 were equipped with radio sets.[35]

Chapter 8

Pre-War Soviet Tanks

The half-measures to modernize the T-38 didn't permit the radical resolution of all the existing problems, so on 19 December 1939 a completely new amphibious tank, the T-40, which was developed in the Design Bureau of Factory No. 37 under the leadership of N.A. Astrov, was put into Red Army service after successful trials (*see* Plate 14). This tank's buoyancy reserve was also insufficient – just 300kg or 5.5 per cent of its water displacement.[1] However, it had a water deflection shield mounted on the front of the tank, which noticeably enhanced its sea-going capability. The individual torsion suspension of the T-40, which was the most advanced for its time, significantly improved its mobility over rough terrain. The powerplant consisted of inexpensive and readily available automotive components, which considerably simplified the tank's manufacturing, reduced its costs, and increased its reliability. Prior to the beginning of the Great Patriotic War, Factory No. 37 managed to produce 222 T-40, of which 50 were equipped with radio sets.[2] The successful chassis of this tank had ample strength to allow the building of heavier vehicles on its basis in the future, such as the T-60, T-70 and T-80 light tanks, and SU-76 self-propelled guns. They lost their former ability to swim, but the practical significance of this vanished due to the increased firepower and armour protection of these combat vehicles.

The amphibious and light tanks played their role in the Great Patriotic War, but the medium tanks made a much more substantial contribution to the Red Army's eventual victory. The T-34 tank made up the lion's share of the latter, so the history of its creation and the men who took part in it should be discussed in more detail. Without this, it is impossible to understand why these tanks became what they were, with all their advantages and shortcomings.

On 15 August 1937 the USSR Council of People's Commissar's Defence Committee approved Decree No. 94 concerning developing a new model of the BT tank of the Christie-type with a combat weight of 13–14 tons, with strengthened sloping armour, a diesel engine, and six drive wheels. The prototype had to be built in 1938 with the aim of switching to serial production in the following year. The fulfilment of the government's order was placed on the shoulders of Tank Factory No. 183, the new name for the Kharkov Locomotive Factory, which was renamed on 30 December 1936.[3] However, the key to the success of this major job, especially in its first stage, was its design bureau, which was renamed from T2K to KB-190 of the 100th Department (which indicated tank production).[4] It was this design bureau that was asked to prepare the project in a limited period of time, and then help turn the design into a real tank.

However, at the time this task was beyond the design bureau's capabilities. As we've already noted, it was a small and not particularly strong team, which worked far away from the leading centres of Soviet tank design and building, and spent most of its time busy with engineering support for the production process of the BT series of tanks. Even though the Kharkov team managed to make gradual improvements to Christie's original model, their own creativity did not fare very well. The majority of the team's engineering designs never reached serial production, primarily because the Kharkov Locomotive Factory had an acute lack of qualified professionals. Moreover the team had little experience, because the tank design group of eight men appeared in the Kharkov Locomotive Factory for the first time only in December 1928. It was headed by the most senior in age among them, the 24-year-old engineer Ivan Nikanorovich Alekseenko.

For a start he was instructed to prepare drawings and bills of material for a manoeuvring (as the medium tanks were called back then in the USSR) T-12 tank, and of course, not from scratch. Engineers of the Moscow Main Design Bureau of the Gun-Arsenal Group under the leadership of V.I. Zaslavsky created a preliminary design for the new tank. They, for their part, also didn't proceed along an untrodden path, but borrowed the overall layout and several technical solutions from the American M1921 and M1922 medium tanks. However, despite the support of the much more experienced and knowledgeable Muscovites, the first effort made by the young collective of Kharkov engineers proved to be, as usual, a clunker. From the end of December 1929 and over the course of the next seven months the prototype

T-12 underwent extensive testing, which resulted in a constant succession of breakdowns, the fixing of defects, and futile attempts to improve a clearly unsuccessful vehicle. On 25 July 1932 it ended with an engine explosion and resulting fire, which knocked the tank out of action for an entire three weeks. The work on an improved model of a medium tank, called the T-24, didn't go much better. It fell constantly behind schedule, despite schedule revisions, but for want of a better tank, serial production had been planned for the T-24 even before the first example was built. The Kharkov Locomotive Factory was instructed in the course of 1931 to produce 300 T-24, and in the following year another 1,300; however, these figures had no bearing on reality.[5] The endless tweaking of its design hampered efforts to get it into production, but it was impossible to get by without them. Here is just one characteristic example: during the first attempt to drive the prototype T-24 tank forwards, it unexpectedly began to move backwards. It turned out that the developers of the transmission had managed to mix up the direction of its turning …[6]

In the circumstances, the decision was made to use up a stock of parts ready for assembly of the T-24 tanks, and with this complete their production, and then shift the Kharkov Locomotive Factory to the mass production of BT tanks. As a result, the first serially produced T-24 appeared only by October 1931, and by the end of the same year another 18 were delivered. They never received authorized guns and went virtually unused by the troops.[7] Their career ended in 1938, when 22 of them were positioned in fortified regions as armoured firing points, and the last two were turned over to a museum of combat vehicles that was created in the Moscow suburb of Kubinka.[8] However, they haven't been preserved up to the present time.

Frustrated by the development of events, Alekseenko vainly tried to fight for his own brainchild. He wanted to get busy with refining and producing his own tank, not someone else's. Getting nowhere and deeply offended, in June 1932 he resigned and moved to Leningrad, where at the time the best cadre of Soviet tank designers worked.[9] There, Alekseenko didn't win any great renown, whereas he was rightly considered the top expert in Kharkov.

However, even before his departure, the management of the Kharkov Locomotive Factory began to search for a qualified design engineer in order to replace Alekseenko, one who was not only capable, but who also had the desire to whip the still raw BT tanks into shape and secure their mass production. The task was not the easiest, because the Soviet Union at the time had an acute shortage of qualified experts, especially in manufacturing. For example, of the 237,000 people employed in the Soviet military industry on 1 October 1929, only 1,897 were engineers, of whom only 439 worked directly in factories.[10] Thus, on average there were 540 other workers per one factory engineer. Moreover, these engineers included not only designers, but also managers, industrial engineers and other professionals. In addition, around half of them had no engineering degrees and belonged to the so-called practitioners, who lacked fundamental engineering knowledge. Even without this, the repressions that had swept through the those engineers who had gained their experience before the Russian Revolution worsened the already hopelessly bad situation with the engineer cadres. Show trials, organised to demonstrate that the numerous miscalculations, mistakes and disarray in the period of the first Five-Year Plan were due to spies and 'wreckers' among the senior professionals who were dissatisfied with Soviet power, were shaking the country.

One such 'scapegoat' was Afanasy Osipovich Firsov. He was born on 8 May 1883 in Berdiansk, but obtained his engineering degree in Germany and Switzerland. In 1911 he found work in Switzerland at the Sulzer brothers' factory that manufactured diesel engines. After the First World War broke out he returned to Russia and continued to work at factories that primarily produced inboard and marine diesel engines. On 30 March 1930 he was arrested for the 'Industrial Party' case that was falsified by the Chekists, and on 23 June of the same year he was sentenced to five years in a concentration camp.[11] Here, one can say, Firsov was lucky: he happened to serve out his sentence not in the notorious Solovetsky Islands, but in one of the special bureaux under the jurisdiction of OGPU. Beginning in 1930, no fewer than 400 innocent engineers like Firsov worked in these shady business establishments; although incarcerated, they were working according to their specialty in relatively tolerable conditions. Primarily they were fulfilling military procurement orders and did so rather successfully. Meanwhile, the arrests of the professionals in the realm of technology, who were few to begin with, led to the disruption of production, the failure to meet vitally important economic plans and the creation of an atmosphere of fear and distrust in the country. Ultimately, this was finally recognized in the Kremlin, and on 23 June 1931 Stalin publicly condemned the harassment of the senior professionals. A small number of them were released and sent to work in military factories, although the history of these shady business operations didn't end on there.[12]

The next political campaign also didn't miss Firsov. At the time he was working in the GKB VOORPO (State Design Bureau of the All-Union Ordnance Complex), where among the other projects the T-19 and T-20 light tanks were being developed, which were intended to replace the MS-1. At the end of May 1931 I.P. Bondarenko, the chief engineer of the Kharkov Locomotive Factory, who two years later became its director, read Firsov's resumé, and realized that this was just the man he needed. Bondarenko began actively to petition that the prisoner be sent to his factory in order to serve out the rest of his sentence, and in the end got his way. On 10 January 1932 Firsov arrived at the Kharkov Locomotive Factory and replaced there Toskin, who had been summoned back to Moscow. He continued his work to bring the BT tanks into serial production, and after Alekseenko's departure from the factory, began to carry out his managerial duties in the T2K Design Bureau. However, only on 1 January 1933 was Firsov officially appointed head of this design bureau and given an apartment in Kharkov, so that finally his family could join him there. Up until this moment, for the course of a full year, he had continued to be treated as a prisoner: he lived in a special barracks on the factory's grounds and went to work and back again in prisoner's garb accompanied by an armed escort.[13]

Firsov left a deep imprint in the history of Kharkov tank building. It is sufficient to say that under his leadership in 1934, for the first time in the USSR, the BD-2 diesel engine was installed in the BT-5 and BT-7 tanks.[14] However, his greatest service was the education that he gave to his young subordinates. He unsparingly shared his experience with them and engrained professional expertise in them. To a large extent thanks to Firsov's unique school, several of them grew to become famed engineers. Meanwhile Firsov himself didn't know much about designing tanks, and didn't have anyone to ask for help. Much had to be done by intuition, while there was never enough time for deep reflection and research into the numerous major problems. After all, he was obliged to be busy with engineering support for the production process, with its inexhaustible flow of urgent questions; the development of new tank models and getting them into production; the building of various test and experimental combat vehicles; and so on and so forth.

Such a situation inevitably led to mistakes. For example, after moving the BT-7 into production and dispatching 687 of them to the troops, in June 1936 reports came flooding back from the army regarding transmission failures. Military acceptance officers even temporarily stopped accepting the ready BT-7 tanks. The root of the problem was identified quickly: the M-17T engines in these tanks had the same 400 horsepower but a maximum torque that was 22 per cent greater than the M-5 engines of the BT-5 tanks, at 220 kg-metre instead of 180 kg-metre.[15] The designers in their haste didn't take this into account and retained the same gearbox for the BT-7. Only its input pair of bevel gears was reinforced. Factory tests didn't reveal any issue: the tank's prototype ran for more than 2,300 kilometres without any transmission problems. However, during these tests, experienced and skilled factory test-drivers were sitting behind the control levers. Careless and often poorly trained army driver-mechanics handled their combat vehicles in a completely different manner, and as a result the transmissions on their tanks barely lasted for 500 kilometres. In order to eliminate this design defect, several variants of a new gearbox with the same overall dimensions were hastily developed. The one prepared by A.A. Morozov under Firsov's direction proved to be the best. The new gearbox had three gears instead of four as before, due to which they managed to strengthen it substantially. This new gearbox immediately went into production and no longer caused any complaints. It was also installed in the previously produced tanks. Nevertheless, Firsov was accused of 'wrecking', and that same summer he was removed from his post. He remained at the factory to work as an ordinary engineer.[16]

Just as before, Firsov readily helped everyone who went to him for advice, but the T2K Design Bureau was in need of a new head, one who would have official power but, most importantly, would enjoy the complete confidence of the authorities. Such a man couldn't be found in the Kharkov Locomotive Factory, so an outsider was brought in: Mikhail Il'ich Koshkin. He was born on 21 November 1898 in the small village of Brynchagi in the Yaroslavl area, and completed three years of schooling in a parochial school. Koshkin participated in the First World War and the Russian Civil War. In 1919 he joined the Party, and in 1921 he was enrolled in the Communist University in Moscow. After completing his studies, in the years 1924 and 1925 he directed a confectionary factory, and then went to do Party work in the city of Vyatka. It was here that his career path abruptly changed: in 1928 the Central Committee of the Communist Party sent 1,000 Communists to study in higher education establishments, and Koshkin was among this group. In 1934 he graduated from the Polytechnic Institute in Leningrad with a specialty in 'Automobiles and tractors', and began work in the same city at Tank Factory No. 185, where he quickly rose to become the deputy head of the design bureau. He took part in designing the T-29 and T-46-1 tanks, which never went into serial production because of their excessive complexity and high cost of manufacturing. However, before this decision was reached, Koshkin was awarded the Order of the Red Star for his success in work.

His faultless biography and his Party membership card served Koshkin well; despite having only 2.5 years of design experience, he was given clearance to work as the head of Kharkov's Design Bureau-190. He was appointed to this post on 28 December 1936. At first Firsov helped him acclimatize to his new position and duties, but this didn't last long. Koshkin's relocation to Kharkov coincided with the beginning of a very dark period in the USSR, which entered history as the epoch of the 'Great Terror'. The Kharkov Locomotive Factory employees and managers also didn't escape it. On 14 March 1937 Firsov was arrested, charged with wrecking, espionage and perpetrating terrorist acts against the Party and government. On 10 December 1937 he was sentenced to be shot, and the sentence was carried out on that very day. The lives of hundreds of thousands of Soviet people were terminated in the same way. It is sufficient to say that in addition to Firsov, of the above-mentioned prominent men in the Soviet tank-building industry, I.P. Bondarenko, V.I. Zaslavsky, O.M. Ivanov and I.A. Khalepsky were arrested and shot in 1937 and 1938. N.M. Toskin was arrested in 1938 and sentenced to 20 years in the Gulag. In 1949 he died in imprisonment.[17] The cruel repression struck not only the directors and managers, but also the simple workers. Engineers and technicians were accused of wrecking only because of mistakes and oversights at work, yet the reason for their errors was primarily their inadequate knowledge and lack of practical experience, or else just trivial haste. The pitiless slaughter of qualified cadres, who were in short supply even without this, negatively affected the results of the tank industry's operations. In 1936 it produced 3,905 tanks, in 1937 only 1,558. Thus, their output fell by 2.5 times and wasn't restored to their previous level until the very beginning of the Great Patriotic War.[18]

After Firsov's disappearance, the co-workers of Design Bureau-190 continued to be summoned to interrogations about his case, and each such summons could end in arrest. Here, Koshkin must be given his due: he fought for his people and defended them against unjustified repression. This greatly helped the bureau; after all, no one was sending new professionals to it, and it was overloaded with urgent projects. Meanwhile, its activity wasn't marked by any particular successes. The first major independent work of the new head was the project started in March 1937 involving the next wheeled-tracked BT-9 tank with sloping armour, a diesel engine, and six drive wheels. Two months later it was inspected by experts of the Automotive-Armoured-Tank Directorate and rejected because it ignored the army's tactical and performance requirements and included crude design mistakes. For example, the suspension arms of its road wheels were not angled towards the rear, as they were supposed to be, but forwards.[19]

The Automotive-Armoured-Tank Directorate was under no illusions about the real abilities of the Design Bureau of the Kharkov Locomotive Factory and took practical steps to improve it. In June 1937 34-year-old Military Engineer of the 3rd Rank Adolf Yakovlevich Dik was sent there with a directive to work on his own variant of the BT-9 tank project. Previously he had never been engaged in designing tanks, but in November 1936 he had graduated with distinction from the Military Academy of Mechanization and Motorization.[20] During his studies, he successfully engaged in academic work and published two articles in the journal *Mekhanizatsiia i motorizatsiia RKKA* (*Mechanization and motorization of RKKA*) about the problems of tank mobility. Then he continued his service as an engineer with the Kharkov Military District's 5th Tank Brigade. In May 1937 the talented and knowledgeable engineer was included on a commission examining the possibility of improving the handling of the T-46-1 tank, but just a month later he received acceptance into the Military Academy of Mechanization and Motorization's post-graduate studies programme.[21] However, instead of continuing his studies in Moscow, he was given the opportunity to realize his academic research results in Kharkov.

Dik's knowledge in the field of tank mobility was particularly needed there, since the serially produced BT tanks were in a need of a substantial improvement in their off-road performance when using wheels. They all had a common design flaw: only the rear pair of their eight road wheels was linked to the transmission, meaning that only a quarter of the tank's weight was used for providing effective tractive power. This was adequate for moving along roads or dry, hard ground with low gradients, but in other conditions the BT tank lost traction when using its wheels. The solution to this vexing problem was to increase the number of drive wheels. The first to venture on this path was the military self-taught inventor N.F. Tsyganov. In 1935–1936 he had managed to build tanks on the basis of the serially produced BT-2 and BT-5 tanks that had gearing for the three rear pairs of road wheels, which turned into drive wheels once the tracks were removed. The forward (steering) pair of wheels when using wheeled movement remained non-powered, since in the Soviet Union at the time they didn't know how to make constant velocity joints necessary for this. For the torque transmission from the engine to the drive wheels, Tsyganov used a complex system of horizontal and vertical drive shafts with a timing mechanism for synchronizing wheeled and tracked movement. The tanks equipped with them, called the BT-2-IS and BT-5-IS in Iosif Stalin's honour, demonstrated splendid off-road capabilities. They were even able to continue moving straight after losing one of their tracks, which substantially enhanced their combat survivability. However, when using wheeled movement, turning the tank with steering clutches led to rapid wear on the solid rubber rims, especially on the outer road wheels, and thus this was permitted only in extreme situations. In ordinary conditions the forward steering wheels were used to make turns. But the primary shortcoming of the BT-2-IS and BT-5-IS was the poor reliability of their transmissions.[22]

The drivetrain for the serially produced BT tanks used so-called 'guitars': special gearboxes for wheeled movement. These gearboxes simultaneously served as suspension arms for the driven road wheels. Their long, flat shape faintly resembled the popular musical instruments, which is why they were given this nickname. In the BT tanks' transmission systems, the guitars directly transmitted torque from the drive shafts of the final drives to the last pair of road wheels, essentially turning them into drive wheels, so they had to be quite long and heavy. Koshkin made an attempt to use them for the gears of all six drive wheels of the BT-9, but they were an awkward fit in the tank's standard hull and increased the tank's weight noticeably. So Koshkin, without further ado, decided to reject the guitar gearboxes and proceed along the path that was first taken by Tsyganov.

The heads of the Automotive-Armoured-Tank Directorate, reluctant to be limited to one type of gears for the drive wheels, which had proved in tests to be far from optimal, instructed Dik to develop a new design for the guitars that would be suitable for the BT-9. However, with his arrival at the Kharkov Locomotive Factory, a sensitive situation arose. The possible success of an entry-level engineer would be evidence of inadequate competence or even negligence on the part of Koshkin and his experts. This might lead to corresponding organizational conclusions, or else to something much worse … So naturally they all sought to hinder the work of the interloper and rival, not least because the improvements to Koshkin's BT-9 variant were continuing at full speed. Instead of the three engineers assigned to assist Dik, he received only two, who were far from the best, and he only got them after a delay. Even so, after just two months of work, he managed to accomplish undoubtedly positive results. The gearboxes he designed, which were half the length, proved to be strong, reliable, and simple to produce and operate. However, Dik didn't stop with this and he also worked out several substantial design improvements. Among these were the possibility of disengaging the gears of separate drive wheels from both within and outside the tank; a longitudinal driveshaft for transmitting the torque effect to the drive wheels; an improved final drive; wheel camber for preventing overloading and damage to their rubber rims; sloped upper side armour plates; an automatic hitch for towing; stiffening of the tank's bottom and installing an emergency hatch there. In addition, he decided to use a five-speed gearbox in the transmission. However, his main contribution became the additional pair of road wheels he proposed, which solved four problems at a stroke:

1. When moving on wheels, the ground pressure of each wheel fell by 20 per cent, which notably enhanced the tank's off-road capabilities;
2. The load on the track links and on all the elements of the road wheels and their suspension fell by the same 20 per cent, which was especially important for extending the lifetime of their rubber rims;
3. The tractive weight of the tank with four pairs of drive wheels of the five available increased to up to 80 per cent of the tank's gross weight with a corresponding increase in tractive power;
4. The tank received an additional allowance for a future increase in weight in the case of necessity.

Koshkin at the time categorically refused to use all these novelties in his project, although in the future some of them would nevertheless appear in the T-34 tank. For example, in 1943 the T-34 began to receive a five-speed transmission, but the sloping upper side armour plates and five pairs of road wheels were used on it from the very beginning. At the same time Koshkin borrowed several of Dik's ideas for his BT-9 variant; for example, he improved the geometry of the suspension, having positioned its springs at an angle from the vertical, and also strengthened both the springs and the final drive gears.[23]

Meanwhile, it was necessary to carry out the aforementioned government decree from 15 August 1937 irrespective of the cadre problems of Kharkov's tank builders. Yet the results of the BT-9 tank's design process demonstrated that for its success, it was necessary to change radically the organization of the factory design engineers' work and to strengthen them with qualified personnel. However, the most important thing was to put in charge of the project a man who would be able to achieve a miracle by completing it on time and with high quality. They appointed Dik, whose performance had splendidly recommended him to this key post. On 28 September 1937 the factory management received an order from the People's Commissar of the Defence Industry to form an OKB (Separate Design Bureau) of up to 100 members headed by Dik, which would be directly subordinate to the factory's chief engineer. The Kharkov factory management was obligated to assign, in addition to auxiliary personnel, eight of its best design engineers to the OKB, capable of leading the design teams. In order to staff them,

30 graduates of the Military Academy of Mechanization and Motorization were to arrive on 5 October, and another 20 on 1 December. Captain E.A. Kul'chitsky, an experienced tank tester, arrived from the Automotive-Armoured-Tank Directorate to serve as the project's main consultant. The OKB was given the task to present to the Automotive-Armoured-Tank Directorate by 1 February 1938 a preliminary design and a mock-up for a tank with three different types of gears for the drive wheels, and by 1 May 1938 – a detailed design with two approved gear systems. By 1 September, the Kharkov Locomotive Factory was to build two prototypes, and by 1 December, complete the testing of them. It was planned to begin serial production of the new tank on 1 May 1939. In total, 22 of the best factory design engineers, 3 engineers from the Automotive-Armoured-Tank Directorate, and 41 students of the Military Academy of Mechanization and Motorization joined the OKB; for the latter group, this would be their graduation project.[24]

On 13 October 1937, Dik received updated tactical and performance specifications for the project's development of a wheeled-tracked tank named the BT-20:

1. Type – wheeled-tracked, with gears for 6 wheels of the Christie-type.
2. Combat weight – 13–14 tons.
3. Armament – 1 x 45mm gun, 3 DT machine guns and a flamethrower for self-defence, or 1 x 76mm gun, 3 DT machine guns, and a flamethrower. Each fifth tank should have an anti-aircraft machine gun.
4. Ammunition load – 130–150 x 45mm or 50 76mm shells, 2,500–3,000 bullets for the machine guns.
5. Armour: frontal – 25mm, conical turret – 20mm, side and rear – 16mm, roof and bottom – 10mm. All the armour is sloped, with a sloping angle of the hull and turret's armoured plates of at least 18 degrees.
6. Speed – the same on tracks and wheels: a top speed of 70 km/hr, a minimum speed of 7 km/hr.
7. Crew – three men.
8. Range – 300–400 kilometres.
9. Engine – BD-2 with a horsepower of 400–600.

10. Transmission – of the wheeled-tracked BT-IS tank type, with the power output for wheeled movement applied after the steering clutches.
11. Suspension – individual; as springs it is desirable to use torsion bars.
12. Install the 'Orion' gun stabilizer and Engineer Povalov's horizontal stabilizer for the turret; install headlamps for night gunnery with a range out to 1,000 metres.[25]

Work went into full swing, but the miracle didn't happen. Indeed, this is understandable, considering the lack of knowledge and engineering skills of the majority of the OKB's staffers, especially the graduate students from the Military Academy of Mechanization and Motorization, who had no practical experience of designing complex combat equipment. All of this was made worse by objective difficulties: there was an acute lack of residential and working accommodation for the arriving men, as well as a paucity of drawing boards, drafting utensils, slide rules and drafting paper. Even the most ordinary pencils and erasers were in very short supply. In addition, his undoubted engineering talent couldn't offset Dik's lack of experience with leading large and complicated projects, especially with such a numerous and motley collective as his OKB. At the same time envy of him quickly spread among the Kharkov Locomotive Factory's managers and employees. Someone wrote an anonymous denunciation of Dik, as a result of which in early December the head of the OKB was removed from his post. Soon he was arrested and sentenced to 10 years in the Gulag, and his name disappeared from official Soviet history. It can't be ruled out that the arrest of the former head of the Automotive-Armoured-Tank Directorate G.G. Bokis on 23 November 1937 had influenced Dik's sad fate. Less than four months later Bokis was shot after being accused of participating in Tukhachevsky's supposed plot against the Party and Soviet government.[26] After all, it was at his personal order that Dik was sent to Kharkov, so this not only deprived him of a powerful sponsor, but also turned him into a protégé of an exposed 'enemy of the people' with all that it implied... On top of everything else, Dik was born to a family of Volga Germans, and just at this time the NKVD was conducting a sweeping 'German operation' that was directed against people of this nationality.[27] Which of these reasons snapped the promising career of the talented engineer is difficult to say with any certainty. Most likely, the combination of them doomed Dik.

Be that as it may, the OKB was disbanded. The Muscovites working there returned to the capital, and the Kharkov workers to their previous departments. However, no one cancelled the government order, and responsibility for carrying it out fell on Koshkin's shoulders. In early 1938, especially for work on this project, he organized and took charge of a new design bureau, KB-24, numbering 24 staffers, the core of which consisted of Kharkov designers from the OKB. N.A. Kucherenko now took charge of KB-190, which continued to work to provide engineering support for serial production. However, time was lost as a result of all these perturbations. The preliminary design and mock-up of the A-20 tank (the name given to the BT-20 within the factory) were late by one and a half months, and they were examined by the Automotive-Armoured-Tank Directorate only on 25 March 1938. Moreover, they simultaneously diverged in several points from the technical and performance specifications: the tank's weight grew to 16 tons, significantly exceeding the target weight, despite the weakening of the frontal armour to 16–20mm and the lack of a flamethrower.[28]

Koshkin fell into an unenviable situation: even without this, the extremely strict deadlines for completing the next stages of the project were approaching inexorably, and the timetable for work had collapsed. Indeed, all of this was accompanied by the repressions that were raging across the entire country, affecting millions of totally innocent people. At the Kharkov Locomotive Factory, in addition to Bondarenko and Firsov, almost the entire management was arrested in the period 1936–1938: the chief engineer F.I. Liashch, the chief metallurgist A.M. Metan'ev, the chief of production M.M. Andrianov, the chief engineer of the capital construction board V.A. Barabekha, and the heads of the following departments: tank – L.I. Zaichik and his deputy K.A. Kulikov; diesel – K.F. Chelpan and his deputy I.Ia. Trashutin; tractor – A.M. Utevsky and his deputy M.A. Merchansky; locomotive – A.I. Dovzhenko and his deputy K.N. Livshits; steel casting – A.M. Shpunt and his deputy Iu.I. Shkroba; autogenous welding – F.V. Savostin; as well as the head of the iron foundry A.P. Semenenko; the head of the mechanical shop P.A. Bobov; the head of Design Bureau-35 I.S. Ber; the head of the design bureau for the fuel injection equipment of diesel production G.I. Aptekman; the head of the motor laboratory V.D. Tiukhtiaev and many other lower-ranking professionals. They were all rehabilitated, but only after a couple of decades.[29] Meanwhile back then Koshkin fully understood that if the project failed, at any moment he could be added to this woeful list. The threat of arrest hung over him like the sword of Damocles.

On top of all this, the volume of work substantially increased with new army requirements. The events that dictated them – the Spanish Civil War – convincingly showed that the system of arming the Red Army with tanks urgently needed not a gradual evolution but a radical renovation. In all 347 Soviet light tanks, the T-26 and BT-5, and 351 Soviet tankers fought in Spain.[30] Among them was the tank brigade commander Dmitry Grigor'evich Pavlov, who was awarded the title 'Hero of the Soviet Union' for his service there. In June 1937, immediately after returning from Spain, he became the deputy head of the Automotive-Armoured-Tank Directorate, and just five months later replaced Bokis as the head of the Directorate. It was just at this time, when Pavlov was standing at the Helm of Soviet tank design, that the new models of tanks were developed and put into RKKA service; together with their immediate progeny, these tanks would have to take on the entire burden of the Great Patriotic War. Undoubtedly, he had a significantly positive influence on the tactical and performance characteristics of these tanks, and on their entire layout and appearance.

Due to his recent, practical combat experience, Pavlov knew all the shortcomings of the Soviet tanks that had been revealed in the combat operations in Spain. Their armour, offering protection only against bullets, no longer corresponded to the demands of the times, when any defence was densely saturated with rapid-firing small calibre anti-tank guns. The 45mm cannon proved insufficiently effective as the tank's main gun, primarily because of the poor explosive and fragmentation effects of its shells. In order to knock out an enemy gun or machine gun, a direct shell hit was required, and it wasn't at all easy to achieve this. Heavier and more powerful shells were necessary also for the destruction of field fortifications. Information that came in about the appearance in France of new types of tanks with anti-projectile armour that reliably protected them against small-calibre anti-tank artillery added fuel to the fire. This was not only due to the thickness of their armour, but also thanks to the sensible sloping of it. It had become clear that the huge park of Soviet tanks which had been built by this time at the cost of enormous efforts on the part of the entire country was rapidly becoming hopelessly outdated. In the circumstances, Pavlov acted swiftly and decisively. In his letter of 23 December 1937 he established new, increased standards for the armour of future Soviet tanks for the RKKA:

– for amphibious tanks: protection against armour-piercing rifle bullets and bullets from light anti-tank guns at all ranges, or not less than 12–15mm of thickness;
– for light tanks: protection against the fire of heavy machine guns and rifles of light and medium calibre at all ranges, or from the fire of a 37mm anti-tank gun at a range of 600 metres, or not less than 20–25mm of thickness;
– for medium tanks: protection from the fire of 37mm anti-tank guns at all ranges of fire and from the fire of 47mm guns at a range of 800 metres, or not less than 40–42mm of thickness; and
– for heavy tanks: protection from the fire of 47mm guns at all ranges, or from the fire of a 76mm gun at a range of 800–1,000 metres, or not less than 60mm of thickness.

When designing the new tanks, the possibility must be provided to increase the level of armour protection at the time of upgrading by at least one step.[31]

The last requirement particularly demonstrates Pavlov's far-reaching vision convincingly. Already he foresaw that the competition between armour and firepower for combat vehicles had just started, and he wanted the new Soviet tanks to be ready for it. The fulfilment of this requirement in the design of the famous T-34 ensured its enviable longevity. Pavlov also didn't forget about increasing the firepower of future tanks. In January 1938 he wrote to the Deputy People's Commissar of Defence for Armaments G.I. Kulik: '... for a breakthrough of contemporary fortified belts of defence, a portion of the medium and heavy tanks must absolutely be equipped with a main gun of no less than 76mm up to 107mm; or with a howitzer of a calibre between 122mm and 152mm'.[32] Just a month later he shared with the students of the Military Academy of Mechanization and Motorization his opinion on the running gear of tanks: 'throughout Europe, they have rejected wheeled-tracked vehicles for two reasons – difficulty of production, repair and maintenance, and they don't yield any particular advantages in combat'.[33] At the same time, in the course of the discussion about what tanks the Red Army needed, tracked or wheeled-tracked, Pavlov supported the idea of a purely tracked tank and proposed building two models, in order to reach a final decision after their testing.[34] He said as much on 21 February 1938 in a report to the People's Commissar of Defence Voroshilov.[35]

Voroshilov listened to the opinion of the country's most famous tanker, and in a memorandum for the Chairman of the Council of People's Commissars V.M. Molotov in the middle of March 1938 wrote: 'There must be one tank designated for actions together with infantry (cavalry) and as part of independent tank formations. For this purpose, it is necessary to develop two types of tanks: one purely tracked; the other wheeled-tracked. Thoroughly test them in the course of 1939 and afterwards adopt the one that will answer these demands in place of the BT and T-26.'[36] On 9 May 1938, after the next discussion of the A-20 tank project in the Automotive-Armoured-Tank Directorate, the paticipants unanimously decided, 'Comrade Pavlov's proposal about the creation of a tracked tank by Factory No. 183 is recognized as viable with a reinforcement of the frontal armour up to 30mm. Adapt the tank's turret to accept a 76mm gun. Crew – 4 men.'[37] The Kharkov engineers also actively spoke up for the tracked option, since it was simpler in both design and production. The final decision to build two prototypes – one purely tracked, the other wheeled-tracked – was adopted at a meeting of the Defence Committee on 27 February 1939. The deadline for their completion was set for 1 June that same year.

Koshkin was the man who would have to carry out all of these more complicated requirements. He showed himself to be a talented organizer and soon managed to get the intensive work of his design bureau up and running, using the carrot and stick approach. According to the stories of his subordinates, Koshkin sometimes threatened those who didn't finish their work on time with a cane.[38] However, it mustn't be forgotten that they had to produce in a very short time an enormous pile of design documents.

After all, in the Soviet planned economy, especially in the pre-war period, it was practically impossible to acquire freely the required items from other organizations. The lion's share of parts and components at each factory had to be designed and produced through their own means. In order to accelerate the job, on 14 December 1938 Factory No. 183 conducted an important reorganization of its design teams. In connection with the ceasing of production of the T-35 tanks and the preparations to produce the T-34, all three design bureaus – KB-24, KB-35 and KB-190 – were merged into one, which was given the name KB-520. Koshkin became the chief designer of the new bureau, and Morozov was promoted to be his deputy.[39]

Work continued, and prototypes of both tanks were ready in time. The purely tracked variant of the A-20 tank initially received the identifier A-20G (from the Russian word for 'tracked'), but as work went on, it changed to the A-32, and then to the T-32. One of its advantages over the A-20 was that there was no need to narrow the forward portion of the hull, necessary for turning the steering wheels, which enabled the expansion of the tank's driving compartment. In addition, the A-32's transmission required fewer bearings (which were in short supply), than did the A-20's. However, the main point was that in distinction from the wheeled-tracked model, it had greater capacity for an increase in the weight, which allowed the design team to meet the army's requirements, to increase the thickness of all of the tank's armour by 10mm, and to give the tank the long-barrelled 76mm gun. No less important was the fact that in the process of testing in July and August 1939, it turned out that the A-32's capacity for further growth was still far from exhausted, so they decided to bring its armour up to 45mm. By comparison, the maximum thickness of the A-20's armour was only 25mm, and it was equipped with just a 45mm gun. Worse, the limited load-bearing capacity of the wheeled-tracked variant's running gear allowed only slight thickening of its armour and by only 5mm at most.[40] It is clear why on 19 December 1939 the Red Army adopted the tracked T-32 with its increased armour of up to 45mm. It acquired a new identifier, which subsequently became world-famous: T-34 (*see* Plates 23–5). In fact, it was adopted *in absentia*, without being produced in finished form and without testing, only on the basis of brief familiarity with the prototype. Such a hasty decision would backfire more than once in the future ...

Aleksandr Aleksandrovich Morozov, a man of extraordinary talent and enormous work capacity, was the lead engineer in the development of the A-20 and A-32 tank projects. It was he who, after Koshkin's death from pneumonia on 26 September 1940, by right replaced him in the post of Factory No. 183's chief designer, and who in the future grew to become the leading creator of Soviet tank designs. However, at the time the 34-year-old engineer didn't have enough theoretical knowledge and practical experience. He was self-taught and had only completed the evening classes of the Kharkov Machine-Building Technical School. In addition, Morozov had some skeletons in his closet: it was he who had headed the development of transmissions in KB-190, and who bore responsibility for the above-described failure with the BT-7's transmission; he knew full well that another mishap might remind the authorities of his previous mistakes and he would be sent in the footsteps of Firsov. In this difficult situation, the inexperienced chief designer and his subordinates had essentially no other alternative but to make maximum use of the technical decisions embodied and proven in the tanks of the BT series. They simply didn't have enough time for seeking and working out fundamentally new designs, and the Kharkov engineers' inadequate knowledge and experience made this exercise too risky.

It isn't surprising that the overall scheme of the T-34 remained the same, except that the fuel tanks moved from between the double side walls into the fighting and transmission compartments. The layout of the engine and transmission compartments, which fully occupied the rear half of the hull, was retained. Because of this, the turret had to be shifted forward, which in turn required the moving of the driver-mechanic's hatch to the upper forward armour plate, thereby substantially weakening it. However, the main difference was the introduction of a nose crossbeam to which the upper and lower armour plates were first screwed and then welded, and the repeated increases in both the turret's armour and the main gun, which inevitably led to the growth of the turret's dimensions and weight. With time, this led to overloading of the tank's front road wheels. For this reason, over the entire history of the T-34's serial production, its frontal hull armour was never thickened. The majority of the T-34's main parts and components were to a greater or lesser degree strengthened versions of those of its predecessor, the BT-7M. For example, the engine was the same diesel V-2, and the Christie-type suspension was retained; only another pair of road wheels was added. The transmission had only a four-speed drive, since the five-speed transmission that was designed in tandem with it exceeded the BT-7's gearbox in size and required new plant equipment for machining its housing. In addition, the old transmission scheme hadn't changed: the shifting of gears was done by the archaic method of axially moving the cogwheels without any synchronizing of them; the final drives were single-staged with an excessive gear ratio, and the drive wheels transmitted torque to the tracks by engaging their horned links with rollers as before. The long-pitch tracks of the T-34 of the first series, fashioned according to the BT model, without sizeable cleats, noticeably worsened the tank's performance in heavy road conditions.

The main differences between the T-34 and the BT-7M were the new shape of the hull and turret, the armour thickness, the armament and the purely tracked running gear. However, the designers borrowed the shape of the T-34's forward hull from the prototype of the BT-SV tank, built in 1937 under the direction of N.F. Tsyganov. He, in turn, in agreement with the task given to him, used as a prototype the hull of the French light ECM-36 tank, which had steeply pitched welded armour plates with a thickness of up to 40mm.[41]

The progenitor of the BT series – Christie's tank – appeared in the 1920s and weighed almost one-and-a-half times less than the BT-7M. Each technical solution had its own limit of use, and the last BT tanks bumped right up against these limits. The T-34 was twice as heavy as the latter, so it isn't surprising that its transmission was a weakness. This was aggravated by the V-2 engine's numerous teething problems. One more major shortcoming of the T-34 tank was its intolerably cramped turret; after all, it had originally been designed to accommodate the 45mm cannon, and the 76mm gun that was installed in its place took up significantly more space. The lack of space within the fighting compartment made the work of the T-34 crew substantially more difficult, the paucity of high-quality observation devices left the crew almost blind, while the acute shortage of radio sets, aggravated by their shortcomings, rendered the crew virtually deaf and mute. All of these defects became apparent in practice from the very beginning of the

T-34's story. The initial field trials of the first two prototypes of this tank, conducted between 13 February and 22 April 1940, ended with the following conclusions:

1. The prototypes of the T-34 tanks presented by Factory No. 183 basically correspond to their tactical and performance requirements.

   In armour protection, firepower and performance in wintry conditions, the T-34 tank is significantly superior to the existing tanks in service.
2. The main shortcomings of the T-34 tank are as follows:
   a) The turret is flawed with respect to the convenience of using the armament, observation and sighting devices, and the ammunition stowage, which makes it impossible to make full use of the artillery system.
   b) The issue of radio communications in the T-34 tank has not been resolved.
   c) The observation devices installed in the T-34 tank do not provide a reliable and sufficient field of vision.
   d) The tank's protection against the penetration of flames of burning fluids is inadequate.
3. The T-34 tank in operation is reliable, and given the elimination of the shortcomings noted in the conclusions regarding the field trials, is suitable for troop operations.

   Without the elimination of the noted shortcomings, the T-34 tank cannot be moved into serial production.
4. The serial V-2 diesel engine mounted in the T-34 tank does not provide a guaranteed 100 hours of service life, although even that is not enough for operational use.[42]

As usual, everything started well and ended badly ... After relatively favourable conclusions in the report about the trials, a lengthy 'List of design changes and modifications to be made in the design of the T-34 tank as a result of the field and proving ground trials' was appended to the report. It consisted of 26 sections that contained a total of 108 items. It can't be said that the creators of the T-34 ignored the criticism. By November 1940 they had managed to make more than 490 changes to its design, of which

266 were design changes and 123 were manufacturing changes.[43] The results of their work received an appropriate assessment at the thorough trials of three serial T-34 tanks, starting on 31 October and ending on 7 December 1940. The testing programme checked the tanks' off-road performance, armament and means of communication, but its centrepiece was a run along the route Kharkov – Kubinka – Smolensk – Kiev – Kharkov that extended for a total of 3,000 kilometres. Some two-thirds of the distance ran along dirt roads and cross-country, and the tanks covered approximately a third of this route with closed hatches. They ran 30 per cent of the total distance at night. The summary report on the results of the trials offers a more than eloquent description of the T-34 tank, but is far from complimentary. For this report, *see* Appendix 1.

This, and other such documents were very disappointing for the Soviet leadership, which from the beginning had placed great hopes on the T-34 tank. To a certain extent, the first two prototypes of the tank with the factory designation A-34 realized their hopes, and this was not coincidental. The most experienced mechanics meticulously assembled them from select parts and components. All their bearings were imported; all threaded joints before assembly were smeared with hot oil, and all mating surfaces with grease. Special attention was given to the outer appearance of this pair of tanks. Here is how one Soviet military officer saw them:

> The quality of the A-34 tank's manufacture is superb. There are no scratches, abscesses or burrs outside ... and the armour surface has been ground. The fitting of the armoured plates to each other is very meticulous – not even the blade of a pocket knife can fit between them. ... The welding seams ... are smooth, with a rounded shape and slick to touch. ... The seats of the crew members have been neatly covered with brown leather.[44]

However, the main point was that test drivers of the highest class were demonstrating them to the authorities. In their skilful hands, the A-34 seemed like a marvel of off-road performance and manoeuvrability. In addition, a team of highly qualified repair workers accompanied these tanks on the test trials, who knew them very well and had spare parts and tools in abundance, in case of the need to restore them quickly to working condition.

This was followed by harsh daily production routines with their unavoidable rush jobs and last minute work marathons; the compulsory replacement of deficit parts with various types of surrogates; the insufficient qualification and low work discipline of many employees; and so forth and so on. The result was the appearance of numerous defects in production, which were quickly revealed in the course of using the tanks in the field. Moreover, the average training of the tankers and their attitude towards their duties were far behind the level of the professional testers. With their own unskilled actions they often worsened the situation with the tanks' dependability, which was already poor enough as it was, so the flow of complaints that were pouring in from the troops was fully justified. The problem of the quality of the T-34 tank became so acute that the decision was made not to resort to half-measures, but to create a different combat vehicle in order to replace it. In the first half of 1941 the bulk of the KB-520's staff was busy with this project, thus the work to improve the quality of the serially produced T-34 sharply slowed. The new tank received the index code T-34M (or the factory code A-43), and in accordance with the army's requirements, it differed from the T-34 by the armour of its turret and front hull, which was increased to 60mm; a three-man turret on a turret ring with a diameter that had been increased to 1700mm; the presence of a commander's cupola that offered 360° vision; a new V-5 diesel engine; a planetary gearbox that had been designed in the Military Academy of Mechanization and Motorization, or an eight-speed gearbox of the regular type with synchronizers; drive sprockets that directly engaged tracks with their teeth; and other novelties. An individual torsion bar suspension on the T-34M replaced the Christie-type suspension with its on-board columns, springs and guide bars. This allowed a 20 per cent increase in available room in the tank's fighting compartment, a substantial easing of the crew's work, the stowage of a larger ammunition load, the elimination of cutouts in the hull sides for the suspension arms, and saved 300–400 kilograms of weight. In addition, the fuel tanks were moved from the fighting compartment to the transmission compartment, further from the crew, and their capacity increased from 465 litres to 750 litres, so the tank's range became 60 to 100 kilometres further.[45] According to a joint decree from the USSR Council of People's Commissars and the Communist Party Central Committee, No. 1216–502ss from 5 May 1941, the T-34M was to replace the T-34 in production from September 1941. It was planned to produce 500 tanks of the new model before the end of 1941, but these plans were disrupted by the Great Patriotic War.[46]

Even before the war started, in addition to the main manufacturer of the T-34 tanks, Factory No. 183, output was up and running in the Stalingrad Tractor Factory. Through the efforts of both, during 1940 and the first half-year of 1941 they managed to deliver 1,225 serially produced T-34 tanks to the Red Army.[47]

The T-35 tank didn't at all correspond to the new requirements put forward regarding the armouring of heavy tanks. The further thickening of the armour of this sluggish giant would bring its weight up to an excessive, ponderous amount, so in July 1937 the Kharkov Locomotive Factory, where the T-35 was being built, was instructed to design and develop a new heavy tank with an armour thickness of 40–75mm and a weight of up to 60 tons. However, the previously mentioned limitations of the Kharkov design bureau and its overloading with work on the prototypes for the T-34 tank made it necessary in April 1938 to include Leningrad engineers from the Kirov Factory and Factory No. 185 in the assignment. The project of the former received the designation SMK, and the latter T-100. In August they received updated tactical and performance requirements for a three-turreted tank weighing 55–57 tons with armour of 20–60mm, armed with one 76mm gun, two 45mm guns and three machine guns, including one anti-aircraft machine gun. The Kharkov design bureau couldn't in fact propose anything viable, so the Leningraders were competing between themselves. On 9 December 1938 their projects were examined at the Main Military Council of the People's Commissariat of Defence, which adopted important decisions. In the first place, in order to keep the tank's mass and dimensions within sensible limits, the number of turrets was reduced to two; in the second place, it authorized the Kirov Factory to include in the competition a project for a third tank with just one turret.

It should be noted that the SKB-2 design bureau of the Leningrad Kirov Factory was noticeably inferior to its rivals from the No. 185 Factory in qualifications. Previously it had never before designed tank projects independently, and it had been kept busy with engineering support for the serial production of the T-28, so the design bureau team had few members. In the dark year of 1937 several of them fell under the steamroller of the repressions, including the bureau's head, O.M. Ivanov. The 29-year-old head of the Military Academy of Mechanization and Motorization's Project-Design Department Zhozef Yakovlevich Kotin arrived on 23 May 1937 to take his place. He didn't take part in routine design work, assigning this to his deputies, but at the same time he looked after his subordinates and he was a talented organizer. Kotin understood the psychology of top brass especially well, and was able to cater to it with the names he gave his tanks. For example, the abbreviation SMK meant Sergei Mironovich Kirov, KV Klim Voroshilov, and IS Iosif Stalin. He managed to get spacious new accommodation for his bureau, and reached an agreement with the leadership of the Military Academy of Mechanization and Motorization about sending six of its graduates to SKB-2 in October 1938.[48] They were the ones who, under the leadership of the much more experienced engineers L.E. Sychev and A.S. Ermolaev, came up with the conceptual design for a heavy tank with a single turret. It was designed and developed on the basis of SMK drafts with the use of certain design features of the Czechoslovakian LT vz.35 tank, which had been painstakingly studied during the trials on the Moscow area proving grounds in Kubinka. These included the vision devices, mirrors, seals and fasteners, as well as the scheme of the planetary transmission.[49]

The idea of a single-turreted tank proved to be so successful that it acquired a path to life. On 31 January 1939 the head of the Automotive-Armoured-Tank Directorate, Pavlov, signed the corresponding tactical and performance specifications, according to which on the following day work began on the preliminary design. At first it wasn't regarded very seriously, and the SKB-2's top experts, headed by Ermolaev, continued to engage in work on the SMK. The lead engineer for the single-turreted tank became the 34-year-old N.L. Dukhov, who had switched to tank design and development only several months before, after designing cars, tractors and cranes. He was put in charge of only five young engineers, but this small group managed to complete the preliminary design in the course of just one month.[50]

This was due largely to the fact that the team borrowed the overall scheme of the armoured hull, torsion bar suspension, optical devices, transmission parts and other components from the SMK. However, instead of the planetary transmission that had been recommended by the Automotive-Armoured-Tank Directorate, because of the lack of time and experience they had to use a regular transmission. In parallel with the output of assembly and detail drawings, parts were produced, and on 31 August 1939 the assembly of the first example of the new tank was completed, named the KV tank in honour of the then People's Commissar of Defence Klim Voroshilov (*see* Plate 21). The single-turreted layout allowed for a substantial reduction in the tank's size and weight in comparison with its twin-turreted competitors, and it was also noticeably superior in armour protection. The KV was protected by 75mm of armour from every direction, which made it virtually invulnerable to the shells of all anti-tank and tank guns of that time. Even before completing the factory tests, the tank went to the front. Together with the prototypes of the twin-turreted SMK and T-100 heavy tanks, it passed through a trial by fire in the course of the Winter War with Finland. In its first combat action on 18 December 1939, the KV tank didn't achieve any particular successes, but it demonstrated excellent survivability, having taken nine hits from 37mm armour-piercing shells. One shell hit the hull front and three struck the right side, but only created impressions 10mm deep in the armour. A hit on the gun barrel left a large dent in it. A hit on the hub of the fourth right-hand road wheel blew off its cover and damaged a bearing. Another three shells damaged the right track. However, the tank was not only not knocked out, it managed to tow a disabled T-28 from the battlefield while under fire, and the damaged barrel of main gun was quickly replaced in the field. The next day Moscow received a report about this, and on the evening of the same day the KV was put into Red Army service by a decree of the Defence Committee. The Leningrad Kirov Factory began to manufacture it instead of the T-28.[51] Up until the end of June 1941, 432 KV-1 tanks were built, of which 25 were produced at the Chelyabinsk Tractor Factory, which back in the autumn of 1940 began to prepare for its role as a back-up for the Leningrad Kirov Factory.[52]

The bloody fighting during the numerous fruitless attempts to breach the Mannerheim Line in the winter of 1939–1940 compelled the Soviet high command to search urgently for new and effective means to break through a defence. Heavy guns, firing with direct laying, were the most suitable for destroying concrete pillboxes. However, to move these guns up to within a sufficient range frequently proved to be problematic, while the gun crews during the attempt would suffer heavy losses from the enemy's return fire. The decision to equip the KV heavy tank, which was virtually invulnerable at that time, with a heavy gun suggested itself. In his letter of January 1938, D.G. Pavlov had been writing about just such a tank. Work to arm the KV tank with a 122mm howitzer began in September 1939, but after the beginning of the war with Finland, at the Red Army's request it was replaced with the slightly shortened 152mm M-10 howitzer, for which concrete-piercing shells were available. The turret ring of the KV's hull proved to be too small to accommodate the 152mm howitzer, so it had to be mounted higher in an enormous turret. However, even then there was barely sufficient room for the howitzer's recoil, loading and four crew members: a tank commander, gunner, loader and breech operator. Before the end of the Winter War, three KV tanks that were so equipped were sent to the front. However, by the time they arrived the Mannerheim Line had already been breached, so they were given the opportunity only to fire at pillboxes that had been abandoned by the Finns. Nevertheless, they managed to combat ordinary field fortifications or clear passages through concrete dragon's teeth with the fire from their gun. The testing of these tanks took place after the end of combat operations. Initially they were called 'KV tanks with the large turret', while the ordinary KV tanks, equipped with the 76mm cannon, were called 'KV tanks with the small turret'. In 1940 the former acquired the designation KV-2 (see Plate 22), and the latter KV-1. Before the Great Patriotic War 204 KV-2 tanks were built, all by the Leningrad Kirov Factory.[53]

The hastiness of the KV-1 project and its acceptance by the Red Army without corresponding testing and debugging led to a range of these tanks' teething problems. Their engines, main transmission components, cooling system, air filters, brakes, running gears, and the turret's traversing and locking mechanisms were especially unreliable. The KV-2 had the same collection of defects, made worse by their heavier weight, so they had even poorer off-road performance and reliability. The first trials, conducted in June 1940, and later the Red Army's use, revealed these problems in full colour. For example, along a paved road, the KV-2 could reach a maximum speed of only 20–21 km/hour instead of the supposed 34 km/hour, and during turns in 2nd gear its engine would die because of insufficient power.[54] The former military acceptance officer at the Leningrad Kirov Factory, Military Engineer 3rd Rank Kalivoda, in a letter about the shortcomings of the KV tank written to the People's Commissariat of State Control in September 1940, came to an impressive conclusion: 'I believe that at the present moment, it is impossible to call this a combat-ready vehicle because of the above-indicated defects. It can be sent to the army only as a training vehicle, not a combat vehicle.'[55]

Initially, it was still not too late to correct these problems; after all, in 1940 the Kirov Factory at first received the assignment to build only 50 KV tanks, so in the course of the year they could improve their design and technology, and only in 1941 switch to large-scale production of them. However, in June 1940, by a decree of the USSR Council of People's Commissars and the Communist Party's Central Committee, the annual production plan was increased up to 230 tanks, and in order to emphasize the importance, it was called a 'Stalin's assignment' – this despite the fact that over the first five months only six KV-1 and four KV-2 had been built.[56] Now, all of the factory's resources had to be focused not on eliminating design shortcomings, but on fulfilling the plan at any cost, including the sacrifice of the product's quality for the sake of its quantity.

In the spring of 1941 the SKB-2 design bureau turned to the resolution of its next urgent problem. It all started with alarming reports from Soviet intelligence in early March 1941 that during the campaign in France the Wehrmacht had used up to 450 heavy tanks, armed with 105mm cannon, and that production had started in Germany of three new types of heavy combat vehicles, among which were super-heavy tanks weighing 90 tons and armed with the same main gun. In addition, the Germans had supposedly repaired 72-ton French tanks and had even begun to form heavy panzer divisions.[57]

All this was just the fruit of the intelligence agents' imagination, or more likely, the product of crafty German disinformation, but the higher Soviet leadership took it more than seriously. Decree No. 548–232ss from the Council of People's Commissars and the Communist Party's Central Committee on 15 March 1941 obliged the Leningrad Kirov Factory from June to switch to the serial production of KV-3 heavy tanks with a weight of 51–52 tons, 90mm of armour, a 76mm cannon F-34 and a 700 horsepower V-5 diesel engine. According to this document, the factory was given the task by 1 May to build prototypes of the KV-1 and KV-2 tanks with add-on armour plates, and a month later to turn to the serial production of such vehicles. In addition, from 20 June teams of factory workers were supposed to begin adding armour plates to the tanks that had already been delivered to the troops. As a result, by mid-July up to 120 KV-1s had been fitted with add-on armour plates 20–25mm thick with a total weight of about 3 tons.[58] An analogous package for the KV-2 proved to be a ton heavier because of the large size of its turret, but the add-on armour plates weren't mounted on them because these tanks were heavily overloaded as it was.[59]

However, this wasn't the end of the matter. On 7 April 1941 the USSR Council of People's Commissars and the Party Central Committee adopted yet another decree, No. 827–345ss. Its demands were to bring up the thickness of the frontal and turret armour of the KV-3 to 115–120mm, to equip it with the powerful ZIS-6 107mm cannon with a muzzle velocity of 800 metres per second, and by the end of 1941 to produce 500 such tanks. On top of this, the Leningrad Kirov Factory was obliged to design a heavy KV-4 tank with the same ZIS-6 cannon, main armour with a thickness of 125–130mm, and the possibility to bring it up to 140–150mm, and produce a prototype of the new heavy tank by 1 October 1941. Finally, by 10 November the factory had orders to build a prototype of an even heavier tank, the KV-5, with a 1,200 horsepower diesel engine. Given the same armament as the KV-4, its turret and frontal hull armour was to be thickened up to 170mm, and its sides up to 150mm.

After receiving the tactical and performance specifications, a genuine crash effort got under way in SKB-2. Almost all of its engineers, individually, in pairs or in small groups on a competitive basis feverishly designed their own variants of the KV-4. As a result, before the beginning of the war, no fewer than 20 conceptual designs with a calculated mass of 82.5 to 107 tons appeared. Between June and August elaboration of the KV-5 design was conducted. Instead of the not yet available 1,200 horsepower diesel engine, it was planned to use two serially produced 600 horsepower V-2K engines. The war brought a stop to all these projects, so all of the time spent on them went in vain. However, the worst thing was that because of them, all the engineering work to improve the KV-1 and KV-2 in the last pre-war months was tossed aside.[60]

As a result of the Soviet people's titanic efforts to build combat vehicles in the pre-war years, an enormous arsenal of tanks was created in the Soviet Union. Over the period until 22 June 1941 the country's industry had delivered 30,120 tanks and tankettes to the Red Army.[61] Even allowing for the fact that some of them were irrecoverably lost in armed conflicts; delivered to other states; written off because of accidents, being hopeless outdated or because of physical wear and tear; as well as for other reason, the Soviet Union had many more tanks than all of the remaining countries of the world combined. The total quantity of tanks and tankettes in the Red Army and in the western military districts on 1 June 1941 is shown in Table 7.

It is necessary to clarify the categories of serviceability of the tanks shown in this table. By orders of the USSR People's Commissar of Defence No. 12–16 on 10 January 1940 the 'Regulations for accounts and records in the Red Army' was put into operation from 1 April 1940. It divided all military hardware into the following categories according to their condition:

Category 1 – new, not yet put into use, meets the requirements of technical conditions and is fully ready for use as directly intended;

Table 7: Tank Park of the Red Army on 1 June 1941.

Type	Model	Number of tanks in the Red Army						Of which, in the western military border districts										
		Total	Category				Percent of operational	Leningrad	Baltic Special	Western Special	Kiev Special	Odessa	Total	Category				Percent of operational
			1	2	3	4								1	2	3	4	
Heavy	KV-1	370	295	73	2	–	99.5	4	59	75	189	10	337	275	60	2	–	99.4
	KV-2	134	125	8	1	–	99.3	2	19	22	89	–	132	124	7	1	–	99.2
	T-35	59	–	48	5	6	81.4	–	–	–	51	–	51	–	42	5	4	82.4
	Total	563	420	129	8	6	97.5	6	78	97	329	10	520	399	109	8	4	97.7
Medium	T-34 ordinary	671	628	42	1	–	99.9	4	30	203	368	30	635	599	35	1	–	99.8
	T-34 with radio	221	217	4	–	–	100.0	4	20	25	128	20	197	195	2	–	–	100.0
	T-28	481	–	292	100	89	60.7	89	57	63	215	50	424	–	283	94	47	66.7
	Total	1,373	845	338	101	89	86.2	97	107	291	711	50	1,256	794	320	95	47	88.7
Light	BT-7M ordinary	509	–	500	7	2	98.2	1	1	4	97	152	255	–	248	6	1	97.3
	BT-7M with radio	181	–	176	5	–	97.2	–	–	36	104	17	157	–	152	5	–	96.8
	BT-7M with AA machine gun	12	–	12	–	–	100.0	–	10	–	–	–	10	–	10	–	–	100.0
	BT-8	2	–	2	–	–	100.0	–	–	–	–	–	–	–	–	–	–	–
	BT-7 ordinary	2,471	8	2,027	299	137	82.4	255	275	234	632	103	1,499	7	1,273	153	66	85.4
	BT-7 with radio	1,881	36	1,545	222	78	84.1	196	296	133	487	100	1,212	6	1,020	143	43	84.7
	BT-7 with AA machine gun	89	3	81	5	–	94.4	–	89	–	–	–	89	3	81	5	–	94.4
	BT-7A	117	4	83	19	11	74.4	12	20	2	31	–	65	–	50	9	6	76.9

	BT-7 with RSMK radio	3	–	3	–	–	100.0	–	–	1	–	–	1	–	1	–	–	100.0
	BT-IS	2	–	1	–	1	50.0	–	–	–	–	–	–	–	–	–	–	–
	BT-5 ordinary	1,277	1	931	119	226	73.0	242	–	88	276	57	663	–	544	60	59	82.1
	BT-5 with radio	399	1	321	34	43	80.7	31	–	88	65	24	208	–	174	16	18	83.7
	BT-5 with diesel	12	–	7	–	5	58.3	–	–	7	–	–	7	–	7	–	–	100.0
	BT-2	580	–	415	112	53	71.6	160	–	68	127	41	396	–	315	63	18	79.5
Light	T-26 ordinary	3,935	446	2,998	172	319	87.5	222	323	701	667	80	1,993	375	1,384	95	139	88.3
	T-26 with radio	3,377	394	2,527	198	258	86.5	222	148	341	722	95	1,528	321	1,007	84	116	86.9
	T-26 with AA machine gun	111	111	–	–	–	100.0	–	11	18	79	3	111	111	–	–	–	100.0
	T-26 with radio & AA machine gun	63	–	60	–	3	95.2	–	–	–	–	–	–	–	–	–	–	–
	T-26 with two turrets	1,261	–	851	152	258	67.5	87	25	211	230	36	589	–	404	72	113	68.6
	Total	16,282	1,004	12,540	1,344	1,394	83.2	1,428	1,198	1,932	3,517	708	8,783	823	6,670	711	579	85.3
	T-40 ordinary	113	100	13	–	–	100.0	1	–	30	70	–	101	100	1	–	–	100.0
	T-40 with radio	17	14	2	1	–	94.1	–	–	14	14	–	14	13	1	–	–	100.0
	T-40 training	2	–	2	–	–	100.0	–	–	–	–	–	–	–	–	–	–	–
Amphibious	T-38 ordinary	1,046	99	576	161	210	64.5	60	76	186	70	46	438	4	270	96	68	62.6
	T-38 with radio	83	5	53	18	7	69.9	1	9	13	5	2	30	–	18	10	2	60.0
	T-37A ordinary	1,933	94	1,109	360	370	62.2	111	57	205	405	149	927	8	434	245	240	47.7
	T-37A with radio	388	18	253	65	52	69.8	7	4	28	87	28	154	4	77	34	39	52.6
	Total	3,582	330	2,008	605	639	65.3	180	146	462	651	225	1,664	129	801	385	349	55.9

Type	Model	Number of tanks in the Red Army						Of which, in the western military border districts										
		Total	Category				Percent of operational	Leningrad	Baltic Special	Western Special	Kiev Special	Odessa	Total	Category				Percent of operational
			1	2	3	4								1	2	3	4	
Chemical and Flame throwing	BT-2 chemical	14	–	14	–	–	100.0	–	–	–	–	–	–	–	–	–	–	–
	BT-7 chemical	1	–	–	1	–	0.0	–	–	–	–	–	–	–	–	–	–	–
	T-26 130	500	10	428	38	24	87.6	12	1	50	113	4	180	10	147	18	5	87.2
	T-26 TT-131	53	–	52	1	–	98.1	–	–	–	26	–	26	–	25	1	–	96.2
	T-26 TU-132	61	–	58	1	2	95.1	3	–	–	26	–	29	–	28	1	–	96.6
	T-26 133	327	2	306	16	3	94.2	67	9	22	67	14	179	2	166	11	–	93.9
	T-26 134	2	–	2	–	–	100.0	–	–	–	–	–	–	–	–	–	–	–
	T-26 BXM-3	308	–	178	34	96	57.8	64	10	38	16	–	128	–	109	13	6	85.2
	T-26 TOS	2	–	2	–	–	100.0	–	–	–	–	–	–	–	–	–	–	–
	T-37A chemical	10	–	9	1	–	90.0	–	–	–	–	–	–	–	–	–	–	–
	Total	1,278	12	1,049	92	125	83.0	146	20	110	248	18	542	12	475	44	11	89.9
Tankettes	T-27 ordinary	2,343	–	1,057	531	755	45.1	–	67	392	368	103	930	–	471	173	286	50.6
	T-27 chemical	33	–	3	6	24	9.1	–	–	3	3	–	6	–	–	3	3	0.0
	Total	2,376	–	1,060	537	779	44.6	–	67	395	371	103	936	–	471	176	289	50.3
Total		25,454	2,611	17,124	2,687	3,032	77.5	1,857	1,616	3,287	5,827	1,114	13,701	2157	8,846	1,419	1,279	80.3

Source: Boevoi i chislennyi sostav Vooruzhennykh sil SSSR v period Velikoi Otechestvennoi voiny. Statistichesky sbornik No. 1. 22 iunia 1941 goda [The order of battle and numerical strength of the USSR armed forces during the Great Patriotic War. Statistical collection No. 1. 22 June 1941] (Moscow: IVI MO RF, 1994), pp. 132–9.

Category 2 –   is or has been in use, fully serviceable and ready for use as directly intended;

Category 3 –   requires repair in district repair shops (intermediate overhauls);

Category 4 –   requires repair in central repair shops or in factories (major overhauls);

Category 5 –   unserviceable. These vehicles were not included in summary lists.

Combat vehicles in Categories 1 and 2 were assigned to the category of operational tanks in the table.

Category 2 also included tanks requiring troop (current) repairs. What this term meant back then was explained in detail in the 'Service manual for use and park service', published by the Main Automotive-Armoured-Tank Directorate of the Red Army in 1938. According to this document, a current repair primarily represented anchoring and tightening loose components and parts done in the process of operating the tank and when carrying out mechanical inspections. It was done as far as was needed primarily by the crew themselves in any conditions under the direction of a technician, using the individual set of tools and spare parts carried by the tank, and it lasted up to 5 to 8 hours. It is today impossible to determine the ratio between fully operational tanks in Category 2, and the tanks that needed current repair.[62] However, this in no way notably changes the overall picture.

Between 1 and 21 June 1941 the western military districts received another 206 new tanks, of which 41 were KV tanks, 138 were T-34 tanks, and 27 were T-40 tanks. They were allocated in the following fashion: 1 KV tank to the Leningrad Military District; 20 KV and 138 T-34 tanks to the Western Special Military District; and 20 KV and 27 T-40 tanks to the Kiev Special Military District. Other than the tanks shown above, there were 1,255 light tanks in the forces of the 16th, 19th and 22nd Reserve Armies and the 21st Mechanized Corps that managed to arrive in their designated areas in the western military districts. The exact number of their operational vehicles is still unknown. However, knowing that the share of serviceable tanks in the troops of the Soviet Second Strategic Echelon amounted to 90.4 per cent, it is possible to assert with a large degree of confidence that among the arriving tanks, 1,135 were operational and ready for use in the role intended for them.[63] Thus, the Red Army had 15,162 tanks and tankettes in the western military districts, of which 12,344 were combat-ready.

Chapter 9

Qualitative Characteristics of the Tanks

In order to compare the tanks according to qualitative criteria, first of all it is necessary to establish their characteristics, determining their strengths and weaknesses to the greatest extent possible. We'll list these features in order of their importance:

1. Availability
2. Firepower
3. Armour protection
4. Mobility
5. Communications
6. Observation
7. Crew comfort
8. Detectability

The most important factor is the first. It is determined, first of all, by the number of tanks capable of carrying out combat tasks within a specified period of time where it is required. The worst tank in the world which manages to show up at the right time and in the right place is immeasurably superior to the best tank which fails to arrive when and where it is needed. In such a case, the best tank in the world becomes completely useless. Moreover, all the resources spent on it will have been wasted. Tanks that timely concentrate on decisive directions in the necessary quantities are capable of deciding the outcome of not only a skirmish, but also a battle, an operation, a campaign, and even an entire war. Thus their presence or absence has not only tactical, but also operational and even strategic significance. However, not all tanks count – only those that are in working order, are supplied with ammunition, fuel and lubricants, and most importantly are operated by well trained and cohesive crews that have mastered how to handle them. Without meeting all these conditions, tanks are little more than useless lumps of metal. Moreover, we're talking not only about tanks, but about armoured *forces*, the main shock strength of which lies in these combat vehicles, operating not alone but as part of elements, units and formations with the support of and in cooperation with other services and branches of the armed forces. A prominent example of the victories achieved by armoured forces, given their proper use, are the triumphal results of the Wehrmacht's blitzkriegs first in Poland, then in Belgium, Holland and France, and later in Yugoslavia and Greece. Meanwhile the failure of Operation Barbarossa, despite its stunning initial successes, demonstrates that the capabilities of armoured forces are not endless, and they are incapable of fully offsetting the decisive strategic advantages of their adversary.

Firepower, armour protection and mobility are the most significant of the tactical and performance characteristics of tanks. It is very important that they harmonically relate to one another and are well balanced. In the period under discussion, the medium tanks showed this balance best of all. In light tanks, as a rule, mobility dominated firepower and armour protection, while in heavy tanks firepower and armour protection dominated mobility. From the point of view of the level of development of these three characteristics and their optimal balance, the undoubted leader among both Soviet and German tanks was the T-34. The heavy KV-1 tank's armour protection plainly exceeded its mobility and firepower. Moreover, the T-34 from March 1941 was armed with the F-34 76.2mm cannon with the long barrel of 41.6 calibres.[1] From the beginning of its production, the KV-1 tank was armed with the L-11 76.2mm cannon. In January 1941 it was replaced with the F-32 cannon of the same calibre. They both had barrels of only 30.5 calibres long, therefore the muzzle velocities of their armour-piercing shells were reduced by 10 per cent, compared to the F-34. Thus, the medium T-34 tank was superior back then to the heavy KV-1 tank in terms of firepower. Only in October 1941 did the KV-1 tank receive the ZIS-5 cannon with the same ballistic performance as that of the F-34.[2] The KV-2's firepower stood in first place, although at the expense of its even greater inferiority in mobility. In essence, it was a heavy self-propelled gun, and was only able to fire from a stationary position. It was even prohibited from moving with a loaded gun 'to avoid slippage of the shell in the chamber from jolts'.[3]

The firepower of the German medium tanks of the time left a lot to be desired. Subsequently the realities of the war forced the Germans to enhance substantially the armament of their tanks and to make them more balanced. Their armour protection was comparatively reliable only in front, although there they lacked rational angles of slope. The mobility of the German panzers that were designed for use in western and central Europe was fine only on roads and hard ground. The light tanks of Czechoslovak production, which equipped the Wehrmacht, especially the Pz.Kpfw.38(t), had an excellent balance between firepower, armour protection and mobility. However, their weight class didn't allow them to reach a high level in the first two characteristics.

The rest of the characteristics listed above have no need for supplementary explanation and will be examined in turn. An analysis of every pre-war Soviet and German tank would take up too much time and space, so attention will be paid primarily to the latest tanks of that period, examining them through the prism of the characteristics listed above.

9.1 Availability

The availability of tanks is determined first of all by the quantity of fully combat-ready vehicles present with the troops. Various factors affect this, such as the generalship of the military commanders, the operational mobility of the tanks, the natural and climactic conditions of their use, and so on. However, to the greatest extent it depends on the presence in the country of the necessary resources, both material and human, for their production. No less important is the correspondence between the technology and materials required for the mass production of tanks and the capabilities of the industry. This correspondence was, perhaps, the T-34's main virtue. The simplicity and ease of manufacture of these tanks enabled the prompt and successful organization of their serial production in several different factories after the war began, despite the harshest conditions of the evacuation and the lack of many necessary materials, tools, equipment and qualified cadres. However, the simplicity of the T-34's design didn't at all mean that it was possible to produce them in any workshop, using whatever was available. On the contrary, the foremost technological achievements of that time were used to build it, including assembly lines, continuous production lines, automatic welding of the hull and casting of the turrets. The wide use of welding, cold forging and casting enabled a substantial increase in labour productivity and reduced the tanks' cost of production. With the beginning of the war, the struggle to reduce the labour inputs to build the T-34 got under way with renewed effort. As a result, the number of thicknesses of the armoured plates and the amount of fasteners used to build the tanks noticeably decreased, and a large number of superfluous parts were discarded. For example, by the beginning of 1942, 5,641 parts of 1,265 items were removed from the tank's design, and by the end of that year this figure reached 6,237 parts. In the process, the list of fasteners was reduced by 21 per cent.[4] The rate of change in the labour inputs to build the T-34 tanks and V-2 diesel engines in the factories of the People's Commissariat of Tank Industry during the war years is shown in Table 8:

Table 8: Reduction in labour input required to produce T-34 tanks and V-2 engines between 1942 and 1945

Product	Factory	Labour input, in man hours					Reduction (%)
		01.01.1942	01.01.1943	01.01.1944	01.01.1945	01.07.1945	
T-34 tank	No. 183	5,300	3,719	3,617	3,251	3,209	39.5
	No. 112	9,000	5,520	5,497	4,439	3,388	62.4
	No. 174	8,092	7,205	4,574	3,209	3,094	61.8
V-2 engine	ChKZ	1,933	1,420	1,129	973	1,036	46.4
	No. 76	–	1,620	1,090	896	831	48.7
	No. 77	–	–	2,024	1,050	1,030	49.1

Note: 'ChKZ' is the Russian acronym for the Chelyabinsk Kirov Factory.
Source: A.Iu. Ermolov, *Gosudarstvennoe upravlenie voennoi promyshlennost'iu v 1940-e gody: tankovaia promyshlennost'* [*State control of the military industry in the 1940s: tank industry*] (Saint Petersburg, Aleteia, 2015), pp. 188, 324.

Extraordinary measures had to be taken in order to maintain the rate of output of tanks in the circumstances of the loss of colossal human, material and manufacturing resources left behind in occupied territories; the mass evacuation of industry; the loss of economic ties; and the overloading of the transport system with military shipments and the interruptions in deliveries of components, parts and materials in connection with this. For example, on 20 January 1942 the State Defence Committee approved 'Conditions for the acceptance of tanks at the tank factories', according to which the military acceptance officers were authorized to 'accept tanks missing clocks, voltmeters and ammeters (with the substitution of an indicator light); speedometers, thermometers (except for one); turret fans (in winter); motors for traversing the turret for the T-34 tank; an intercom system (with the substitution of signal lights); and spare containers and radio sets in those cases when these devices and parts were temporarily unavailable in the factories.'[5]

All these and other similar measures helped the T-34 to become the most-produced tank of the Second World War. Yet another of its important advantages was its relative simplicity of operation, which made it possible in short periods of time to train crews for them in sufficient numbers to take advantage of the enormous output of tanks produced by the industry. The qualification requirements for these crews fully corresponded with the not-very-high level of human resources available to the Red Army at the time. The T-34 was also simple to fix, which eased the difficulties of repair work with the limited means at hand in field conditions.

However, the unrestrained pursuit of quantity unavoidably led to a decline in the quality of the tanks. There were several reasons for this, but the main one was the human factor. It mustn't be forgotten that the average educational level of the USSR's population at that time was low, and its technical knowledge was even lower. This is especially marked in comparison with the Germans, who had grown up and been educated in a country saturated with various types of vehicles and mechanisms that were part of the daily life of each individual. For example, per capita there were almost 30 times more cars in private hands in Germany than altogether cars in the Soviet Union on the eve of the war.[6] Thus the training of German factory workers, as a rule, didn't have to start from scratch because they already had various technical knowledge and skills from childhood. In contrast, for many Soviet people back then even the ordinary bicycle was a curiosity, and they had never heard of household appliances. After the beginning of the war, this situation became substantially worse, as many experienced engineers, technicians and workers departed for the front or ended up in occupied territory. For example, of the 17,988 workers and 3,591 engineers and technicians who worked at the lead manufacturer of the T-34 tanks – Factory No. 183 – only 2,859 workers and 1,456 engineers and technicians were evacuated to the Urals. In addition to them, 119 white collar workers and 800 students of the factory apprenticeship school travelled from Kharkov to Nizhny Tagil, but they couldn't compensate for the acute lack of qualified cadres.[7]

Women and adolescents went to work in the factories, but even they were far from enough to meet the multiplying needs of the wartime economy. Poorly educated peasants from around the entire country, including remote areas of Central Asia, where many people didn't even understand the Russian language, were drawn into the production of complex combat equipment. According to the account of Iu.E. Maksarev, the director of tank factory No. 183 in Nizhny Tagil the majority of the employees starting work at the factory didn't know any vehicles more complicated than a dray cart.[8] There wasn't enough time to train them properly, so they had to master new specialties while working on the production lines.

They laboured for 11 or more hours a day, with no weekends or vacations, at times in unheated workshops. There were also, as a rule, no normal conditions for rest, because the majority of the people were quartered in overcrowded barracks without any conveniences, which were sometimes quite distant from the factory. For example, the workers of Factory No. 77 had to walk to work in any weather for more than 10 kilometres each way, since no transport was available. The meagre wartime rations were inadequate for nutrition, and in the first quarter of 1943 at Factory No. 112 alone more than 1,000 people (or 4.5 per cent of the entire labour force) fell sick with dystrophy from malnutrition, and over two weeks of February 1944 at Factory No. 76, 14 workers died from this illness at their workstations. Because of the intolerable conditions, each year the turnover at the factories of the tank industry reached 20–25 per cent, and approximately 45 per cent of those who left deserted.[9] Nevertheless, the hungry and exhausted people found a way to meet and even exceed the stressful wartime production norms. Yet the lack of knowledge and experience, and the acute shortage of means to mechanize manual labour, exacerbated by the striving to produce an ever greater amount of tanks, frequently led to flagrant violations in the production process. For example, some tank assemblers drove the majority of bolts three-quarters of the way in with a sledgehammer, and only then screwed in the bolts to the end using the few remaining threads. It isn't surprising that the quality of the tanks produced in wartime, especially in the first half of the war, left much to be desired.

However, the matter didn't end with the production of the maximum possible number of tanks. They still had to be given crews; kept constantly supplied with fuel and lubricants, ammunition and spare parts; given routine maintenance and an effective evacuation procedure; while a system for repairing tanks and getting them back into service after breakdowns and combat damage had to be established, along with a fast transportation system for moving tanks in order to save time and conserve their service life; and so on. The amount of work necessary in order to maintain the tanks' combat-readiness to a great extent depended on their reliability, longevity, ease of maintenance, reparability, and finally on the qualifications and conscientiousness of the people working with the tanks, especially their crews. In a word, tank availability wasn't just a technical problem, but also an organizational problem associated with the human factor.

In this field, the Wehrmacht at the beginning of the war held a significant advantage over the Red Army. Of course, the RKKA had on the eve of the war a manifold superiority in numbers of tanks, but this was neutralized by the superiority of the Germans in mobilization, deployment, organization, mobility, handling, training and combat experience of the invading army, as well as in its leadership. The Germans' effective system of supply, which made it possible to launch attacks with their mobile forces to a never-before-seen depth and shortened the necessary operational pauses between these attacks, must also be mentioned. The Wehrmacht's tanks also demonstrated impressive reliability. For example, by the end of October 1941 the Pz.Kpfw. II tanks in the 6th Panzer Division had covered on average 11,500 kilometres, the Pz.Kpfw.IV tanks 11,000 kilometres, the Czech Pz.Kpfw.35(t) 12,500 kilometres, and they had retained their combat-readiness even after this.[10] Of course, over this time they were repaired more than once, but in any case this is an outstanding achievement for tanks of that time. It also mustn't be forgotten that the Pz.Kpfw.35(t) had long since been taken out of production and spare parts for them were lacking, because manufacture of them had also ceased. Thus the German repair teams had to cannibalize some of these tanks.

The acute lack of material resources for producing new equipment forced the Germans to make enormous efforts to restore damaged or disabled tanks back to combat readiness. They took great pains to establish an effective system of repairing equipment in field conditions. In the Wehrmacht's panzer forces, such a system had been created in peacetime, thoroughly fine-tuned in training exercises, and was successfully functioning at the front. Moreover, it continued to improve, flexibly adapting to the constantly changing military environment. Each panzer company had a maintenance detachment of 19 men led by a non-commissioned officer. At first their primary equipment was a light 1-ton half-track prime mover and a lorry that carried spare parts. Later they received a second prime mover and two shop lorries. The panzer regiments had a maintenance company that numbered between 120 and 200 men depending on the regiment's composition and the types of tanks that armed it. The company consisted of a headquarters, two maintenance platoons, a recovery platoon, a weapons and radio repair section, as well as a spare parts section. The maintenance companies were each equipped with eight shop lorries, 12 heavy 18-ton half-track prime movers, four tank transporters, two wreckers with 3-ton traversable lever cranes, two blacksmith's shops, two electric generators on trailers, machine tools, other tools and fixtures, equipment for gas and electric welding, and so on. Maintenance platoons that numbered between 50 and 120 men were attached to separate panzer battalions. In addition to the authorized subunits, the Wehrmacht also had separate maintenance and recovery companies, kept in the reserve of the OKH, which were attached to army groups or armies for use on the most important sectors of the front. The company maintenance detachments dealt with repairs that were not too labour-intensive, requiring up to a half a day, in the majority of cases, to complete. For more serious work, disabled panzers were evacuated to the field repair shop, deployed on the basis of the regiment's maintenance company. Its personnel and equipment allowed it to work on up to 30–40 tanks simultaneously. Usually repairs there took up to two weeks, although sometimes this stretched to a month if they were waiting for the arrival of spare parts.[11] In especially difficult cases, the tanks had to be sent back to tank repair factories far to the rear, which could put them back into service even after very heavy damage. However, only about 5 per cent of the damaged tanks underwent such major overhaul, the overwhelming majority of them being repaired at the front.[12] Through the rapid return to service of damaged combat vehicles, even during intensive battles, the Germans often succeeded in keeping the panzer units and formations at an acceptable level of combat effectiveness. Repaired panzers served as a substantial source of replenishments for the Wehrmacht throughout the entire Second World War. Their number was especially significant when the Germans were on the offensive, when the battlefield remained in their possession and no one could interfere with the evacuation of disabled armour.

In contrast, the technical and service support for the Red Army's armoured forces left a lot to be desired. They were equipped with only 41 per cent of their lorries, 34.7 per cent of their mobile repair workshops, 28.2 per cent of their charging stations, and 18.5 per cent of their mobile gas tanks, according to their wartime authorized tables. At the same time, the motorized transport had no reserves of tyres because of the unplanned expenditure of them in the course of combat operations in Mongolia, Poland and Finland. Moreover, in the first half year of 1941, only 37 per cent of the annual requests were allotted to tyres. However, there is one by no means unimportant detail here. When calculating the shortage of auxiliary equipment in the pre-war Soviet armoured forces, it is necessary to take into consideration that the total number of tanks amounted to 61.4 per cent of their wartime authorized strength. Thus, the relative shortage of auxiliary equipment compared to the tanks present in the units was approximately 1.5 times less than the absolute; however, this improved the generally cheerless picture by not very much. The lack of spare parts for all types of equipment was especially acute. In the Soviet Union, priority attention was generally paid to the output of the main product, while completely inadequate care was taken over keeping it supplied with spare parts. In 1941 the production of spare parts for the T-28 tanks and M-5 and M-17 motors was completely halted, and reduced for the T-37A, T-38, T-26 and BT tanks. This happened because by this time they were no longer being built, and all the resources of the tank industry were devoted to producing the T-40, T-34 and KV tanks, to preparing the production of the T-50 tank, and also to the manufacture of spare parts for the new tanks. Meanwhile, in 1941 the funds allotted for the production of spare parts for tanks amounted to just 46 per cent of the calculated needs, and for automobiles and tractors it was 54 per cent.

There was not only a shortage of spare parts, but not even enough of the most needed materials, machine tools and tools, so the equipment repair plan in the first half-year of 1941 was fulfilled by only 45–70 per cent.[13] In addition, a substantial proportion of the reserve of spare parts that had been accumulated for the most numerous Soviet pre-war tanks, the T-26 and the BT series, was expended during the war with Finland. As a result, by the end of June 1941 the Red Army had just 32 per cent of the spare parts needed for the T-26 in peacetime, 18 per cent of those needed for the BT, T-37A and T-38 tanks, 4 per cent of those needed for the KV tank, 10 per cent of those needed for the T-34 tank, and 26 per cent of those needed for the V-2 diesel engines.[14] And in the war, the Red Army had to deal with a vastly larger volume of repair work than in peace time.

The design of the T-34 was superbly suited for mass production, but in use it was not nearly as good. The tanks built in the first years of production required numerous adjustments and frequent work to service their systems and components. For example, after each hour of engine operation it was necessary to lubricate the water pump's shaft by rotating the handle of the grease gun by 1–2 turns; to make matters worse, the grease gun was mounted on the engine compartment bulkhead far away from the driver-mechanic. After each 100 kilometres of march, it was necessary to grease mechanisms in 16 places by hand; after each 250–300 kilometres, or after 10–12 hours of engine operation – another 6 places; after each 500 kilometres, or 25 hours of engine operation – another 13 places; and after each 1,000 kilometres, or 50 hours of engine operation – 38 more places. In the summer it was necessary to flush the air filter and change its oil after every 10 hours of engine operation, and in the winter after 20–25 hours of engine operation.[15] In real combat conditions, it was practically impossible to carry out all these numerous procedures regularly, especially considering the driver's extreme fatigue because of the hard work required to drive the tank. As a result, the V-2 engine provided less power and failed sooner. Modifications of this engine were installed on the BT-7M, T-34 and KV tanks, but it was still quite raw and not all its teething problems had been resolved yet. Despite the Automotive-Armoured-Tank Directorate's requirements to ensure a guaranteed life of at least 200 running hours between engine overhauls, the T-34's engine at the time reached on average only 100–120 running hours, and the KV's engine even less than that, just 80–100 running hours between engine overhauls.[16] However, their V-2 engines could run so long when used flawlessly under perfect conditions, but in practice they rarely lasted more than 70 running hours.

The V-2 engine of the T-34 and KV tanks, given all its early problems, was still quite promising, but their transmissions were archaic. In a memorandum to Stalin on 16 May 1942, the head of the Military Academy of Mechanization and Motorization's Department of Tanks, Professor N.I. Gruzdev, and his deputy A.I. Blagonravov wrote openly and bluntly:

In the realm of design and especially regarding the transmission components (engine clutch, gearbox, steering clutches with brakes and final drives), our KV and T-34 tanks have lagged too far behind.

There is no substantial difference between the transmission of the T-18 tank (1929–1930) and the transmissions of our contemporary tanks.

The obsolescence and primitiveness of our design approaches in the realm of designing transmissions leads in the final analysis to a sharp reduction in the number of vehicles that take part in combat; the vehicles all too often are not so much being used, as being tinkered with and repaired without any sort of damage from enemy fire.

It is sufficient to point to the actions of the KV tanks on the Kerch Peninsula, where in just one operation on 27–28 February, of the 36 KV tanks designated for combat, 20 were disabled because of the grinding down of the bearing of the revolving gear cluster of the reduced rear gear and first gear.

… in the 39th Tank Brigade during the fighting from 27 February to 5 March 1942, the losses from enemy fire amounted to 1 KV tank and 2 T-34 tanks, but the losses due to transmission failure amounted to 5 KV tanks and 3 T-34 tanks.

… In short, in the light of the present-day designs of Allied and captured German tanks, the conservatism and obsolescence of design thought in the realm of tank transmissions is indisputable.[17]

For those who always like to blame the engineers for everything, we'll point out that the flight of design thought is always and everywhere restricted by production capabilities, and in the pre-war USSR they were less than modest. Thus, the developers of the T-34's gearbox, despite all their wishes, were unable to rework this mechanism substantially, since only one special machine tool was available at the Kharkov Locomotive Factory to bore out its housing. This machine tool had been given to the factory in order to produce the BT-5 tank, and from then on all of the gearboxes of the Kharkov tanks were forced to follow the same design scheme and keep the same distance between shafts.[18] The T-34's engine clutch was also a direct descendent of the analogous component of the BT tanks, and inherited from them the principle of dry friction of steel against steel without any friction pads. This worked well enough on the BT light tanks, but the T-34 was in a heavier weight class, and immediately problems arose with warping of the disks of the engine clutch. Despite all the efforts of the design and manufacturing engineers, they were unable to rid the T-34 tank of this problem right up to the very end of the war.

Almost all the main systems and components of the T-34 from pre-war production suffered these and other problems due to design, engineering or manufacturing causes. They were described in detail in each account about the testing of these tanks. The chaos of the war's beginning not only aggravated them, but also added new problems. As a result, the low reliability of the T-34 at that time was a serious shortcoming. They also didn't excel in service life, but at the front this wasn't in fact necessary. The new tanks received a factory guarantee of 1,000 kilometres of operation, though in fact the true figure fell far short of this; the majority of them simply didn't last long enough to exceed even their limited service life. According to the account of the well-known former armoured fighting vehicle design engineer L.I. Gorlitsky, the average lifecycle of a tank or self-propelled gun in the Red Army at the front was rarely longer than three to seven days of combat operations. Over this time they managed to take part in at the most just two or three attacks and to fire anything from half to all of their ammunition load from their main guns.[19] So the requirements for quality, reliability and longevity of service life of a tank differ substantially between peacetime and wartime. Any vehicle must have sufficient reliability within the limits of its anticipated period of service. The somewhat lower quality of tanks during wartime can be justified, moreover, if because of it the man–hours spent to build them and the expenditure of scarce materials are reduced, which means more of them can be produced.

However, for the T-34 tanks that were built on the eve of the war and especially in the first half, this reduction in quality went far beyond permissible boundaries.[20] For example, over 10 days of combat operations in July 1941, of the 102nd Tank Division's 15 T-34 tanks, 7 were disabled by transmission failures before even having travelled 1,000 kilometres. Of the 69 T-34s examined at Moscow-area repair bases between 20 August and 10 September 1942, the reason for 22 of them (or 32 per cent) being out of service was not combat damage, but failure of the engine or running gear.[21] It was not without reason that Stalin angrily told the Military Commissar of the Main Automotive-Armoured-Tank Directorate N.I. Biryukov on 5 June 1942: 'The main defect of our tanks is the fact that they can't conduct lengthy marches' because of the unreliability of their transmission systems; he demanded that they be improved.[22] According to the results of the war, in the USSR they came to a blunt conclusion: 'It should be noted that the quality of the assembly of domestic armoured fighting vehicles was in some cases unsatisfactory, which significantly shortened their service lives and contributed to the high loss of personnel in the 1942–1943 period.'[23]

However, there was yet another substantial reason for the excessive losses of Soviet tanks in the first half of the war. It was mentioned in the report of Scientific Research Institute-48, 'Porazhaemost' tankov Krasnoi Armii i prichiny vykhoda ikh is stroiia' (Vulnerability of the tanks of the Red Army and the reasons for their being disabled), which was written on the basis of the analysis of 178 T-34 tanks that had been sent back to the rear for repair. The quality of their armour was recognized as fully satisfactory, but it recommended enhancing their survivability first by increasing the quality of their mechanisms and running gear, and secondly, by a fundamental improvement in the combat training of the crews.[24] It is understandable why: the influence of the human factor on the results of using equipment, especially equipment as complex as tanks, was and remains decisive.

It was only in the second half of the war, primarily thanks to the reserves of weight and space in the T-34's chassis, that Soviet designs and manufacturing engineers were able to improve these tanks with respect to the majority of the main indicators, including reliability and length of service life, and did this while the pace of production output grew relentlessly. The T-34s at the end of the war were much superior to and quite different from those which started it. A decisive turning point in the level of quality of the serially produced Soviet tanks took place in the middle of 1943. As Chart 1 illustrates, failures in quality happened even later, but they were more temporary than of a systemic nature.

Chart 1: Percentage of serially produced Soviet T-34 tanks that covered 300 kilometres during test trials without breaking down.

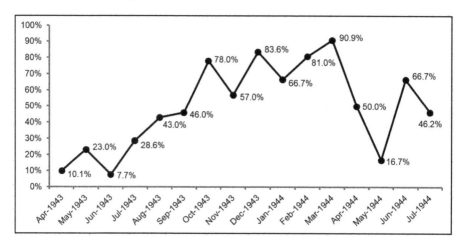

Source: TsAMO, f. 38, op. 11389, d. 18, ll. 15–25; as cited by *Glavnoe avtobronetankovoe upravlenie: Liudi, sobytiia, fakty v dokumentakh, 1943–1944* [*Main Automotive-Armoured-Tank Directorate: Men, events, facts in documents, 1943–1944*] (Moscow: GABTU, 2006), p. 700; ibid, op. 11355p, d. 361d, ll. 92–4; as cited by *Glavnoe avtobronetankovoe upravlenie: Liudi, sobytiia, fakty v dokumentakh, 1944–1945* [*Main Automotive-Armoured-Tank Directorate: Men, events, facts in documents, 1944–1945*] (Moscow: GABTU, 2007), p. 109.

The reliability of the KV tanks didn't even reach the level of the T-34; in addition to its design and manufacturing defects, its engine and transmission system were hopelessly overloaded. In addition, the Red Army lacked sufficiently powerful prime movers capable of towing these heavy tanks, let alone dragging them out when they got bogged down. What this problem created can be learned from a report by the commander of the 32nd Tank

Division, Colonel E.G. Pushkin, regarding the combat operations over the period from 22 June to 14 July 1941:

> Repair and evacuation means for the KV tanks were lacking. The available Voroshilovets tractors were unable to ensure evacuation; the tractors for towing the KV tanks broke down from the excessive overload. Very frequently the towing of a tank with another tank took place, and after 10–15 kilometres the towing tank would also break down (the engine clutch would fail, the gears would stop shifting, or the steering clutches would become ruined). The KV tanks (from this experience) can be towed by the Voroshilovets tractor only along roads. On tilled soil, peat deposits or boggy terrain, a KV tank can only be towed by two tractors.[25]

It isn't surprising that, according to the results of the testing of Lend-Lease tanks on the scientific-research proving ground of the Red Army's Main Automotive-Armoured-Tank Directorate in the summer of 1942, the following conclusion was made: 'The American M3 Medium and M3 Light tanks have exceptionally fine reliability in operation.'[26] Without at all diminishing the merits of the US combat vehicles, we'll note that everything is relative. Undoubtedly, the American tanks made such a favourable impression on the experts of the Main Automotive-Armoured-Tank Directorate because of their striking contrast with the unreliability of the Soviet tanks that were well known to them.

At the same time, despite widely circulated opinion, the situation regarding the serviceability status of the Soviet tanks of the old types on the eve of the war was not so bad. This was not least because the service life of the carburettor tank engines produced in the USSR in the 1930s was not at all short. For example, the engine of the T-35 heavy tanks had a minimum time between major overhauls of 300 operating hours, the engine of the medium T-28 tanks 400 operating hours, the engine of the light BT-2 and BT-5 tanks 450 hours, the engine of the most numerous light BT-7 and T-26 tanks 600 hours, and the engines of the amphibious T-37A and T-38 tanks and of the T-27 tankette 800 hours.[27] However, the quality of their manufacture left much to be desired. The point is that since 1927, the Soviet leadership had been whipping up 'war hysteria' in the country, in constant anticipation of an enemy attack, for which there was no real basis. Thus from the early 1930s, the production of tanks grew at a feverish pace. As a result, by the beginning of the Second World War the USSR had far more tanks than the rest of the world put together, although a significant share of them were outdated, especially with respect to reliability and armour protection.

Even so, the majority of the tanks that were produced in the 1930s still had operational capability by the beginning of the war. This was ensured by an all-encompassing system of conserving the service life of combat vehicles that had existed for many years in the pre-war Red Army. On 13 May 1933 Order No. 046 from the USSR's Revolutionary Military Council appeared, entitled 'On the operating procedure of the combat vehicles in the RKKA's motorized and mechanized forces', which divided all the tanks, tankettes, armoured cars and six-wheeled vehicles that were available to the troops into three categories. In the first of these belonged 50 per cent of the combat vehicles arming each unit. They had to be kept in full combat readiness as an untouchable reserve, and the use of them was authorized exclusively with the permission of the People's Commissar of the Army and Navy at the direction of the head of the RKKA's Directorate of Mechanization and Motorization and the commanders of the military districts. Even then, this was only for manoeuvres, field exercises and inspections according to the programme approved by the People's Commissar, and could expend no more than 50 hours of engine operation a year. Another 25 per cent of the combat vehicles belonged to the second category. They were allowed to be used only for drill and tactical training of units, with a total expenditure of up to 100 engine hours per vehicle per year. The remaining 25 per cent of the combat vehicles belonged to the third category and were designated for all types of combat training, gunnery, driving, and tactical exercises, and so on. Their maximum expenditure of engine operating hours could not exceed 200 hours.[28] Later on, even these norms, which were meagre from the beginning, were significantly cut. On 20 October 1937 there appeared the People's Commissar of Defence's Order No. 0167 'On the operating procedure of the automotive-armoured materiel of the RKKA in peacetime'. In accordance with this document, each tank in the first category was allowed to expend no more than 20 hours of engine operation each year. In 1938 approximately

15–17 engine hours of this allowance were spent in the Leningrad Military District for team building.[29] Such restrictions had an adverse impact on combat training for the crews.

Three years later, on 24 October 1940, new 'Provisions on the operating procedure of tanks, tractors, automobiles and motorcycles in the Red Army in peacetime' were put into effect by People's Commissar of Defence Order No. 0283. This divided the vehicles, according to their intended roles, into combat and auxiliary types. All the vehicles that had armour or weapons (both firearms and chemical weapons) were assigned to the combat category, which included tanks, armoured cars and prime movers, artillery or machine-gun self-propelled mounts (both wheeled and tracked), and motorcycles armed with machine guns, as well as artillery tractors designated for towing guns. In their turn, all the authorized combat vehicles equipping the units of the RKKA were split into two parks: combat and training–combat. In the process, all the best, operational and fully equipped tanks with a sighted–in and functioning weapon, and with a service life of not less than 75 engine hours until the next intermediate overhaul, were assigned to either a park of combat vehicles or the untouchable reserve. As a rule, these were tanks of the latest production series, not more than five years in age. They were maintained at full combat readiness in conservation and periodic use, expending no more than 30 hours on the engine of each vehicle per year. Tanks of the untouchable reserve, of which at times the units had more than the authorized number in order to provide the mobilization deployment of the army, were also stored in such conditions. However, unlike the vehicles of the combat park, their use was forbidden.

A very close eye was kept on those tanks standing in storage. They were constantly guarded by armed sentries, and even their own crews could gain access to them only with the written authorization of the unit commander. Periodically, but not less than once every two months, the combat readiness of these vehicles was checked personally by the commander of the formation or separate unit. The plan of utilizing the service hours of the combat vehicles, compiled by the commander of the formation or separate unit, was approved by the head of the military district's Automotive and Armoured Troops. The service hours were only spent in training the units and formations in tactical exercises, mobile camps and gunnery exercises for the subunits. To remove the combat tanks from storage was permitted by an order only after the start of combat operations.

The tanks of the training-combat park were kept separately. They included the older and worn-out vehicles, which served for the daily combat training of the tankers. At the same time, in military schools all available tanks were assigned to the combat-training park. Despite their relatively intense use, the combat-training tanks were also maintained in a condition of complete combat readiness. Their operation was authorized only within established norms. After each use in the field, regardless of the time of day and the weather, it was requisite to bring them back up to full readiness – to refuel them, grease them, clean them up, and only then put them in storage. When combat-training vehicles were sent away for repair, it was forbidden to replace them with combat vehicles. After their return to the unit from a major overhaul, they were sent to the combat park, and in place of them, at a special order to the units, the combat tanks with the most operating hours on their engines were converted to combat-training vehicles. Thereby the number of vehicles in the combat park remained unchanged.[30]

In the process, putting it mildly, service hours were stingily assigned to combat training in the Red Army. Nothing was spared on the mass production of new tanks, but a strict economizing of resources was made the cornerstone of their use. The need for thorough training of tank crews was plainly underestimated. For example, on 1 June 1941 there were just 70 KV and 38 T-34 tanks in the combat-training parks of the western border military districts; all the remaining tanks of these types – 469 KV and 832 T-34 – were in storage. It is not surprising that by the eve of the war in the western border military districts, they had had time to teach not more than 150 crews for the KV tanks and only approximately as many for the T-34 tanks.[31] Thus, less than a quarter of these most advanced combat vehicles received tank crews that were trained for them. It was planned to work out the field repair and service manuals for the T-40, T-34 and KV tanks only by November 1941.[32] Even instructions on operating the new tanks weren't delivered to the units, because by order of the General Staff, they were considered 'top secret' combat vehicles. Thus, the documents for them were kept in the headquarters of the mechanized corps 'under seven seals' and were handed out to the tankers only while conducting exercises, under signed receipt, and it was forbidden to take notes about them. The crews of the tanks of older types, as a rule, handled their combat vehicles much better than did their colleagues who fought in the T-34 or KV tanks.

Yet even the best equipment is useless without people who know how to use it properly. Thus there is no sense in arguing about the advanced combat qualities of the latest pre-war Soviet medium and heavy tanks, if there were not enough men to make use of them in practice. It is just as senseless to discuss the combat potential of the tank units, based only on the scrupulous tabulation of the numbers of their combat vehicles. After all, the tanks don't fight by themselves, and the tankers who are handling them, and their level of training and preparation, have a much stronger influence on the outcome of a battle than do the nominal technical and performance characteristics of their tanks. Poorly trained men are doomed to defeat in a clash with seasoned and skilful opponents. One of the numerous examples of this was described in a report by the head of the Southwestern Front's Directorate of Political Propaganda Brigade Commissar Mikhailov on 8 July 1941:

> In combat the KV tank demonstrated exceptionally high qualities. The enemy's medium anti-tank artillery can't penetrate its armour.
>
> The large losses of the KV tank is explained first of all by the poor technical training of the crews, their low knowledge of the tank's hardware, and the lack of spare parts. There were cases when crews were unable to fix the problems with immobilized KV tanks and blew them up.[33]

In addition, the soldiers' lack of preparation was immediately recognized by the enemy, giving them greater confidence in their own strength. Germany's Chief of the OKH Staff Franz Halder noted the low level of training of the Soviet tank drivers at the beginning of the war in his war diary on 12 July 1941.[34] This isn't surprising; after all, the majority of the driver-mechanics of the latest Soviet tanks in the 8th Mechanized Corps, for example, had just three to five hours of practical driving experience.[35] Moreover, the crews of the heavy tanks had done the majority of their training on T-27 tankettes, which were almost 20 times lighter than the KV-1. The People's Commissar of Defence Order No. 0349 'On preserving the heavy and medium tanks' from 10 December 1940 authorized their use for this purpose:

With the aims of preserving the hardware of the heavy and medium tanks (T-35, KV, T-28 and T-34) and keeping them in constant combat readiness with a maximum number of service hours, I am ordering:

1) All tank battalions (training and ordinary) of heavy and medium tanks by 15 January 1941 to be equipped with T-27 tankettes, allocating 10 tankettes for each battalion.

  Conduct all tactical exercises of these battalions in the T-27 tankettes.

  In order to train the personnel of the heavy and medium tanks on driving and gunnery, and in order to forge cohesion in the units and formations, the expenditure of the following service hours on each heavy and medium tank engine is authorized:

  a) of the training-combat park – 30 engine operating hours each per year;
  b) of the combat park – 15 engine operating hours each per year.

  Cover all of the remaining quantity of service hours, indicated for combat training according to Order No. 0283 of the People's Commissar of Defence from 24 October 1940, by use of the T-27 tankettes.[36]

In the first place the outdated and obsolete T-27 tankettes were sent to units equipped with the most expensive KV tanks, so it was there that such a practice was most common.

There is nothing surprising about the mechanical illiteracy of many Red Army soldiers. More than two-thirds of the USSR population at the time lived in rural areas. The level of education and overall development of the conscripts from these areas were as a rule impermissibly low. The lack of experience with handling machinery and mechanisms among the majority of the new recruits was especially telling when they wound up serving in the armoured troops. Inexperienced recruits weren't accustomed to observing rules about handling complex and unfamiliar combat equipment, didn't understand the importance of keeping it properly maintained, and frequently made crude mistakes when using it. For example, in the Baltic Special Military District's 3rd Mechanized Corps, a third of the training-combat T-34 tanks had burned out engine clutches owing to improper operation by 11 May 1941. Meanwhile, on 23 May 1941 five of the latest T-34s in the Western Special Military District's 6th Mechanized Corps had been rendered unserviceable when the tankers filled their fuel tanks with petrol instead of diesel fuel.[37]

Even authorized fuel could cause tank engine failures, if it contained impurities. This happened most often because of dirty containers used when transporting it. The requirements of the purity of the fuel for the diesel engines were particularly high, so it was recommended to conduct refuelling through a funnel with a mesh filter, supplemented by a doubled piece of silk.[38] However, in practice, in order to accelerate this task, the men often ignored this rule, which led not only to clogging of the fuel filter, but also to the failure of the expensive injectors of the high-pressure fuel pump.[39] Yet the tankers' haste was understandable, because as much as 72 minutes had to be spent on the refuelling of the T-34 tank.[40]

The pre-war system of preparing qualified cadres for the Red Army's armoured forces suffered from serious inadequacies and couldn't handle the requirement to staff the enormous number of brand-new units and formations with personnel in the shortest possible time. A report from the 6th Army's head of the Automotive-Armoured-Tank troops Colonel V.N. Dedov at the beginning of the war commented: 'The crews for the KV and T-34 tanks and on the Voroshilovets tractors in their majority have little experience and are unable to fix even the smallest mechanical problems.'[41]

The numerous flaws in the RKKA's tank logistics and repair systems, the tanks' insufficient reliability, the unsatisfactory training of the tanker cadres at every level and the unskilled use of the tanks by the Soviet command in the initial period of the war all led to the fact that, as a rule, the tanks almost never showed up at the right place at the right time. Meanwhile those that did manage to reach their designated place usually lost their accompanying infantry and artillery on the way there; left without support, they were quickly destroyed by German infantry and artillery.

A significant portion of the Red Army's tanks in the first weeks of the war were not lost in combat. A characteristic example is that of the 8th

Mechanized Corps, the units of which over the first four days of the war, while carrying out contradictory orders from the higher command, marched about 500 kilometres along the roads and lost in the process approximately 50–60 per cent of their materiel even before making direct contact with the enemy.[42]

In the summer of 1941 many Soviet tanks were simply left abandoned by their crews after suffering mechanical failures, which couldn't be fixed because of the lack of repair teams and spare parts; or after running out of fuel, which couldn't be brought up in time; or after getting bogged down and waiting in vain for prime movers to tow them out. Today it is difficult to determine just where the desperately needed mobile repair shops, fuel tankers, lorries and prime movers went: were they cut off by German forces? Were they destroyed by Luftwaffe airstrikes? Did they get lost somewhere on the roads because they didn't know their way around? Or did they ever exist at all? We just don't know. However, there is every justification to assert that the Germans, with their competent actions, took advantage of and amplified the defects of the Soviet armoured forces, which had been embedded in their organization from the very beginning. Even the experience of the 1939 Polish campaign plainly demonstrated that the command of the two tank corps that participated in it lost control over their units and didn't know how to keep them supplied with fuel even in the absence of organized enemy resistance. Since that time, the Red Army never truly learned how to conduct manoeuvring combat actions effectively. Attempts to develop this difficult ability came at a high cost in blood in a war against a skilled and ruthless adversary.

9.2 Firepower

The firepower of tanks is determined by the ability of their armament to destroy the designated targets. However, to start with, it needs to get a hit on the target, and here much depends on the capabilities of the sights. In this field the Germans were surely leading; their Zeiss optics served as the benchmark throughout the world. The TZF4 and TZF5 telescopic sights with anti-reflective coating (and their modifications) that equipped the German tanks at the beginning of the war had a magnification factor of 2.4–

2.5 and a field of vision of 23.5–25°.[43] In 1941 the Red Army's T-34 tank with the F-34 cannon and the KV tank with the ZiS-5 cannon were equipped with the TMFD-7 telescopic sight. It had the same magnification factor of 2.5, but its field of vision was only 14.5°, which means that at the same range the Soviet gunner saw through his sight about a third of the area the German gunner could see. Accordingly, it was much more difficult for the Soviet gunner to spot a target, especially considering the insufficient transparency of the TMFD-7 sight, which only allowed 39.2 per cent of the light that hit it to pass through it. In addition to the telescopic sight, the T-34 and KV tanks had the periscopic PT-4-7 sight with a magnification factor of 2.5 and a field of vision of 25.5°. However, its light permeability was even worse – just 26.3 per cent.[44] The limited transparency of the Soviet tank sights was a result of the lack of anti-reflective coating, which was mastered in the USSR only after the war, as well as the low quality of the domestic optical glass and bonding adhesives. Given good light, it allowed the gun to be aimed at a target at a range of 800 metres, which corresponded to the maximum range at which tank battles played out early in the war. However, in low light conditions (in twilight, in fog, or given rain or snow) the German tankers had a substantial advantage in combat. In normal conditions, thanks to their high-quality optics, they had the ability to take aim at a range of up to 1,500 metres. Thus, due to the quality of their sights, the Wehrmacht's panzers could employ their main gun at almost twice the range of the Red Army's tanks.

Accurate aiming is still insufficient to guarantee a hit. Much depends on the design and quality of production of the gun barrel, which pre-defines the direction and size of the dispersion of projectiles. As was found in the summer of 1942 during comparison tests between Soviet, German, Czechoslovak, American and British tanks, the Pz.Kpfw.III's 50mm gun demonstrated the best accuracy and precision. The worst gun, according to these characteristics, was the 45mm cannon of the Soviet light T-70 tank – the very same gun that equipped the T-26, BT-5, BT-7 and BT-7M tanks.[45]

The results of a hit on the target to a great extent depended on the calibre and muzzle energy of the tank's gun. From this point of view, at the beginning of the war the T-34 and KV tanks with their long-barrelled 76mm guns had an undoubted advantage over the German tanks. The armament of the other Soviet tanks also basically corresponded to the demands of that time. However, it isn't the gun that strikes the enemy target, but its shell. It is here that one more weakness of the Soviet tanks was concealed. It first became known in the spring of 1940 after test firing at a German Pz.Kpfw. III tank that had been captured in Poland the preceding autumn. The test unexpectedly revealed a very unpleasant fact: the German tank's 30mm of face-hardened armour proved equivalent to the Soviet homogeneous 'IZ' type with a thickness of 42–44mm. The main Soviet tank and anti-tank 45mm gun at that time was unable to penetrate it from a range of 400 metres, yet theoretically this thickness at a right angle should have been vulnerable to it at a range of more than 1 kilometre. Further tests six months later only confirmed the previous results. As it turned out, the standard 45mm BP-240 armour-piercing shells were heat-treated to such a degree of hardness that they became too fragile and shattered when striking hard armour even before they had time to penetrate it. Steps were taken to eliminate this defect. Already produced shells were fixed by applying Gartz's undercut localizers (essentially rather simple circular grooves cut into the shell's body (*see* Figure 17b)), named in honour of their creator. The concept was simple and effective: they prevented the spreading into the body of the shell of cracks, which arose in its head when striking armour. In the process, the head would disintegrate down to the level of the localizers, while the rest of the shell would remain intact and continue penetrating the armour. The modernization of the 45mm armour-piercing shells began during the Great Patriotic War, in the autumn of 1941, but at the beginning of the war they were able to penetrate the armour of the German medium tanks only from close range, and even at that range, only in certain areas.[46] Moreover, testing conducted in the USSR in the summer of 1942 demonstrated that even the improved Soviet 45mm armour-piercing shells were still inferior in strength and penetrative capability to their German, Czechoslovak and American 37mm analogues.[47] Indeed, as will be shown, the shortcoming was not at all a matter of chance, but was of a systematic nature.

There was a different problem with the 76mm armour-piercing shells: these were in catastrophically short supply, because for a long time it was thought that the 45mm guns were fully adequate for countering any enemy tanks. The mass production of 76mm armour-piercing shells in the USSR didn't get up and running until 1939, but it didn't go smoothly and there simply wasn't enough time to accumulate sufficient reserves of them. The primary reasons for this included the shortage of high-quality alloyed steel for shell bodies and various mass production defects, especially at Munitions Filling Factory No. 55 in Pavlograd, Ukraine. There, over the first 10 months of 1940 the military acceptance officers accepted only 20,000 76mm armour-piercing shells despite an annual plan of 155,000 shells. In December 1940 this factory failed to supply a single shell, although it was supposed to deliver 28,000. At the same time, back in mid-July 1940, 107,000 bodies of 76mm armour-piercing shells were left corroding under the open sky in the factory grounds, and approximately a third of them had reached a point of complete unsuitability. All this was not only the fault of the plant workers. The armour-piercing shells were equipped with MD-5 base detonating fuses, which had insufficient triggering capability, and so required a more sensitive explosive agent than cast TNT. However, there was no mass production of hexogen in the Soviet Union back then, and the filling of shells with TNT using the compaction method had only just begun to be mastered, so the roots of the problem with the armour-piercing munitions are more than obvious.[48]

The armour-piercing pointed shells used by the Wehrmacht were equipped with fully effective heads of high hardness, which were welded to their bodies with electric resistance welding (*see* Figure 17c).[49] This design guaranteed to prevent the penetration of cracks from the shell's head into its body, significantly increasing its strength and penetrating ability. However, manufacturing of shells with weld-on heads required high precision in the mass production's machining process, which was unattainable in Soviet industry of that time. Special high-performance welding machines were also unavailable. Therefore the bodies of the Soviet BP-350A 76mm armour-piercing shells were turned out in one piece, and were subject to spotty hardening (*see* Figure 17a). In contrast to the German shells, they had blunt-nosed heads and were optimized for penetrating face-hardened armour. According to the thinking of the developers, the shell's blunt-nosed tip, when striking armour, was supposed to bite into it, pivoting the shell towards becoming more perpendicular to the armour surface, and to shatter the hardened layer of the armour, after which it was to fragment or snap off. The bulk of the shell body, which wasn't as hard as the blunt-nosed tip and thus was less brittle, would remain intact and complete the penetration of the armour. However, experience demonstrated that this design had serious defects. The mushroom-shaped nose of the shell actually weakened the shell body, and at the same time caused an enormous headache for the manufacturing engineers. Because of it, the penetrative capability of the shells sharply fell. The Main Artillery Directorate of the Red Army commented back then:

> The existing design of the 76mm armour-piercing shell according to drawing No. 2-03545, which is presently in mass production, is unsatisfactory with respect to the strength of the bodies, and moreover, is very complex to produce.
>
> If in the period of development, these shells of mass production still passed testing, then over the recent time (1939–1940), in connection with the improvements that have occurred in producing armour plates, the shell's design has become weak, especially in its cavity.[50]

In the summer of 1942, the BP-350B 76mm shell began to arrive in the Red Army, although mass production didn't begin until March 1943.[51] It had a much simpler shape and, thanks to the Gartz undercut localizers, better armour-penetrating capabilities as well, although it was still inferior in this respect to its foreign counterparts. On paper at least, things didn't look so bad. Let's compare, for example, the performance characteristics of the authorized Soviet and American armour-piercing shells of medium calibre, which are presented in Table 9.

Test firing using a captured German Tiger tank conducted at the end of April 1943 spoiled this favourable picture. It turned out that the BP-350B shell fired from the T-34's main gun couldn't penetrate the Tiger tank's 82mm of side armour after normal impact even at a range of just 200 metres. In contrast, the 75mm gun of the American M4A2 Sherman tank firing with the M61 shell penetrated this armour at a range of 400 metres, and the M72 shell from a range of 625 metres, despite the fact that, as Table 9 shows, the BP-350B was superior in muzzle energy by 10 per cent to the M61, and by 18 per cent to the M72. However, the body of the Soviet shell lacked the

Table 9: Technical characteristics of Soviet and American armour-piercing shells of the first half of the war.

Tank	Country	Main gun			Armour-piercing shell			
		Model	Calibre, mm	Barrel length in calibres	Model	Weight, kg	Muzzle velocity, m/s	Muzzle energy, kJ
T-34	USSR	F-34	76	41,6	БР-350Б	6.505	662	1425.4
M4A2 Sherman	USA	M3	75	40,1	M61	6.786	619	1300.1
					M72	6.323		1211.4

Source: TsAMO, f. 38, op. 11377, d. 12, l. 24. R.P. Hunnicutt, *Sherman. A history of the American Medium Tank* (Navato, CA: Presidio Press, 1978), p. 562.

necessary strength and shattered when striking armour, while the American M72 shell under similar conditions remained intact and only deformed a little bit.[52] The inferior quality of the Soviet armour-piercing shells was further revealed in the next round of tests at the end of 1944. The commission that conducted them came to the conclusion that: 'the American 76mm armour-piercing shell penetrates the armour of German Tiger H tanks from a range 2–2.5 times greater in comparison with the armour-penetrating capability of the domestic 85mm armour-piercing shells.'[53] Note that the comparison was between the American M62 76mm armour-piercing shell and the Soviet BP-365K 85mm armour-piercing shell, which had almost 40 per cent greater muzzle energy. It is no coincidence that the head of the Department of Self-propelled Artillery of the Red Army's Main Armoured-Tank Directorate, General-Major N.N. Alymov, acknowledged in a memorandum on 25 July 1945: 'As is known, the domestic armour-piercing shells with respect to their quality proved somewhat worse than the quality of the armour-piercing shells of the Allied armies and of the enemy's army. This situation was confirmed by testing of the domestic, Allied and enemy's armour-piercing shells at the Scientific Research Armour proving grounds.'[54]

However, the primary problem wasn't the quality of the 76mm armour-piercing shells, but the acute shortage of them. The leading plant for their production before the war was Factory No. 73 in Stalino (present-day Donetsk). It wasn't especially efficient, and completely botched the attempt to get the high-volume output of shells up and running quickly. The high rejection rate of cast steel and difficulties in mastering heat-treating technology and the production of ballistic caps all hampered the factory. Meanwhile, Moscow Factory No. 70 and Leningrad Factory No. 77, which were capable of producing 40,000–45,000 76mm shell bodies a month, were switched to producing different goods.[55] Even over the course of the final pre-war peacetime month, Factory No. 73, despite a planned production of 21,000 76mm armour-piercing shells, didn't deliver a single one. In June 1941 there were plans to produce 47,000 76mm armour-piercing shells, but the timetable of their production (as of 19 June 1941) was hopelessly behind schedule.[56] Obviously, industry didn't wish to waste time mass producing a complex and already outdated product, which in the near future was going to be replaced by something better.

Meanwhile the artillery command had, at the beginning of 1941, a little more than 20,000 armour-piercing shells for the 76mm guns in its possession, or just 2.6 shells per long-barrelled gun. Although by the beginning of the war the situation had improved somewhat, complete resolution of this long-standing problem was still far away. On 1 May 1941 the USSR had 132,000 76mm armour-piercing shells. Accordingly, each long-barrelled 76mm gun on average had just 12 shells, or 15 per cent of the required number. At the same time, the situation in certain border military districts was even worse: in the Western Special Military District there were 9 armour-piercing shells per 76mm gun and in the Leningrad Military District less than 1. The Baltic Special Military District was provided with such shells at the average level, while the Kiev Special Military District had 1.5 times more. Meanwhile the Odessa Military District received 34 armour-piercing shells for each 76mm gun.[57] As a result, the divisional 76mm guns, let alone the T-34 and KV tanks, weren't supplied with armour-piercing shells even according to minimal requirements. In the course of May, another 18,000 such shells were produced, but this was a drop in the bucket.[58] Therefore the nearly fully equipped 7th Tank Division of the 6th Mechanized Corps didn't have a single armour-piercing shell for its 51 KV and 150 T-34 tanks.[59] As for the other guns, besides the 45mm and 76mm, the Red Army at that time also lacked armour-piercing shells. The acute shortage of the necessary ammunition substantially reduced the Soviets' ability to fight successfully against the German panzers.

The war consumed a huge amount of ammunition. On 2 July 1941 the armoured forces' leadership requested 292,00 76mm armour-piercing shells within the next three months. State Defence Committee Decree No. 299ss of 28 July 1941 determined the front's need for 76mm armour-piercing shells at 250,000 for August and another 400,000 for September. However, there was no way to acquire so many. Soviet industry couldn't immediately switch over to a wartime footing and was unable to meet the front's needs. Prior to the war, only the three aforementioned factories – Nos. 73, 77 and 70 – were engaged in the production of shell bodies for the 76mm armour-piercing shells. The first was evacuated to the Urals at the end of September 1941 and temporarily ceased production, while the Leningrad factory at the beginning of the same month was cut off by the German blockade. The Moscow factory that remained alone managed to get mass production under way only in December 1941. The munitions filling factory No. 55 also had to be evacuated to Nizhny Tagil, Novosibirsk and Kopeysk in August 1941.[60] Other factories were drawn into the manufacture of this vital yet complex product, but they weren't able to get it up and running quickly. In addition, the acute lack of shells was aggravated by the enormous problems of delivering them to the front because of the widespread disorder in the transportation system at the beginning of the war.

Out of necessity, the commander of the Western Front, Marshal Timoshenko, on 9 July 1941 ordered, 'Given the absence of armour-piercing shells, when shooting at medium and heavy tanks, aim for their tracks.'[61] Indeed this is understandable, since it was impossible to penetrate the main armour of medium, much less heavy, tanks with ordinary ammunition of small and medium calibre. For example, on 28 July 1941 the Southern Front's artillery commander, General-Major Ustinov, reported that, in the 12th Army, all of the 76mm M1938 mountain guns, as well as all the 76mm divisional guns of the same calibre, 'had no armour-piercing shells, and firing at the tanks with high-explosive shells didn't have any effect. There were instances … [when] after six direct hits, the tank continued moving.'[62] Therefore in 1941 the T-34 and KV tank crews frequently had to fire old shrapnel shells at the enemy tanks. Their fuses were set to detonate instantaneously upon impact. Their body was essentially a hardened steel vessel, which served as a container for shrapnel balls, and when striking an object it worked like a die punch. At a range of 400 metres these shells were capable of penetrating armour with a thickness of 30–32mm and were suitable for use in combat against light tanks.[63] They could effectively penetrate the

Czech Pz.Kpfw.38(t) and German medium tanks with reinforced frontal armour of 50–60mm only in the side.

The troops had no armour-piercing shells for the 152mm gun of the heavy KV-2 tank because it was intended not for tank-to-tank combat but for destroying strong fixed positions. In fact, it didn't even need special anti-tank ammunition. A hit from the massive 40-kilogram bunker-busting 152mm shell on any German tank of that time resulted in its guaranteed destruction. However, there wasn't enough ammunition for these powerful combat vehicles. For example, the Kiev Special and Odessa Military Districts only had 10–15 per cent shells for their KV-2 tanks, while the tankers of the Leningrad, Baltic Special and Western Special Military Districts didn't have any.[64] Moreover, the KV-2 tank crews hadn't been trained to fire at enemy tanks, since they were being prepared for completely different tasks. In addition, it was quite problematic to hit a relatively small, moving target with the gun of the KV-2 because of its low muzzle velocity and extremely slow rate of fire.

The DT machine guns that equipped the Soviet tanks also had their own problems. Designed on the basis of the DP-27 light machine gun, they inherited from them a slow practical rate of fire because of the light gun barrel and the lack of belt feeding. After two or three long bursts of fire, the DT overheated, and its bullets became unstable: they not only flew with a large dispersion, but they also tumbled in the air.[65] It is no surprise that the tankers in combat preferred to fire their main guns. As a rule, having expended all their shells, the Soviet tanks came out of battle with their ammunition load for the machine guns almost untouched.[66]

In short, the armament of the Soviet tanks seemed impressive only on paper. In reality, its effectiveness left much to be desired.

9.3 Armour protection

A tank's armour is intended to protect the crew, on-board supplies and components from enemy-inflicted damage. However, during its development it was impossible to get by without compromises, since any attempt to cover a combat vehicle with armour that makes it invulnerable to powerful artillery leads to an unacceptable rise in the tank's weight and a loss of mobility. Thus by the beginning of the Great Patriotic War, both sides were striving to ensure protection against at least the most popular light anti-tank guns of the period with a calibre up to 37–45mm.

It was just such requirements that were applied to the T-34's design. It was no coincidence that its armour proved to be a tough nut for the German shells to crack, not only due to its thickness of up to 45mm, but also because of the large angles of its slope from vertical. It amounted to 60° for the upper front hull armour, which increased its equivalent thickness up to 90mm. However the placement of the driver-mechanic's hatch and the machine-gun mounting significantly weakened the strength of the T-34's front armour. In addition, its protective properties were noticeably lower in the zones of thermal tempering in the vicinity of weld joints. This was particularly substantial in the event of full strength penetration welding, in which the metal is welded through to its entire thickness. Such seams jointed the T-34's hulls and its welded turrets. In the process, because of overheating the armour around the weld joints and burning-out of the carbon and alloy elements in it, the strength of the armour fell by two to four times. As a result, 37mm armour-piercing shells could penetrate the front hull of the early T-34 in the vicinity of the nose crossbeam and in other places where welded parts came together.

Later, the vulnerable zone in the nose of the tank expanded. Immediately after the beginning of the war in July 1941, the design bureau of Factory No. 183 was tasked with simplifying the design of the T-34 in every possible way, with the aim of maximally increasing its production. One of the directions this work took was to get rid of the special screw rivets used to attach the front armour plates to the nose crossbeam prior to final welding. The purely welded form of the nose assembly noticeably decreased the labour input for its manufacture, but assembly became considerably more difficult. The crossbeam, which was heat-treated for high hardness and had a complex shape, was becoming significantly warped during welding, due to high internal stresses and local heating. Because of this, parts of the nose assembly were moving apart while being welded and thus hindering the process. In order to reduce the twisting of the beam, its hardening had to be kept to a minimum. As a result, the hardness of the nose assembly fell so far as to make it vulnerable to penetration by 37mm armour-piercing shells.[67] The nose crossbeam was dropped only on the T-34/85, and not from the beginning of its production, but after the war ended.

German armour-piercing shells also sometimes penetrated the T-34's cast turret, but for a different reason. The main advantages of casting are high labour productivity and lower production costs of items with a complex shape. The French first mastered the use of cast armour back in the mid-1930s. At the end of 1940 the USSR began to switch from welded T-34 turrets to cast turrets. In order to preserve the strength of the armour, the thickness of the turret's walls was increased to 52mm instead of the former 45mm. However, the same MZ-2 steel was used there, which was not intended for casting. The casting of it resulted in an uneven thickness and a heterogeneous structure, in which hollows, gas bubbles and microporosity appeared, which weakened the armour locally. Only at the beginning of 1944 did they begin casting the turrets for T-34/85 tanks from 71L steel intended for this purpose.

Other areas vulnerable to 37mm armour-piercing shells were the vertical parts of the hull on the sides of the tank, but they were covered by the road wheels and screening terrain, which in the European theatre of operations reached a height of about a metre. The vision devices of the driver-mechanic could also be struck successfully. However, it wasn't easy to hit these weak places, especially on a moving tank. This is illustrated by the statistics collected by the engineers of the Scientific Research Institute No. 48 in the summer of 1942 on the basis of 154 knocked-out T-34 tanks; only 32 per cent of the hits by German 37mm armour-piercing shells on these tanks led to full penetration of their armour.[68]

The welding of the T-34's hull armour had one more extremely undesirable result. The remaining stresses in the welded armour following this process were so great that after a certain amount of time, cracks with a length of up to 300mm and sometimes greater appeared there. As a rule, they were discovered too late, when the tanks were already at the front. However, they appeared not only as a result of welding; irregularities in the processes of cutting, welding and the heat treatment of the armoured plates also made their contribution to the appearance of the cracks. However, perhaps the main reason for the cracks was the low quality of the armour. The point is that the USSR at the time didn't have enough precise instruments to control the temperature and chemical composition of the metal in the furnaces, and thus the smelting was frequently a matter of guesswork. In the conditions of a deficit of experienced smelters, and the haste in carrying out plans, this led to impurities in the armour with harmful contaminants such as phosphorous and sulphur. From the very beginning of the serial production of the T-34, there was an on-going struggle against cracks. As early as 15 May 1941 the Deputy People's Commissar of Medium Machine Building, A.A. Goregliad, reported a success to the Deputy People's Commissar of Defence, G.I. Kulik: '... the percentage of hulls, having tears [meaning cracks in the armour] has dropped from 90 per cent in October 1940 to 50 per cent in March 1941'.[69] Nevertheless, in the summer of 1942 up to 45 per cent of Factory No. 183's armoured hulls, and up to 89 per cent of Uralmash's armoured hulls, had cracks. By the end of the year the rate of this defect had dropped to 10 per cent, but it was never totally eliminated during the whole war. Meanwhile, cracks in the armour led to extremely unpleasant consequences. For example, once an armour-piercing shell broke off a chunk of armour that was approximately one metre square from the side of a T-34.[70]

The seams of the KV heavy tanks were not made with full strength penetration welding because in the Soviet Union at the time they still hadn't learned how to weld thick armoured plates together that way. In the KV tank's case, it was first necessary to join them with rivets, including special screw rivets. For this it was necessary, when assembling the first KV tanks with armoured plates of 75mm thickness, to drill 1,100 holes with a diameter of 25–30mm, and then tap thread in 600 of them. After this, shallow weld seams were made in the places where parts came together in order to seal them. This approach preserved the quality of the armour, but it was very time-consuming and labour-intensive. By the end of September 1940 two-thirds of the screw-rivets and one-third of the regular rivets were replaced by welding, but it was still impossible to manufacture KV tanks in large numbers.[71] Even so, at the beginning of the war the KV's armour protection was sufficiently reliable even without a significant sloping of its plates, due to their thickness. The ordinary armour-piercing shells of the German panzer and anti-tank guns couldn't penetrate it and simply ricocheted away. The best they could do was damage the running gear of this tank and immobilize it, or jam the turret with a hit in its turret ring. However, from close range the APCR (armour-piercing, composite rigid) 37mm shells were able to penetrate both the side and rear of a KV tank without add-on armour plates. The German Pak 38 50mm anti-tank gun presented an even greater threat.

According to Soviet data, its armour-piercing shells from close range could penetrate its armour from the side and rear, while the APCR 50mm shell could penetrate its armour from any direction.[72] In order to destroy a KV tank from medium or long range, the Germans would bring up 88mm Flak guns or 105mm K.18 corps guns.

The information of the experts at Scientific Research Institute No. 48 is convincingly confirmed by Table 10.

The armour penetration capability in the table corresponds to the hit of a shell at 30 degrees to normal. At a right angle to the surface the shell's armour penetration capability increased by approximately 20 per cent, but when encountering the armour at an angle of 45°, it decreased by approximately 40 per cent relative to the tabular values. The likelihood of a hit is given for a target 2 metres high and 2.5 metres wide, which corresponds to the head-on dimensions of the majority of the tanks of that time. In the process it was assumed that the range to the target was determined correctly, and the distribution of hits was centred on the target. The proving ground's probability of a hit was obtained empirically during the tests, while the actual probability of a hit was calculated by means of doubling the proving ground's dispersion values. It was very close to the average results obtained during gunnery exercises and in combat, if the soldiers conducting the fire remained calm. Pzgr.40 was the German designation for the APCR shells.

The figures in Table 10 plainly demonstrate that the T-34 and KV tanks from the very outset of the Soviet–German war were far from invulnerable to the Wehrmacht's tanks and artillery, as it seems to many people who have only superficial knowledge on this topic. Even the numerous German 105mm light field howitzers represented a definite threat to them, especially from close range.

Soviet statistics regarding the losses of T-34 tanks to German guns from the beginning of the war until September 1942 speak quite eloquently on this matter: 4.7 per cent of them were knocked out by 20mm shells, 10 per cent by 37mm shells, 61.8 per cent by 50mm shells, 10.1 per cent by 75mm shells, 3.4 per cent by 88mm shells, and 2.9 per cent by 105mm shells. The calibre of the shells that knocked out the remaining 7.1 per cent of these tanks could not be identified.[73] Yet the German Army that invaded the Soviet Union on 22 June 1941 had 14,459 37mm and 1,047 50mm anti-tank guns.[74] Including the German and Czech tank guns, the Germans at that time had on the Eastern Front 15,523 37mm and 1,754 50mm tank and anti-tank guns. Of course, it must be taken into account that the share of 50mm guns in the Wehrmacht during the relevant period was constantly growing, while the share of the 37mm guns was falling. However, the difference in their effectiveness is fully apparent, and it is all too clear which guns presented the main threat to the T-34. Nevertheless, initially the T-34's armour protection was not the best but still satisfactory: up until September 1942 only 46 per cent of all the shells that hit these tanks fully penetrated it. This situation deteriorated substantially in the latter half of the war after the Wehrmacht's mass employment of long-barrelled 75mm and 88mm tank and anti-tank guns. From the summer of 1943 87–99 per cent of the German shells were piercing the armour of the T-34 tanks after hitting.[75]

In Germany's armour industry, only rolled armour plates were used to produce tank hulls and turrets. They rarely used castings, for instance, to produce gun mantlets. In general, rolled armour is 10–20 per cent stronger than cast armour of the same thickness, since the equalization of structure and correction of internal defects occurs in the process of rolling so the steel becomes tougher. Loads on the welding joints in the German tanks were not borne by the welds, but by milled interlocks on the joined plates, which allowed them to make the seams shallower and to lessen their negative effect on the armour at these joints. In order to enable this, a large amount of preliminary machining on the edges of the armour plates was necessary, which required a large quantity of machine tools and, in the final account, a rise in the man-hours and costs of the tank. Moreover, interlocking joints were not amenable to automatic welding and required the use of hand labour of highly qualified electric welders who welded both on the inside and outside of the joint. However, Germany's armour industry had plenty of machine tools and skilled professionals, so the volume of output was limited primarily by the lack of raw materials and the restrictions on training crews, and the Germans went ahead and used this technology. In a word, the multiple examinations of German tanks by experts of Soviet Scientific Research Institute No. 48 throughout the course of the war didn't once reveal cracks in their hulls or turrets.[76]

Table 10: Characteristics of the German weapons that were used against Soviet tanks at the beginning of the Great Patriotic War

Gun	Calibre, mm	Barrel length, in calibres	Ammunition Designation	Weight, kg	Muzzle velocity m/s	Characteristics		Range of fire, metres				
								100	500	1000	1500	2000
Anti-tank rifle Pz.B.38	7.92	L/137	S.m.K.H.	0.0145	1,175	Armour penetration, mm		30	25	*	*	*
						Probability of a hit, %	On-range	n/a	n/a	n/a	n/a	n/a
							In field	n/a	n/a	n/a	n/a	n/a
Tank cannon Kw.K.30	20	L/55	Pzgr.	0.148	780	Armour penetration, mm		20	14	9	*	*
						Probability of a hit, %	On-range	100	100	81	n/a	n/a
							In field	100	87	37	n/a	n/a
			Pzgr.40	0.100	1,050	Armour penetration, mm		40	20	*	*	*
						Probability of a hit, %	On-range	n/a	n/a	n/a	n/a	n/a
							In field	n/a	n/a	n/a	n/a	n/a
Anti-tank gun Pak 35/36 and Tank cannon Kw.K.35/36	37	L/45	Pzgr.	0.685	745	Armour penetration, mm		35	29	22	20	*
						Probability of a hit, %	On-range	100	100	90	47	n/a
							In field	100	95	47	15	n/a
			Pzgr.40	0.368	1,020	Armour penetration, mm		64	31	*	*	*
						Probability of a hit, %	On-range	n/a	n/a	n/a	n/a	n/a
							In field	n/a	n/a	n/a	n/a	n/a
Anti-tank gun Pak 36 (t)	47	L/50	Pzgr.	1.650	775	Armour penetration, mm		52	47	40	35	*
						Probability of a hit, %	On-range	100	100	100	94	n/a
							In field	100	100	89	59	n/a
			Pzgr.40	0.825	1,080	Armour penetration, mm		100	58	*	*	*
						Probability of a hit, %	On-range	n/a	n/a	n/a	n/a	n/a
							In field	n/a	n/a	n/a	n/a	n/a

Weapon	Calibre (mm)	Barrel	Ammunition	Projectile weight (kg)	Muzzle velocity (m/s)		53	43	32	24	*
Tank Cannon Kw.K.38	50	L/42	Pzgr.	2.060	685	Armour penetration, mm	53	43	32	24	*
						Probability of a hit, % — On-range	100	100	100	99	n/a
						Probability of a hit, % — In field	100	100	96	71	n/a
			Pzgr.40	0.925	1,050	Armour penetration, mm	94	55	21	*	*
						Probability of a hit, % — On-range	n/a	n/a	n/a	n/a	n/a
						Probability of a hit, % — In field	n/a	n/a	n/a	n/a	n/a
Anti-tank gun Pak 38	50	L/60	Pzgr.	2.060	835	Armour penetration, mm	67	57	44	34	*
						Probability of a hit, % — On-range	100	100	100	98	n/a
						Probability of a hit, % — In field	100	100	95	68	n/a
			Pzgr.40	0.925	1,180	Armour penetration, mm	130	72	38	*	*
						Probability of a hit, % — On-range	n/a	n/a	n/a	n/a	n/a
						Probability of a hit, % — In field	n/a	n/a	n/a	n/a	n/a
Tank cannon Kw.K.37	75	L/24	K.Gr.rot.Pz.	6.800	385	Armour penetration, mm	41	38	35	32	30
						Probability of a hit, % — On-range	100	100	98	74	30
						Probability of a hit, % — In field	100	100	73	38	n/a
Flak gun Flak.18/36/37	88	L/56	Pzgr.	9.500	810	Armour penetration, mm	98	93	87	80	72
						Probability of a hit, % — On-range	100	100	95	77	58
						Probability of a hit, % — In field	100	98	64	38	23
Field Howitzer le.F.H.18	105	L/28	Pzgr.	14.000	395	Armour penetration, mm	56	52	48	45	*
						Probability of a hit, % — On-range	100	100	97	76	n/a
						Probability of a hit, % — In field	100	98	63	32	n/a
			Pzgr.	14.000	470	Armour penetration, mm	63	59	54	50	46
						Probability of a hit, % — On-range	n/a	n/a	n/a	n/a	n/a
						Probability of a hit, % — In field	n/a	n/a	n/a	n/a	n/a

Notes: n/a – Data not available; * – beyond effective range; On-range – test fire under controlled conditions on a firing range; In field – during actual combat use.

Source: T.L. Jentz, *Tank Combat in North Africa: The Opening Rounds* (Atglen, PA: Schiffer Publishing Ltd, 1998), pp. 48–9, 58.

The German medium panzers of that time had heterogeneous frontal armour with a surface layer of very high hardness after carbonizing and proper heat treatment. The rest of the armour plate had much greater ductility. One more distinctive feature of the German armour was differentiation. Only the first series of the Pz.Kpfw.III and Pz.Kpfw.IV were protected on all sides by evenly thin anti-bullet armour. The chassis didn't allow the Germans to thicken all the armour equally; they weren't designed for the weight this would require, so the Germans at first began to increase primarily the frontal armour, where the tank would most likely be hit by enemy shells. At the same time, the armour was positioned vertically or with only slight sloping, which didn't provide a perceptible increase in its anti-projectile strength. The evacuation hatches were another shortcoming. They were cut into the sides of the turret, and on the Pz.Kpfw.III into the lower hull sides between the lower and upper track runs, and seriously weakened them. However, the aforementioned shortage of 76mm armour-piercing shells, which the Red Army experienced throughout the entire first year of the war, eased the life of the German tankers. If these were available, the T-34 and KV-1 could both successfully penetrate the side and rear armour of the German panzers from almost any realistic combat range. However, this wasn't true for the 50–60mm thick frontal armour on some of the Wehrmacht's tanks, where much depended on the range of fire and the angle of the shell's hit.

A distinctive feature of the Czech tanks was the extensive use of rivets for assembling hulls and turrets, whereas Soviets and Germans used welding for this. Each of these manufacturing procedures has its pros and cons. The advantages of welding are its higher labour productivity and the watertightness of the joints, which is very important for tanks intended for operations under a variety of conditions. However, in the process, as we've already discussed, this frequently weakens the protection quality of the armour in the area of the welded seams. Moreover, in the event of a shell hit, the cinder build-up on the inside of a welded seam, together with the spalling, would fly into the faces of the tank crew members, inflicting painful wounds and even blinding them at times. Riveting is more time-consuming and requires highly-skilled assemblers, especially in order to make its joints waterproof. The Czechs had no lack of experienced and skilled rivet drivers, so the hulls of their tanks were waterproof to a level one metre above the ground.[77] The rivets themselves were made from special steel and had adequate resistance to bullets and shell fragments.

The armour of the Czech tanks had been designed for protection from small-calibre shells and had been heat-treated to a high hardness. However, such hardening was inadequate against medium-calibre shells. This was shown in the summer of 1942 on the Soviet proving grounds in Kubinka and Kazan, where test firing was conducted against captured tanks with armour-piercing and high-explosive fragmentation shells. The trials demonstrated that a 76mm high-explosive fragmentation steel shell fired from the gun of a T-34, when striking the hull or turret of the Pz.Kpfw.38(t), shattered and cracked open its frontal armour plates with a total thickness of 50mm from a range of not less than 950 metres. At the same time, the shell's fragments and pieces of the armour would strike the crew and tank's components. German armour of the same thickness in analogous situations proved to be sufficiently ductile and shellproof, and didn't develop cracks. The test experts came to the conclusion: 'The hull armour of the Czechoslovak Praga 38T tank (the name given to the Pz.Kpfw.38(t) in the Soviet Union) is very brittle, easily cleaves and produces large cracks.'[78]

9.4 Mobility

A tank's mobility is determined by its capability of moving under its designated conditions, both on the battlefield and on the march. Its main characteristics include its maximum and average speeds, acceleration, manoeuvrability, off-road performance, ability to overcome obstacles, and range. The average speed of a tank on the march includes the time spent on refuelling and necessary maintenance. Factors rarely mentioned in the reference books noticeably affect this. For example, in the summer the air filter on the KV tank had to be cleaned or replaced every 1 to 1.5 hours when moving in a column.[79] An air filter clogged with dust would lead to a loss of engine power, and then to the complete disablement of the tank. The T-34 tank's filter was no better, and its cooling system couldn't handle its task in summertime conditions. For example, in 1941–1943, when the air temperature was above 25° C, the T-34's engine would overheat after 12 minutes running at 400 horsepower. In these conditions it could continually generate only 315 horsepower, which limited the tank's speed to 30 km/hour.[80] The KV tank's cooling system also didn't allow it to move even at an average speed in summertime, because in the process the temperature of the water in its engine would increase to 105° C, which is above its boiling point, and its oil to 115° C.[81]

The maximum speed on level ground to a great extent depends on the vehicle's power-to-weight ratio, but for a tank, in distinction from a race car, this isn't so important. The transmission transfers the engine torque to the drive wheels, and the average speed of a tank in real conditions largely depends on its effectiveness. In the aforementioned memorandum to Stalin, Gruzdev and Blagonravov cited examples of how the backwardness of the Soviet tank transmissions affected their mobility:

> In addition to the high percentage of vehicles being disabled because of transmission failures, the maximum and average speeds of our tanks, despite the high specific power of the engines, are lower than those of the Pz-III and ChMKD [Pz.Kpfw.38(t)] tanks.
>
> Take, for example, the fact that the Pz-III tank's power-to-weight ratio of 15 horsepower generates a maximum speed of 70 km/hour, while the T-34 tank's power-to-weight ratio of 18 horsepower generates a maximum speed of only 45 km/hour. ...
>
> On the Matilda tank [a British tank delivered to the Soviet Union via the Lend-Lease programme] with the planetary transmission, the number of horsepower per ton of weight is almost twice less than that of the KV tank (7.6 horsepower per ton, versus 13.3 horsepower per ton), and yet there is no perceptible difference in the average speed of these vehicles on the battlefield.[82]

However, even the most powerful engine in combination with the most up-to-date transmission is unable to ensure a tank's high mobility on the battlefield. After all, it is fighting for the most part on rough terrain, and there the suspension system has a decisive influence on its speed. At the same time it determines to a great extent the crew's comfort and the effectiveness of fire when on the move. The most progressive suspension at the time we are discussing was the independent torsion bar suspension with shock absorbers on the Pz.Kpfw.III tank. However, its counterpart, the Pz.Kpfw.IV, was unlucky with its suspension, even though it was given serious attention during the development of this tank. Five different types of suspension were tried on the two prototypes of this tank, until they decided on the scheme of four support wheels and eight bogie wheels, interlocked in pairs. A one-quarter elliptic multi-leaf spring on each pair of bogie wheels served as the flexing element. The use of shock absorbers for a multi-leaf spring suspension isn't mandatory, since the damping in them occurs due to the interleaf friction when the springs bend up and down, so the Pz.Kpfw.IV tank had no shock absorbers. Its suspension remained practically unchanged throughout this tank's long service life.

The story of how and why this occurred is interesting and instructive. One of the test options was the torsion bar suspension, which was ahead of its time. It had very low internal friction, thus the need immediately appeared for the rapid damping of the rocking of the tank's hull, which inevitably arises when moving cross-country. The shock absorbers used for this were usually installed on the outer road wheels, where they brought to a stop the tank's rocking most effectively. Not having enough experience with torsion bar suspension at the time, Krupp's engineers installed them on each road wheel, and it seems they chose shock absorbers with an insufficient energy-absorbing capacity, which became overheated on the move and broke down. The suspension turned out to be plainly unsuccessful. Because of this negative experience, Krupp's chief tank designer, Woelfert, developed a strong prejudice against torsion bar suspension, and from then on always spoke out against its use.[83]

One of the main advantages of an independent suspension is the large vertical movement of the road wheels, allowing it to adjust better to uneven terrain, especially when moving at high speed. With this design, cases of suspension 'bottoming' – when its lever arm slams into its stop, thereby transmitting the shock to the tank's body – happen much more rarely. Note that the Soviet T-34 tank with its individual Christie-type spring suspension allowed a full 215mm range of motion for the first road wheel, and 250mm for the remaining road wheels.[84] The range of motion of the Pz.Kpfw.III's road wheels also approached 250mm, but that of the Pz.Kpfw.IV was just 100mm.[85] Tanks with an individual suspension more than once demonstrated their enviable survivability on the battlefield after taking serious damage. For example, on 10 March 1940 a KV-2 tank triggered a Finnish land mine and lost two of the forward road wheels on both sides, but was still able to cover 8 kilometres under its own power and safely return to friendly lines.[86]

Christie's suspension had undoubted merits. Its large diameter road wheels allowed it to get by without return rollers (which support the top run of the track), offered better protection for the tank's sides, and reduced the resistance of the rolling motion. The bearings of the large road wheels rotated rather slowly, which increased their serviceable life. At the same time the heavy weight of the unsprung parts reduced the ride comfort. However, the main disadvantage was that Christie's suspension took up too much room in the tank's interior. Ultimately, this in fact forced the rejection of it. Another serious flaw in the T-34's suspension was the absence of shock absorbers, because of which the tank kept strongly swaying in reaction to speed changes, bumps and hollows for a long time. Incidentally, all Soviet tank suspensions of that time suffered from this shortcoming.

Even so, the Red Army's tanks, as a rule, were noticeably superior to their German opponents in cross-country performance, especially in conditions of soft soil, mud or deep snow. Thus, the T-34 could assuredly negotiate a snow blanket with a depth of 0.5–0.6 of a metre.[87] The important factor here was the low ground pressure of the tracks, while that of the Wehrmacht's medium tanks proved too high for the conditions of Eastern Europe. Czech-produced combat vehicles stood out in this regard. In comparison trials of captured tanks on the Kazan proving ground in the summer of 1942, the Pz.Kpfw.38(t) several times easily made it through a swamp 100 metres wide, in which the Pz.Kpfw.III (judging from the description, an updated Ausf.F or G model) became hopelessly stuck.[88]

However, for genuinely good off-road performance, the low ground pressure should be combined with secure contact between the ground and the tracks, but here the early T-34 tanks fared less well. They were equipped with stamped tracks with a smooth external surface, inherited from the BT tanks, but widened to 550mm. Yet the first cast tracks, which appeared in September 1940, differed little from their predecessors in traction quality. Therefore in the first field tests of the T-34 tank in February–April 1940, it was unable to climb slopes steeper than 15–16° with deep snow or wet loamy soil. In the same conditions on a cross slope of 15°, the tank hopelessly slid in the direction of the inclination.[89] Only in the second half of September

1941 did they begin to equip the T-34 with cast tracks with well developed grousers, which substantially enhanced their off-road performance on soft or waterlogged soil, snow and ice.[90] However, by the spring of 1942 all the factories that were building T-34s produced their own tracks for them, which were non-interchangeable with the others.[91]

Rarely was attention given to the tank tracks, yet at the same time they had a prominent effect on the development of world tank building. For example, Christie in his famous tanks made it possible to switch from tracked movement to wheeled movement not only in order to break the speed record. At that time, tank designers and builders around the world were striving to resolve the difficult problem of extending the service life of the tracks. They only were lasting for hundreds, or sometimes dozens of kilometres, which was plainly inadequate because after all the tank doesn't only fight. First of all it needs to reach the battlefield, which it often has to do under its own power. Thus, the operational mobility of combat vehicles depended directly on the lifetime of the tracks, which was frequently too short. For example, in the first half of the 1930s the Soviet 45th Mechanized Corps over one day of training exercises lost up to a quarter of the tanks that were participating in it because of broken tracks.[92]

A radical solution for the problem was found thanks to an invention by Englishman Robert Hadfield. Back in 1882 he created the first steel alloy in the world with high manganese content, which after heat-treating acquired exceptional durability and resistance to impact forces. At the end of the 1920s in Great Britain they began to cast tank track links out of such steel, which was named after its inventor. This measure, together with the case-hardening of the connecting pins, allowed an increase in the service life of the tracks of the Vickers Mk.E to 4,800 kilometres.[93] In addition, it was a track of the simplest design, having open single-pin joints with dry friction. The Czech tank builders achieved an even more impressive result in this field. The tracks of their LT vz.35 tanks were able to last for 6,500 kilometres.[94] This was an outstanding result for that time, when even a run just a quarter of that length was considered an enviable outcome.

In the USSR they decided to adopt the British method of producing high-quality tank tracks. For this purpose, in 1932 two young Soviet engineers – Vasin and Nikonov – were sent to Great Britain for the purpose of studying foundry practice. After returning, the first of them at the end of 1934 took charge of a new foundry at the Kharkov Tractor Factory, which in the following year began to produce cast track links made from Hadfield steel for the T-26, T-28 and T-35 tanks.[95] The end objective of this work was discussed in from the head of the Automotive-Armoured-Tank Directorate, Pavlov, to People's Commissar of Defence Voroshilov dated 21 February 1938:

> The weakest point of the existing T-26 and BT tanks is the running gear and in particular the tracks. In the new design, the weaknesses of the existing tanks must be eliminated.
>
> …
>
> When the running gear (including the tracks) of a purely tracked tank operates no less than 3,000 kilometres, we can reject the wheeled-tracked type of tank.[96]

However, the Soviet Union was unable to achieve the level of quality of the British tracks prior to the war. Despite the Main Automotive-Armoured-Tank Directorate's demands to ensure a service life of 3,000 kilometres for the T-34's tracks, Factory No. 183 agreed to give a warranty for only half this distance. However, it didn't even achieve this, as a letter written by Korobkov, a Military Engineer of the 1st Rank of the Main Automotive-Armoured-Tank Directorate, to Goregliad on 15 March 1941 indicates: 'The quality of the tracks with respect to their mechanical strength still remains quite low. … The experience of using the tanks in the troops, according to complaint reports, also confirms the low quality of the tracks. There are cases of broken tracks after just 8–10 hours of operating the vehicle.'[97] Even at the end of the war, the service life of Soviet tank tracks did not exceed 1,000 kilometres.[98]

The operational radius of a tank is restricted first of all by the range of movement on one fuel refill. Here, diesel engines have an undoubted advantage over petrol engines due to their better fuel economy, so tanks that are equipped with such engines have noticeably better range than their petrol counterparts. For example, the BT-7M excelled with a record distance of march along paved roads: 630 kilometres on tracks and 1,250 kilometres

Plate 1: A German Pz.Kpfw.I light tank and a column of German infantry on a Soviet country road. The summer of 1941. (*Author's archive*)

Plate 2: A German Pz.Kpfw.II light tank rides along a country road past a wounded and surrendered Red Army soldier. The summer of 1941. (*Author's archive*)

Plate 3: A German Pz.Kpfw. III medium tank from the 3rd Panzer Division knocked out and captured by the Red Army. The summer of 1941. (*Author's archive*)

Plate 4: A tank factory in Germany. In the foreground is tank "Neubau Fahrzeug". 1940. (*Bundesarchiv*)

Plate 5: A German Pz.Kpfw. IV medium tank stuck on the bridge near the Lepel (Belorussia). 4 July 1941. (*Bundesarchiv*)

Plate 6: A German Kl.Pz. Bef.Wg command tank participating in Operation Barbarossa. The summer of 1941. (*Author's archive*)

Plate 7: A German assault gun passing a Soviet village. September 1941. (*Bundesarchiv*)

Plate 8: German Pz.Kpfw.35(t) light tanks from the German 6th Panzer Division. The summer of 1941. (*Author's archive*)

Plate 9: A German Pz.Kpfw.38(t) light tank captured by the Red Army. The summer of 1941. (*Author's archive*)

Plate 10: A Soviet "Renault-Russky" light tank at a military exercise. (*Author's archive*)

Plate 11: Soviet MS-1 (T-18) light tanks. (*Author's archive*)

Plate 12: Soviet T-37A amphibious tanks captured by the Germans near Brest (Belorussia). June 1941. (*Author's archive*)

Plate 13: A Soviet T-38 amphibious tank captured by the Germans. July 1941. (*Author's archive*)

Plate 14: A Soviet T-40 amphibious tank and a BT-7 light tank knocked out near the Ukrainian village of Sitnoye. July 1941. (*Author's archive*)

Plate 15: A knocked-out Soviet T-26 light tank and T-34 medium tanks from the 57th Tank Division stuck in the flood plain of the Drut river near Tolochin (Belarussia). July 1941. (*Author's archive*)

Plate 16: Soviet BT-2 light tanks armed with twin machine guns burning near Dubno (Ukraine). June 1941. (*Author's archive*)

Plate 17: Soviet BT-5 light tanks captured by the Germans. The summer of 1941. (*Author's archive*)

Plate 18: A knocked-out and burnt Soviet BT-7 light tank, which managed to crush a German 37mm anti-tank gun. The summer of 1941. (*Author's archive*)

Plate 19: A knocked-out Soviet T-28 medium tank with add-on armour captured by the Germans in Ukraine. The summer of 1941. (*Author's archive*)

Plate 20: A Soviet T-35 heavy tank and a T-27 tankette in a parade. 1937. (*Author's archive*)

Plate 21: A Soviet KV-1 heavy tank with add-on armour from the 108th Tank Division. September 1941. (*Author's archive*)

Plate 22: A Soviet KV-2 heavy tank from the 2nd Tank Division stuck in a creek after fighting with tanks of the German 8th Panzer Division near the village of Sheta. 24 June 1941. (*Author's archive*)

Plates 23 & 24: Two views of a Soviet T-34 medium tank with add-on armour after its front fuel tanks detonated. (*Author's archive*)

Plate 25: A Soviet T-34 medium tank after its front fuel tanks detonated. (*Author's archive*)

on wheels! Even so, these paper figures were never verified in practice, and in fact couldn't be checked. They were calculated, based on the nominal expenditure of fuel per kilometre of march and the total capacity of the tank's fuel tanks. As already mentioned above, it was not recommended for the BT-7M to move on wheels at all, so it makes no sense to talk about its operational range on them. In fact, it was also hardly able to cover 630 kilometres on tracks on one refill of fuel because of teething problems and the low quality of manufacture of the V-2 engines. Their main shortcoming back then, in addition to their short service lives, was their increased consumption of fuel, and especially oil, which was many times higher than usual norms. The operational range of tanks equipped with them, including the T-34 and KV, throughout the first half of the war was often limited not by fuel but by oil, and in reality they never achieved their paper estimates. So if in fact Soviet tanks of that time were superior to the German tanks in real operational range, it wasn't by much.

9.5 Communications

Communication is a most important and irreplaceable instrument for organizing combat actions and commanding troops. The creators of the German panzer forces from the very beginning recognized the need to equip the panzers with radios, without which successful independent operations, effective coordination of efforts, and timely mutual assistance are impossible. All German tanks without exception were equipped with either two-way radios or Fu2 receivers only. Transmitting radios were not initially installed in all tanks, not only for reasons of economy. There was the justified concern that crews with two-way radios would jam the airways with empty chatter, which might drown out important messages and orders. Therefore in the years 1940–1942 only around 45 per cent of the Wehrmacht's tanks had transmitting radios.[99] These included the combat vehicles of the panzer company and platoon commanders and their deputies, which were equipped with Fu5 very high-frequency radio sets in addition to Fu2 receivers. The panzer battalion commanders and their deputies used special command tanks, which had the more powerful Fu6 very high-frequency radio sets instead of the Fu5. The command tanks of the commanders of panzer

Table 11: Basic characteristics of German panzer radio sets at the war's outset

Type	Power, watts	Frequency range, kilohertz	Communications range, kilometres		Comments
			Voice	Key	
Fu2 EU	–	27,200–33,300	–	–	Receiver
Fu5 SE10u	10	27,200–33,300	2–3	3–4	In motion
Fu6 SE20u	20	27,200–33,300	3–6	4–8	In motion
Fu7 SE20u	20	42,100–47,800	70	80	To aircraft in flight
Fu8 SE30	30	835–3,000	10	25	In motion
			40	70	Stationary

Source: T.L. Jentz, *Panzertruppen: The Complete Guide to the Creation & Combat Employment of Germany's Tank Force, 1933–1942* (Atglen, PA: Schiffer Publishing Ltd, 1996), pp. 272–3.

regiments and divisions, as well as those of their deputies, had long-range Fu8 shortwave radio sets, in addition to the Fu6. For communications with Luftwaffe aircraft, the forward air controllers used the very high-frequency Fu7 radio sets. The basic characteristics of the standard German panzer radio sets of the initial phase of the war are shown in Table 11.

The range of the Wehrmacht's tank transmitters corresponded to the reliable reception of the signal from both sides. The Germans skilfully used radio communications and fought collectively. If a German panzer wound up in a difficult situation, others would quickly arrive to help it.

The design of the first serially produced Soviet tank, the MS-1, from the beginning made no provision for the mounting of a radio set, and its operating manual made no mention of a radio.[100] It is hard to say with any certainty whether this is explained by the underestimating of the importance of radio communications or simply the banal lack of resources. However, in 1930 a rear bustle for accommodating a radio appeared in the turret of the MS-1, and just a year earlier the Scientific Research Institute of Communications received an assignment to work out the corresponding apparatus of three types simultaneously: for ordinary tanks and for tanks of the company and platoon commanders. However, the initial tank radio sets couldn't be installed in the spot assigned for them because of protruding parts within the turret.[101] In 1932 the 71-TK tank radio set appeared, and two years later its modification the 71-TK-1 was put into Red Army service. In 1935 it was replaced by the updated 71-TK-3 radio set, which was installed on the overwhelming majority of serially produced Soviet tanks equipped with a radio before the war and at its beginning. It worked at a frequency range of 4000–5625 kilohertz and had 3–5 watts of power.[102]

Meanwhile, the development of contemporary means of communication in the RKKA lagged behind the rapid growth in its ranks. Radio sets equipped only command tanks and heavy tanks. Even among the latest T-34 tanks of pre-war production, only one in four received a radio. The rest had to rely on primitive signal flags and flares, for the use of which a special small hatch was installed in the turret. Unlike the German panzers, the Soviet tanks didn't have any receivers, since they cost almost as much as the transmitters, were complicated and awkward to use, and required special training for the users, but there weren't enough resources for this.

One distinctive feature of the Soviet radio-equipped tanks produced in the 1930s was the mounting of a hand-rail antenna on their turrets; these were clearly visible from a distance and immediately revealed them as command tanks. The experience of the fighting in Spain and at Khasan and Khalkin-Gol demonstrated that the enemy sought to knock out any tanks with antennae, first, and thereby deprive the tankers of command and control. Therefore in 1939 the decision was taken to remove the hand-rail antennae from all the tanks and replace them with rod antennae, which were less noticeable and cheaper. However, there wasn't enough time to implement this important measure fully before the war broke out.

The quality of Soviet radio sets left much to be desired. For example, in an account of the field trials of the T-34 tank in February–April 1940, it was noted: 'The 71-TK-3 radio set mounted in the tank doesn't satisfy requirements given for tank radio sets due to reasons of the device's large dimensions, complicated operation, and the inability to tune out interference when using the radio.'[103] At first glance the radio had excellent paper figures: it had a range of 18 kilometres when the tank was moving, and 25 kilometres when the tank was stationary with its engine switched off.[104] However, in reality the maximum range was obtained only by one-way reception or via a telegraph key. Reliable two-way telephone connection became stable at a range of not more than 4 kilometres.

Soviet experts conducted comparative trials of a German radio set (by all evidence, a Fu5) with the 71-TK-3 Soviet radio set. The account of these tests, signed on 11 October 1940, ended with more than eloquent conclusions:

> The radio set of the German tank provides a reliable two-way telephone connection when moving and standing still, including at the maximum range indicated by the manufacturers. ... The operator was able to connect by telephone even at a range 30 per cent greater than the indicated maximum range, while the radio set of our tank at maximum range ensures only reliable reception. The transmission range on our tank is significantly lower in comparison with the datasheet specifications. ...
>
> A positive quality of the two-way radio of the German tank is the fact that it ensures reliable communication in movement, whereas the quality of reception significantly drops during movement of the BT tank, right down to the complete loss of contact. ...
>
> Judging by all basic characteristics, the radio set of the German tank is superior to that installed in the domestic tank. I consider it useful to conduct the design and development of a new type of tank radio on the basis of the available German models.[105]

Yet there wasn't time to complete the design of a domestic analogue of the German radio sets before the war began. Even the domestically produced communication equipment wasn't supplied to the troops in sufficient quantities. However, the chronic shortage of radio sets was far from the Red Army's only problem, because even the available sets could not always be used. For example, a report on the combat training of the 8th Mechanized Corps' 15th Tank Division in January 1941 noted: 'The 30th Tank Regiment in the course of the first phase didn't have a single 71-TK radio available for training (they'd all been stored away). The radio operators of the first year of service have only started classes on audible reception; the radio operators of the second year aren't working on radios and don't know how to transmit or pick up a signal using a telegraph key.'[106] Moreover, in other units many of the radio operators had unacceptably low proficiency, were unable to master equipment that was far too complicated for them, and as a result of unskilled use of the radio quickly broke it. There were even cases of deliberate sabotage of the radio sets by the tankers, who were trying to conceal their own technical illiteracy by pointing to the wretched quality of the equipment entrusted to them. Speaking honestly, they had some justification for this, because the 71-TK-3 was excessively complex and inconvenient for use. It was difficult to tune because of poor selectivity, especially at great range and when in movement. The frequency drifted, especially when the tank was jolting, and required frequent tuning. It required a genuine master of radio communications to work it, and such men were few and far between in the troops. There was also an acute lack of qualified people able to repair radio sets.

In addition to all the above, Soviet tankers in radio-equipped tanks frequently lacked the basic abilities of command actions and preferred to operate independently. They didn't call for help from comrades, even when this was justified, and possibly thereby substantially reduced their chances of success in combat. What then could be said about the tanks without radios, which were literally deaf and dumb?

Problems with communications weren't limited to contacts with the outside world. The intercom system for communications between the T-34's crew members barely worked, while inside the tank, when the engine was running, there was an unbelievable rumble, which drowned out any attempts to converse. According to the recollections of a driver-mechanic who served in one: 'Communications were handled by the feet, which is to say I had the boots of the tank commander resting on my shoulders; he would push my left or right shoulder, which let me know whether to turn left or right, and if he wanted to stop, he'd tap my head.' Meanwhile, the loader was excluded from the intercom, and received commands in a totally unique manner: 'A fist would be put under the loader's nose, and he already knew that this meant an armour-piercing shell, while splayed fingers meant a fragmentation shell.'[107]

9.6 Observation

Good observation substantially increases the tanks' chances of success in combat. It is especially important to allow the commanders as wide and as deep a field of vision as possible. At the beginning of the war all German medium tanks were equipped with a commander's cupola with a 360° field of vision, positioned in the centre of the aft section of the turret. This enabled them to see in every direction with minimal dead zones along the sides of the tank. They not only had the ability to keep track of the encompassing situation thanks to their liberation from all other duties, except command functions, but also possessed superb optical devices for this. This enabled them in the majority of cases to detect the enemy more quickly, and before they were spotted, and therefore gave them a perceptible advantage from the very outset of combat.

The first serially produced MS-1 tanks in the USSR also had a commander's cupola. Instead of optical devices for observation, it had ordinary vision slits which left the tank commander vulnerable to small fragments and bullet splashes. Moreover, subsequently the commander's cupola disappeared for a long time from Soviet tanks, and they effectively became blind.

This especially concerned the T-34, so we will take a closer look at it from the point of view of observation. Initially, it was planned to install a periscope in this tank's wide turret hatch. It was designed by S. Porfir'ev and provided all-round visibility. However, in 1939 Porfir'ev was arrested on suspicion of espionage, a move which was followed by the rejection of all of his designs. Instead, the T-34 received a hastily engineered 'device of an all-round panoramic view'.[108] However, the site for it was chosen at the time when the 45mm gun was planned for the turret. After its replacement with the 76mm gun with its much larger breech end, the place for the tank commander could only be in front of and to the left of the optical device. After testing done on the T-34 at the end of 1940 it was found that this rendered it extremely awkward to use the device, and in the early spring of 1941 it was rejected. In the absence of anything better, the tank commander, in order to observe the battle, had to use the periscopic sight with its narrow field of vision and plainly insufficient speed of scanning. In addition, he had a static mirror periscope with a narrow field of vision to the left. The loader and driver-mechanic had restricted sectors of view through mirror periscopes analogous to the commander's, but only in one direction: the former to the right and the latter straight in front. At the same time it was difficult for the commander and loader to use their vision ports located in the sides of the turret due to the 76mm gun's bulky breech. However, the most deprived crew member with respect to vision was the T-34's radio man/machine gunner. He could peer out in front through a small aperture in order to aim his ball-mounted machine gun. This aperture wasn't much larger than a keyhole, yet his eyes were approximately a half-metre away from it. It isn't surprising that the radio operator saw almost nothing outside the tank, especially when it was moving.

The view through the T-34's periscopic vision devices left much to be desired. They were equipped with mirrors made of polished steel, which because of the poor hermetic sealing of the device's body often fogged up in the summer, iced over in the winter, and over time oxidized. This is not mentioning the fact that polished steel reflects only 60–65 per cent of the light in comparison with a glass mirror, so 2.5 times less light passed through such periscopes just because of the pair of steel mirrors installed in them. The lenses of the vision devices had even larger shortcomings. According to the recollections of one T-34 driver-mechanic, 'the shatterproof glass on the hatch of the driver-mechanic … was made from wretched yellow or green Plexiglass, which produced a completely distorted, waving view. To identify something through such safety glass, especially in a jolting tank, was impossible. Thus the war was fought with slightly open hatches.'[109] This was confirmed by British experts, who tested and studied a T-34 that was built in June 1942. They described its periscopes: 'The quality of the glass is poor and it contains many bubbles and flaws.'[110] Of course, the discussion was about the vision devices of wartime manufacture, the quality of which perceptibly fell. However, here are the conclusions of a commission on the results of field trials of the T-34 from 22 April 1940:

The vision devices installed on the T-34 tank do not allow observation and driving the tank (with closed hatches).

1) The vision devices have a large dead space.
2) In wintry conditions they do not provide a view.

a) The device becomes covered with snow and mud (both the driver-mechanic's and the one in the turret).

b) Fogging of mirrors and glasses leads to their icing.

3) Cleaning from dust and precipitation is not provided.

4) When firing, the protective glass of all the devices cracks.

5) When test firing at the vehicles with a 37mm shell at one side of the turret, all of the mirrors were disabled with the very first hit.

6) On the basis of the above-listed shortcomings, it is considered that the design of the vision devices is unsatisfactory.

Design new vision devices with the objective to eliminate the above-listed shortcomings.

The next day a representative of Factory No. 183, A.A. Morozov, answered all these comments in writing: 'At the given time, the factory cannot propose another design for the vision devices.'[111]

The factory workers nevertheless reacted to the justified criticism of the military men; following the path of least resistance, they replaced the glass mirrors of the vision devices with polished steel mirrors, which correspondingly degraded their clarity. Moreover, the first combats showed that after two to three rounds fired by their own cannon, the safety glass of the driver-mechanic that was already blurry became coated with powder residue. In the spring of 1941 the periscopic panoramic PTK device was installed in the T-34's turret for the loader; this device was used at that time on all the other Soviet medium and heavy tanks, as well as on the latest T-26 tanks. However, in use it was difficult to determine the direction in which the device was pointed, so the observer easily lost his bearings.[112] However, there was nothing better, and only in 1943 were they replaced by prismatic MK-4 observation devices (Gundlach periscopes) copied from British tanks.[113]

In June 1941 a German 37mm anti-tank gun at close range hammered 24 shells into a T-34, but in the end only managed to jam its turret.[114] This testifies not only to the reliability of the T-34's armour protection, but also to the completely unsatisfactory visibility from this tank. After all its crew, despite their efforts, was unable to detect and destroy its adversary. Moreover, the battlefield was left in German possession.

Other Soviet tanks at the beginning of the Great Patriotic War also lacked a commander's cupola, and the quality of their observation devices was just as poor as in the T-34. Very quickly the Germans became aware of these shortcomings and didn't fail to take advantage of them. In the summer of 1941 a German instruction pamphlet on ways to counter Soviet tanks recommended firing at them with ordinary machine guns, starting at a range of 800 metres, in order 'to force the tank to close the hatches'.[115] Indeed, it is understandable why: as soon as the tankers took cover from the machine-gun fire and began to use the authorized observation devices, their ability to spot and destroy their enemies decreased sharply. In contrast, the Germans not only had a much greater chance to come out unscathed, but also to knock out the enemy tanks.

In the winter of 1942–1943, the OKH summarized the experience of combating the Soviet tanks in a special order, which stated in particular, 'The main weakness of the Russian tanks: the poor conditions for observation. Anti-tank guns should exploit this weakness for opening surprise fire at tanks from close ranges.'[116] Economizing on visibility for the Soviet tanks cost their crews dearly ...

9.7 Crew Comfort

Comfort for the crew is necessary for creating favourable conditions for them when on the march and in combat. It allows the tankers to conserve their strength before entering combat and to fight more effectively. Comfort factors include an adequately spacious fighting compartment and driver's compartment, equipped with effective ventilation; the thoughtful positioning of devices and controls; the ease of handling the levers, grips and pedals; the implementation of ergonomic guidelines when designing the battle stations for the crew members; a good suspension, which prevents the transmission of sharp blows and jolts from rough, uneven terrain to the tank's hull and the quick damping of its swaying and so on.

However, everything starts with the proper allocation of the crew's duties, and this proved to be one of the main weaknesses of the T-34. Its commander, along with carrying out his primary responsibilities, worked as the gunner. In practice this joint role deprived him of the ability to do everything he was supposed to do, especially in combat. After all, he simultaneously had to direct his crew's actions, observe the battlefield, locate targets and threats, determine the range to them, conduct fire at them with the main gun and co-axial machine gun, follow the actions of the other tanks of his platoon, especially the platoon commander's tank, and carry out commands given by signal flags and flares. To do all this in the heat of battle is physically impossible for one man, especially given the shortcomings of his observation devices. Meanwhile the platoon commander in his radio-equipped tank, in addition to all else, was to receive orders from his company commander and make them known promptly to the combat vehicles subordinate to him, with the help of those same primitive flags and flares. In addition, he had no opportunity to correct something if they didn't notice or understand his signals. As a result, the tanks tended to drift together into a clump instead of attacking in a deployed combat line at proper intervals, and thus interfered with one another and presented an excellent target for the German anti-tank gunners. They didn't even have the ability to warn each other about a spotted threat. Instead of concerted actions, the Soviet tanks wound up by themselves and virtually fought alone. As the saying goes, united we stand, divided we fall…

The commanders of the Soviet light tanks, as well as of the German tanks of the same weight class, also worked as gunners, but this was an unavoidable consequence of their smaller crew. However, even in the medium T-28 tanks, as well as in the heavy T-35 and KV tanks, the commanders also had to be busy with secondary jobs – they carried out the functions of the loaders and machine gunners. In the USSR, of course, it was recognized that the overburdening of tank commanders with duties that were not inherent to their role seriously weakened the effectiveness of their combat vehicles. On 6 November 1940 the People's Commissar of Defence Timoshenko requested in a letter to Voroshilov: 'It is necessary to give the tank commander, starting from the separate tank and on up the chain of command, the possibility of complete and continuous observation over the battlefield, the situation, and the tanks subordinate to him, freeing him completely of the duties of gunner or loader.'[117] However, this wasn't done before the war, since they were planning that the T-34 would soon be replaced by the T-34M, in which this problem would be resolved. Later, however, this had to be set aside, for a long time.

The point is that in order to free the tank commander from the responsibility of firing the turret's main gun and co-axial machine gun, room had to be made for a third man in the turret – a gunner. In the first several dozen T-34, there was no room for one, because the turret was so cramped. It is sufficient to say that their commanders and loaders had to work in a space that was 450mm (17.7 inches) wide, which was 50mm (1.97 inches) less than the minimal requirement for a tanker wearing a summer uniform.[118] Later the turret was widened by another 160mm (6.3 inches), so the width of the space for the commander and loader grew to 530mm (20.9 inches).[119] This was barely sufficient only for summertime, because after all a man in winter uniform had an average width of 600–630mm (23.6 to 24.8 inches).[120]

The main problem with widening the turret was never in fact resolved, because the volume of the fighting compartment is largely determined by the interior diameter of the tank's turret ring. On the German Pz.Kpfw. III it was 1,520mm (59.8 inches), and on the Pz.Kpfw.IV 1,680mm (66.1 inches).[121] On the T-34 tank it was just 1,420mm (55.9 inches), and on the KV-1 and KV-2 1,535mm (60.4 inches). The Pz.Kpfw.III tank, however, was equipped with a 37mm gun or 50mm gun, and the Pz.Kpfw.IV with the 75mm gun with relatively short ammunition, whereas the T-34 and the KV-1 had a 76mm gun and the KV-2 a 152mm gun; thus it becomes clear why the German crews had much more room than the Soviet crews. The hasty evacuation of the industry that was conducted in the USSR in 1941 and 1942 was accompanied by the inevitable loss of manufacturing equipment, especially bulky machinery. For example, they were unable to evacuate the unique turning-and-boring mills from Kharkov, which were capable of machining turret rings with a diameter larger than 1,500mm, and in the USSR such machine tools weren't produced. That was the main reason why the two-man turret was kept for a long time on the T-34. It was only after the Soviet Union received the necessary machine tools in February 1944 through Lend-Lease that the serial production of the T-34/85 began;

this had a three-man turret with an internal diameter of the turret ring of 1,600mm (63 inches).[122]

The cramped nature of the fighting compartment was far from the only inconvenience for the T-34's crew. It took 26 seconds to traverse the turret with its L-11 main gun 90° manually, but a complete revolution of the turret required 384 turns of the handle with a force of 3.5–4.5 kilograms. This was on a horizontal surface; an incline of 10° increased the required force to 20–28 kilograms. When on an incline of 15° the force reached 45–50 kilograms, and on a 16° slope it was difficult to traverse the turret even with a power drive, where in the process the 165 amp fuse periodically burned out.[123] Moreover, it was extremely inconvenient to use the turret's power drive, and not only because it had two fixed speeds; it turned the turret in jerks and didn't allow for accurate aiming. In order to reach the control knob for the power drive, the gunner had to take his eye away from the sight. Thus, the turret had to be traversed blindly, so the necessary direction had to be guessed, and then the gunner would have to search for the target in the sight's narrow and blurry field of vision. Therefore in a combat situation the tankers preferred to traverse the turret manually despite all its shortcomings. Moreover, in the first half of the war the tanks that were produced often had no power drive for the turret. All of this adversely affected the tanks' ability to fire quickly and accurately, as described in a letter from the Deputy Head of the Main Automotive-Armoured-Tank Directorate, General-Lieutenant B.G. Vershinin, to the People's Commissar of the Armour Industry, I.M. Zaltsman on 8 March 1943:

> One of the main design flaws of the T-34 tank, which significantly reduces its combat power, is the low rate of fire, low speed of aiming, and low accuracy of the tank's fire.
>
> Comparative gunnery tests between the T-34 and foreign tanks that were conducted by the Scientific Research Institute of Armour on the proving ground of the Red Army's Main Automotive-Armoured-Tank Directorate demonstrated that the rate of fire and accuracy of fire when on the move is significantly lower from the T-34 than from the foreign tanks.

The main reasons for the T-34's lower rate of fire and accuracy of fire are:

1. The awkward mutual arrangement of the turret's traversing mechanism, the gun's elevating mechanism and the sight, which makes aiming the gun at a target difficult. When aiming the gun, the gunner's hand that is turning the handwheel of the gun's elevating mechanism interferes with the hand that is turning the handwheel of the turret's traversing mechanism. The latter, moreover, bumps into the gunner's chest and forces him to break away from the sight. The gunner loses the target and spends excessive time to find it again.
2. The low speed of the turret's traverse and the need to apply strong force to turn it, especially on slopes.
3. The poor visibility from the tank, which makes it hard to find targets.
4. The small diameter of the turret ring, which cramps the work of the loader.

The Technical Directorate has repeatedly raised the question of eliminating the indicated shortcomings; however, up to the present day virtually nothing has been done about it.[124]

Still one more factor that worsened the T-34's combat rate of fire was the placement of the lion's share of its stored ammunition on the floor of the fighting compartment. Even though the bottom of the tank offered the best protection against enemy fire, the loaders had to bend over for each shell, and then raise it over a relatively long distance to the gun's breech. The absence of a rotating floor in the turrets of all the Soviet tanks other than the T-28 and T-35 further complicated the loader's work. Because of this, in combat the loader had to be constantly on the alert and move quickly in order not to be sent flying by the gun's breech during a turn of the turret, or not to be struck by the recoil after a shot. Such compulsory gymnastics didn't at all contribute to an increase in the tank's rate of fire. It is no surprise that the actual rate of fire of the T-34's main gun, which was revealed in the course of field tests at the end of 1940, didn't exceed two or three shots per minute. Only after improving its ammunition stowage in May 1941 was it able to achieve four shots per minute.[125] Yet at this time, on paper at least, its rate of fire was twice that.[126]

The heavy KV tanks had their own range of problems with turning the turret, since they had almost the same traversing mechanism as the T-28 medium tank's main turret, which weighed around 3 tons. Yet the KV-1's turret weighed 7 tons, and the weight of the KV-2's turret even reached 12 tons, which was aggravated by a lack of balance. As a result, the turning of the turret by hand required excessive force, while the electric motor of the power drive lacked adequate power and the stop locks couldn't hold the turret in place. If the tank wasn't level, all of these problems stood out even more.[127]

The German tanks were much more comfortable for their crews. Among their considerable advantages were articulated telescopic sights, the eyepiece of which remained stationary relative to the gunner when raising or lowering the gun barrel. This gave him the ability to fire not only more accurately but also more rapidly. The use of an electric firing key on the German tank guns served the same purpose. It required special ammunition, but plainly improved the rate and accuracy of fire in comparison with the manual firing mechanism used in Soviet tanks. Moreover, the foot-operated firing switch of the T-34's cannon was not particularly reliable, and the effort needed to depress the pedal approached 40 kilograms. Soviet front-line veterans persistently requested its replacement with an electrical trigger of the type used in German assault guns or the British Matilda and Valentine tanks, which were delivered to the USSR by Lend-Lease.[128]

The presence of a suspended floor, which rotated with the turret, and on which the loader stood, contributed to increasing the rate of fire of the Wehrmacht's medium tanks. Thanks to this support under his feet, the loader remained stationary relative to the gun, despite the turret traversing. The Pz.Kpfw.III was perceptibly superior to the T-34 in weapon manoeuvrability, as well. Its two-speed traversing mechanism enabled the turning of its turret by 90° within 13 or 19 seconds (depending on the speed used). For a complete revolution of the turret, it required correspondingly 164 or 244 turns of the handle with a force of 1.3 to 1.5 kilograms.[129] Thus, the turret of the Pz.Kpfw.III could be turned manually twice as quickly, and with a third of the effort, as the T-34's turret. However, this tank lacked a power drive for traversing the turret. This shortcoming was somewhat offset by a secondary handwheel, with which the loader could assist the gunner and accelerate the turret's traverse.

It is noteworthy that the Pz.Kpfw.III always proved victorious in every trial of tanks conducted in the USSR with respect to their rate of fire. It also, in the opinion of Soviet experts, was constantly recognized as the most comfortable for the crew. Undoubtedly, the location of the turret close to the tank's centre of gravity in order to minimize the amplitude of its longitudinal rocking played a large role in this. In the Soviet tanks of this time, the turret was shifted towards the front of the tank, which noticeably increased the amplitude of oscillation in the fighting compartment because of its distance from the centre of gravity. The turret was positioned just as optimally on the Pz.Kpfw.IV as it was on the Pz.Kpfw.III, but its suspension was much less successful. This begs the question: why was the Pz.Kpfw.III tank removed from manufacturing in 1943, while the less comfortable and unexceptional Pz.Kpfw.IV tank stayed in production until the very end of the war? The main reason was the large diameter of the Pz.Kpfw.IV's turret ring, which allowed its firepower to be increased substantially while retaining adequate work space in the fighting compartment. One more significant advantage of this tank was the electric drive for traversing the turret, which was equipped with its own twin-cylinder motor. This allowed an acceleration of its turning from 0.08° a second to 16° a second and was suitable for accurate aiming even with the tank's main engine off.[130]

For the normal work of any tank's crew, adequate ventilation of the fighting compartment is necessary. First of all, it must quickly remove the highly-toxic propellant fumes that result from firing. In the T-34 tanks of the early production series, ventilation was completely inadequate for a reason already known to us. When the 45mm gun was replaced with the 76mm gun with its much longer breech, the breech block wound up not directly below the vent fan but far behind it, where fan operation was much less effective. This was revealed in the very first trials on 22 February 1940 and was reflected in the conclusion written after they ended:

A check of the air's fouling with CO [carbon monoxide] when firing yielded the following results.

When firing 10 rounds from the main gun in the course of 2 minutes, the concentration of CO in the turret with the ventilator on and the engine running: after 5 shots 0.071 mg/litre; after 10 shots – 0.21 mg/litre.

When firing 10 rounds from the main gun in the course of 7 minutes and 15 seconds with the ventilator and engine off: after 5 rounds – 0.99 mg/litre, after 10 rounds – 1.52 mg/litre.

When firing 3 drums of ammunition each from two machine guns in the course of 6 minutes, the concentration of CO in the turret was 0.024 mg/litre. ...

With the ventilator on and the engine running, the concentration of CO becomes significantly lower, but doesn't reach health standards (0.02–0.03 mg/litre).[131]

The low practical rate of fire of the T-34's main gun somewhat reduced the consequences of the poor ventilation, but once in a while the tankers became poisoned by propellant fumes, sometimes even to the point of death.[132] The situation perceptibly improved only in 1944 with the T-34/85, where two ventilators were mounted in the rear portion of the turret roof.

The problems with the Soviet tanks' transmissions that were described by Gruzdev and Blagonravov in the above-mentioned memorandum to Stalin not only negatively affected their reliability and mobility; it also made them significantly difficult to handle: 'The timely (rapid) shifting from low gear to high gear in our tanks demands an experienced driver with a long service record, while in the Pz. III, Matilda and ChMKD [Pz. Kpfw.38(t)], the shift from one gear to the next requires less time and less expertise; accordingly, in a short time one can master the driving technique.'[133]

In addition, the T-34 in the first half of the war had only four gears – plainly inadequate for matching the tank's range of speeds with the engine's range of rpms; especially because a diesel engine's range of rpms, as a rule, is noticeably more limited than that of a petrol engine. In the ideal scenario, after shifting to a higher gear, the engine's rpms corresponding to its maximum power (in the V-2 engine, 1,800 rpms) should fall down to the rpms corresponding to its maximum torque (in the V-2 engine, 1,100–1,200 rpms). But in the T-34, the V-2 diesel engine's revolutions fell so precipitously in the process that it almost dropped to its minimum sustainable rpms (in the V-2 engine, 600 rpms), where its torque was much less than the maximum.[134] Given the slightest delay in shifting gear or significant road resistance, the engine would stall and die. Loss of movement in combat conditions meant the tank became a sitting duck, so T-34 crews fought as a rule in second gear, with no gear shifts and without fully exploiting its speed capabilities.

Criticism was also prompted by the difficult handling of the transmission, which was characteristic not only of the T-34. Thus the driver-mechanic of the BT-7M had to apply between 24 and 60 kilograms of pressure on the pedal of the engine clutch, and 55–65 kilograms of force on the levers of the steering clutches. To shift the levers of the T-34's steering clutches required the same amount of force, but with the help of a pneumatic servo actuator this dropped to 10–20 kilograms of force and even less. However, the pneumatic servo actuator proved too expensive and difficult to produce and service; in addition, it wasn't very reliable. At the end of the summer of 1940, it was replaced by a mechanical booster, which lowered the required force on the levers of the steering clutches to 15–30 kilograms.[135] Yet the T-34's gear shift still required up to 40 kilograms of force.[136] The point is that in order to shift to a different gear, it was necessary to move large and heavy cogwheels along the castellated shaft in the axial direction. However, there were no means to synchronize the cogwheels before engaging them in gear, other than bullhead teeth. The cogwheels' speeds were equalized only through the friction of their sides between each other, so they had to be pressed tightly together. Moreover the gearbox was located more than three metres away from the driver-mechanic and had no devices that would ease its use. The complex actuator mechanism, using shifting gears with selector rods, articulated linkages and lengthy pull rods that sagged, stretched, went out of alignment and frequently jammed, aggravated the situation.

One can find out how all this looked in practice from the numerous recollections of Soviet veteran tankers. Here is one of the most characteristic: 'You couldn't engage the gear stick with one hand; you had to give it an assist with the knee.' A former T-34 radio operator corroborates this:

One of my tasks was to help in shifting gears. The T-34/76 had a four-speed transmission. It took enormous effort to shift gears. The driver-mechanic would shift the lever in the needed position and begin to pull it, and I would grab it and pull on it together with him. After some spell of jittering, it would engage. A tank march consisted entirely of such drills. Over the time of an extended march, the driver-mechanic would lose 2 or 3 kilograms of weight: he'd be totally exhausted.[137]

In this connection, the account of General Colonel of Tank Forces V.S. Arkhipov is interesting; during the war, he commanded the 53rd Guards Tank Brigade:

Once our medics conducted an experiment – they weighed approximately 40 tankers before and after a 12-hour battle. It turned out that the tank commanders over this time lost on average 2.4 kilograms of weight, the gunners on average 2.2 kilograms of weight, the radio operators on average 1.8 kilograms of weight. But the driver-mechanics lost more than the others – on average 2.8 kilograms and the loaders on average 3.1 kilograms of weight. So on halts the men would fall asleep instantly ...[138]

9.8 Detectability

Detectability is determined by the intensity of the tank's physical fields, making it perceptible to contemporary means of detection. During the Second World War this related to its geometric dimensions, painting, level of noise and weight; after all, the heavier the tank, the greater the distance at which it can be detected due to shaking of the ground when moving. In this area, the German tanks had an advantage, chiefly because they were significantly quieter and lighter in comparison with the T-34 and KV. The noise a tank makes substantially affects how noticeable it is, especially in closed terrain, at night, or in low visibility conditions. The T-34 was very noisy, first of all because of its 500 horsepower engine, which didn't have a muffler. In addition to the roaring of the powerful diesel when moving, there was the clattering of the large-link tracks with horn-roller meshing, accompanied by the characteristic jingling of its tracks' connecting pins against the special cam, which ensured they stayed in place. Even the heavy KV didn't make such a din, because its propulsion system used small-link tracks, which were directly engaged by drive sprockets. When moving along a road, a T-34 could be heard from a half-kilometre away, while the German Pz.Kpfw.III was audible only from a distance of 150–200 metres. In addition to the sound, in dry weather the T-34 was betrayed by the high plumes of dust kicked up by its exhaust pipes directed downwards.

A tank's detectability can be reduced by the application of various camouflaging measures and means that match the surrounding terrain, light and time of year. One of the most effective of these means is digging it in. However, this has one major shortcoming – it is labour intensive. For example, in order to dig a pit for a medium T-34 tank, it was necessary to excavate 27.5 cubic metres of soil, and for a heavy KV tank 35 cubic metres. According to regulations, the tank crews had to expend 7.5 to 8 hours for such a job. At night, the time required doubled, and in winter time, with frozen soil, the time tripled.[139] Thus, in a real situation, the tankers could only dig their tanks into positions that were chosen well beforehand, which gave them enough time to accomplish the task.

However, in the majority of cases on the battlefield, they had to adapt as far as possible to the terrain features, and success depended on the maximum depression angle of the tank's main gun. Attention wasn't usually paid to this, but it is important; after all, when this angle increases, not only does the dead zone around the tank decrease, but even more importantly a gun angled downwards allows the tank to fire from the reverse slope of a hill in a hull-down position behind the hill crest. In Germany they duly appreciated the importance of this technical parameter, the increase of which substantially expanded the tactical possibilities for their combat vehicles, so by the beginning of the war the guns on all of the Wehrmacht's tanks could lower 10° below the horizontal. The design engineers of the Soviet tanks were more concerned about decreasing the height of their turrets, which becomes possible for the price of small angles of gun depression. Indeed, whereas on the BT-5 and early BT-7 with the cylindrical turrets, the gun's maximum angle of depression reached 8°, on the BT-7 with the conical turret, this angle decreased to just 5°. The main guns on the BT-7M, T-28, T-35, T-34,

KV-2 and KV-1 with the F-32 cannon also had a maximum depression of 5°. Only the KV-1 with the L-11 gun had an angle of depression of 7°, and the T-26 with the conical turret 6°.[140]

Smokescreens are an effective means of concealing combat vehicles on the battlefield. In order to create them, German tanks at the beginning of the war were equipped with a smoke candle rack, which was mounted on the tank's rear and held five candles that could be dropped from the inside. Of course, with respect to flexibility and convenience, the use of this device fell far short of the later multi-barrelled smoke grenade launcher mounted on the tank turret. Nevertheless, it enabled the Wehrmacht's tankers, covered by smokescreens, to manoeuvre on the battlefield in relative safety or leave if necessary. The tanks of the Red Army of that time had nothing similar.

Chapter 10

The Survivability of Tanks and Crews

There are four basic principles for ensuring the survival of a tank on the battlefield:

1. Avoid detection.
2. It the tank is detected, avoid being hit.
3. If the tank takes a hit, prevent penetration of the armour.
4. If the armour is penetrated, ensure survival of the crew and prevent the tank suffering fatal damage.

The first two principles relate to the tank's active protection, and the latter two to its passive protection. We'll take a look at them in order:

1. To remain undetected, it is necessary first of all to decrease the noticeability of the tank to a minimum as already discussed.
2. It is possible to avoid being hit by minimizing the area of the tank that is exposed to the enemy and the amount of time that the enemy can see it. This can be achieved:
   a) by skilful use of the terrain and cover;
   b) by artful manoeuvring so as not to expose the tank's side, which presents a significantly larger area and, as a rule, weaker armour to enemy fire, than its front;
   c) by maintaining a high speed on the battlefield; or
   d) by decreasing the tank's dimensions.
   The tank's technical features affect the last two points, primarily its power-to-weight ratio and the quality of the transmission and suspension, as well as its height, width and length. However, to a much larger degree everything depends on the crews themselves, their knowledge of combat tactics and their ability to master the handling of their combat vehicle.

If decreasing the tank's dimensions can lessen the probability of a hit on the tank by a matter of percentages, then the masterful exploitation of the terrain and cover combined with intelligent and rapid manoeuvring on the battlefield can reduce it by many times more.

3. Only a tank's designed protection can prevent a shell that hits it from penetrating into its interior. (We have previously discussed the armour protection on the German and Soviet tanks.)

4. Even if the armour is penetrated by a shell, that still doesn't necessarily mean the tank's total demise.

We'll discuss this in more detail. For a start, we'll examine the main damaging factors of anti-tank ammunition. Primary among them in the period of our concern were the full-calibre, armour-piercing shells, the rear cavities of which were filled with small, but sufficiently powerful bursting charges. In addition to them, full-calibre solid armour-piercing shells – or so called solid shot shells – were also used. Armour-piercing shells penetrate armour due to their high kinetic energy. If it is sufficient, then as a rule, a shear plugging of the armour occurs, the diameter of which is approximately equal to the calibre of the shell itself. The after-penetration effect of an armour-piercing shell with a bursting charge depends on its remaining kinetic energy and the blast effect of its explosive. A solid shot has no blast effect, naturally, so its after-penetration effect is perceptibly lower than that of a shell with a bursting charge. However, it has greater kinetic energy, and accordingly better armour penetrating capability due to its larger inherent weight, because the specific density of an explosive charge is less than that of the metal of the shell's body.

There are also other factors that enhance the potency of a shell's effects. For example, often as a result of their penetration, so-called secondary fragments are often created within the tank. These are various pieces of the armour, parts and components that form as a result of their destruction, as well as unanchored objects. All this gets thrown around within the tank as a result of the influence of the shell's kinetic energy and the armour plug punched out by it, as well as the blast effect of an armour-piercing shell with a bursting charge. The secondary fragments multiply and intensify the damage inside the tank, and also substantially increase the probability of injuring or killing the crew, so efforts are made to reduce their number to a minimum. Ideally, the result of the penetration of armour would be the appearance of one single plug that hasn't been fragmented. However, in practice, fragments that have been chipped away or broken off from the armour surrounding the shell's penetration frequently add to it. In order to prevent their creation, there are efforts to make the armour, especially its inner surface, as malleable as possible without sacrificing its resistance against shells. Other steps to decrease the severity of the consequences of the armour's penetration include eliminating unsecured items within the tank and increasing the strength of both elements of the tank's design and its parts and components, which when being destroyed turn into lethal secondary fragments. This is particularly important for the fighting compartment and driver's compartment, where the tankers are positioned.

It is necessary to add that even when shells strike a tank yet fail to penetrate the armour, they sometimes nevertheless do damage to its crew and mechanisms. The main reason for this is the insufficient malleability of the interior surface of the tank's armour, which as a result of the enormous stress caused by an impact that wasn't able to penetrate the armour leads to spalling, the fragments of which are capable of not only damaging the tank, but also causing serious wounds and injuries to the tankers. This was typical of the T-34's armour, especially of its cast turrets in the first half of the war. Heat treated for high hardness to its entire depth, it was prone to create secondary fragments. Remnants of moulding compound and burn-on from the casting process that haven't been cleaned from the rear surface, surface defects of the rolled armour and dross from the welding seams are further sources of increased danger to the tankers. Blown free by the impact of a shell against the armour, they inflict painful wounds to a tanker's exposed skin or the skin under their summer uniforms, and can even blind them.

As a result of the process of penetrating the armour and the conversion of the shell's kinetic energy into heat during the process, the shell and the plug of armour (or its fragments, if it breaks into pieces) become heated to extremely high temperatures and acquire igniting capabilities. In the case of an armour-piercing explosive shell, the incandescent gases created during the explosion of the charge spread with extremely high velocity and pressure and add to their effect. Within any tank there are always items that are flammable. First and foremost there are the fuel and lubricants and the propellant charges of the stored ammunition, but there are also various rubber and plastic articles, paint, rags and the uniforms of the tankers, especially the winter uniforms. The very worst consequence of a fire in a tank is the detonation of the on-board ammunition and fuel storage, which results in the tank's complete destruction. However, even without this, a burned-out tank becomes totally disabled and must be written off, since as a result of the lengthy effects of high temperatures during a strong fire, the tank armour loses its hardness and thus its protective qualities. In addition, because of the uneven heating of the burning tank, the hull and turret become irreversibly deformed, which is virtually impossible to correct. There is no sense in repairing such a tank, because it is much cheaper and faster to build a new one.

In the designs of their tanks the Germans took adequate measures in order to prevent fires. First of all, this included isolating the fuel tanks from the crew members. For example, the Pz.Kpfw.III's fuel tank was in the engine compartment, separated from the fighting compartment by an internal firewall. Another such wall separated the fuel tank from the engine.[1] On the Pz.Kpfw.IV the fuel tanks were located beneath the floor of the fighting compartment and were additionally protected by fireproof panels above them.[2] Moreover, this section of the tank is usually shielded by folds in the ground when in combat and a direct hit on it is less likely.

In the Soviet tanks the situation with fire safety was much worse. For example, in the vehicles of the BT series, the fuel tanks were positioned between double walls in the area of the engine compartment and occupied a significant portion of the hull's side profile. This created an unacceptably high likelihood that a shell hit would result in the ignition of at least one of them. In the T-34 that replaced them, the four fuel tanks (two upper with a capacity of 105 litres each and two lower with a capacity of 55 litres each) were placed right in the middle of the fighting compartment (*see* Figure 18). Two more T-34 fuel tanks with a total volume of 145 litres were located in its transmission compartment.[3] All three fuel tanks of the KV tank, with a total capacity of 600–615 litres, were also positioned along the sides of its fighting compartment.[4]

The decision to place them in such an unsuitable place was taken as a result of the serious misjudgment of the combustion hazard of diesel fuel, although its flammability is significantly lower compared to petrol. The physics of this natural occurrence is rather simple. The fuel itself doesn't burn, only its fumes do, thus the flammability of any fuel is characterized by two basic parameters:

1. The flash point: the lowest temperature of fuel at which its fumes create a mixture with the oxygen in the surrounding air, which combusts when it makes contact with an ignition source. Sustained burning in the process doesn't yet arise because of the insufficient rate of fume production. On average, the flash point of various sorts of petrol is within the limits of –30 to –45° C., while that of diesel fuels is between 30° C. and 80° C.

2. The ignition point: the lowest temperature of fuel at which its fumes are produced at a sufficient rate to burn steadily after ignition from an external source. The ignition point of petrol is just 1–5° C higher than its flash point, while the analagous difference for diesel fuel is between 30 and 35° C.

Thus petrol easily ignites at a temperature above –25° C, while for diesel fuel the suitable conditions for ignition are created at much higher temperatures – at least 60° C., and for some types more than 115° C. These figures clearly explain why, when bringing a flaming torch close to an open container of petrol, it immediately ignites, but when rapidly plunging the same torch into a container of diesel fuel, the flame is extinguished. In the latter case, the torch simply doesn't have time to heat up the diesel fuel to its flash point and dies when submerged in it because of the lack of oxygen necessary for burning. However, a hit by a shell or secondary fragments in a fuel tank filled with diesel fuel creates completely different conditions. Let's analyse the main possible scenarios of this event:

1. When solid shot, shell fragments or pieces of armour strike a full fuel tank, they penetrate and create a fuel spillage. In the process, a fire rarely results because the solid shot, high-speed fragments and pieces which pass right through the penetrated fuel tank simply don't have enough

time to ignite the fuel over the very short time it takes to pass through it. In this case the fuel tank even serves as a supplementary defence against fragments and pieces that lack the energy to penetrate right through it. They also, as a rule, aren't capable of igniting the fuel.

2. When an armour-piercing shell with a bursting charge strikes a full fuel tank and explodes either inside it or in direct proximity to it, the result is the total destruction of the fuel tank and the splashing of the fuel contained in it with its subsequent ignition.

3. When a solid shot, shell fragments or pieces of armour strike a fuel tank that is only partially full of fuel, they penetrate it. If the fuel tank is penetrated above the fuel level, but there are few fumes, then the solid shot, fragments or pieces pass completely through it and don't cause a fire. If the penetration is below the fuel level, then the likelihood of fire depends on the correlation between the amount of fuel left in the tank and the amount of thermal energy transmitted to the fuel by the fragments or pieces. A small quantity of fuel in these conditions may ignite.

4. The most catastrophic consequences result when an armour-piercing shell with a bursting charge explodes in a fuel tank that is only 10–25 per cent full of fuel. In this instance an aerosol mixture of tiny drops of fuel and air forms, adding to the fuel fumes already within the fuel tank. The requirements for generating such a lethal cocktail are high temperature and abruptly increasing pressure created by the bursting charge's blast effect. In order to trigger the mechanism of detonation of the mixture, this charge must be equivalent in power to not less than 50–100 grams of TNT, which at that time corresponded to an armour-piercing shell with a bursting charge with a calibre of 75mm and higher. The capacity of the fuel tank for creating the optimal conditions of mixing for detonation should amount to no less than 100 litres. In fuel tanks with a volume of 30–50 litres, there is no noticeable amplification of the shell's blast effect. However, in the event that it happens, the detonation of the fuel tank increases the blast effect of the shell that explodes in it by two to four times. Thus, the explosion of a T-34 fuel tank, caused by the hit of a 76mm BP-350A armour-piercing shell, which contained 155 grams of TNT, was equivalent to the force of the explosion of a 152mm BP-540B armour-piercing shell with an explosive charge of 480 grams of TNT. As a result of a fuel tank's

explosion, the armour plate closest to its origin would be ripped from the hull along a welding seam and blown to one side. The tank's turret, which usually gets blown off by detonation of the on-board ammunition, would remain in place in this event. Even the shells in the tank, despite the detonation taking place next to them, would often be left in their stowage racks. A conflagration virtually never resulted, and moreover, the fire that had already started would instantly die out. This is easily explainable: the powerful shock wave created by the fuel tank's explosion extinguished the flame, and the available oxygen within the tank would instantly and completely burn out. A diesel fuel tank itself after a detonation inside it would disappear without a trace, having been blown apart into dust. Yet the explosion of an analogous fuel tank with petrol inside it was approximately 1.5 times weaker and wouldn't cause the destruction of the tank hull's welding seams. After the Germans introduced the use of shaped charge shells at the front at the end of 1941, cases of explosions of the T-34's fuel tanks, which were filled only 25 per cent or less with fuel, began to be noticed from the effects of the explosive jet. However, only the diesel fumes contained in the fuel tank itself would detonate in this case. The resulting effects were equivalent to a charge of 30–50 grams of TNT, which would kill the entire crew, but the tank's body would remain intact.[5]

As is clear from the description of the dynamics of a fuel tank's detonation and its consequences, all this fully corresponds to the process that occurs during the triggering of a contemporary fuel-air explosive, which is sometimes called a 'vacuum bomb'. The speed of detonation approaches 1,500–1,800 metres per second, and the pressure up to 15–20 atmospheres. In the process, the mass velocity of the gas stream moving in the direction of the blast wave achieves 600–800 metres per second.[6] It was this incredible force that tore apart the full strength penetration welded seams of the T-34's hull (see Plates 23–25). Tankers inside these tanks in such cases were killed instantly, with scarcely any time to sense anything.

Here it must be added that the Wehrmacht's 37mm, 47mm and 50mm armour-piercing shells had insufficient explosive effect in order to cause the detonation of the T-34's fuel tank. At the beginning of the war, really only the shells of the 88mm Flak 18/36/37 gun could trigger it, as could the 105mm K.18 cannon, which wasn't encountered so frequently at the front line. However, the penetration of the T-34's armour by guns with a calibre of up to 50mm also frequently had tragic consequences for their crews. A hit by a small calibre armour-piercing shell with a bursting charge on one of the fuel tanks in the fighting compartment, as a rule, meant the immediate ignition of the resulting spilled and spattered fuel directly among the tankers. In such circumstances, their chances of survival were very low. However, this isn't all. The probability of the outbreak of a fire in the T-34's fighting compartment also substantially increased as a consequence of the constant leakage of fuel from the fuel tanks positioned there. Most often the leak didn't come from the tanks themselves, but from the rubber-canvas hoses and fittings that connected them. As a result, there were puddles of fuel on the floor of the fighting compartment, which easily ignited both from shells that penetrated the armour, as well as from the red-hot secondary fragments that resulted from the penetration. Moreover, ammunition boxes were stowed on the floor of the T-34's fighting compartment, and the consequences of their ignition are not difficult to predict. However, this was not the worst scenario for the crews. The diesel fuel that seeped from the fuel tanks soaked into the tankers' uniforms, which also became impregnated with fuel and lubricants during refuelling, repairs and maintenance, and when wiping the grease from shells while loading them aboard the tank, etc. Such cloth ignited very easily and it was virtually impossible to smother the flames. Burning diesel fuel caused much more serious burns to the men than did petrol. When petrol gets on the skin, first of all its fumes burn, so tankers who bailed out of burning tanks with petrol engines not infrequently got away with comparatively light burns. Blazing diesel fuel, unlike petrol, adheres tightly to the skin, burns much more slowly than petrol, and leaves deep burns on the body right up to the point of charring. It is no coincidence that special incendiary mixtures like napalm, which are intended to stick where they land, burn for a long time and at the same time reach a very high temperature, are made from heavy types of fuel, including diesel fuel.

A fire in the tank's fighting compartment and driver's compartment leads to an agonizing death for the men who aren't able to bail out in time. The chances of saving the tankers' lives increase if they have the ability to quickly abandon their burning vehicle. In the German tanks of the period under discussion, each crew member had his own hatch, so according to statistics, in the case of a tank catching fire, often the entire crew was able to get out, and in the worst case just two of the five crew members would not be able to escape. The German design engineers went so far as to weaken the sides of the turrets of their medium tanks by adding hatches to them, in order to give the crews a better chance in an urgent evacuation. However, the main point was that the Werhmacht's tankers, in the majority of cases, had sufficient time to bail out of their tanks, because fires usually began in the engine compartment and didn't always spread to the fighting compartment, and if they did, they didn't do so immediately. For the T-34, the statistics were much worse. The fires in them often started in the fighting compartment because of the fuel tanks located there. From a burning tank, in the worst case no one managed to bail out, and in the best case, two might have been able to save themselves, usually the tank commander and driver-mechanic.[7]

In the T-34 the driver-mechanic had the best chance of survival. In the first place, he was seated rather low and was partially screened from enemy shells by folds in the ground. Secondly, he was protected by a 45mm thick frontal hull plate, sloped at an angle of 60° from vertical, which was equivalent to 90mm of armour. The opening for the driver-mechanic's hatch weakened the frontal armour, but on the other hand he was able to clamber quickly out of the tank through it. The radio operator and loader, however, had to wait for their turn to bail out, because they didn't have their own hatches; wait, even when they were just seconds away from an agonizing death or a maiming injury from flames. The situation was no better with evacuation from the KV tanks, which had just two hatches for the five or six crew members. Moreover, the hatches sometimes became jammed because of the deformation of the hull or turret as a result of a shell's hit. Therefore some tankers before a battle didn't fasten the hatches, but instead lashed their covers with straps from within the tank into partially open positions. Hatches in this case loudly clapped when on the march and permitted shrapnel to enter the tank, but on the other hand the crew had a better chance to escape. Emergency escape hatches on the bottom of the vehicle appeared on Soviet tanks shortly before the war, and the BT-7M received them first. However, they weren't suitable for an emergency abandonment of the tank. For example, in order to open the emergency hatch on the T-34, first six hex nuts had to be loosened, followed by the disengagement of six bolt bars, before the safety catch could be released, and only then could the hatch cover be dropped free.[8] All this took on average 2.5 minutes, and around another minute was required for a trained crew of four men to exit through the emergency hatch.[9] Hardly anyone could survive in a burning tank that long ... Moreover, in the event of a fire in the tank's work space, it was frequently impossible to use the emergency hatch – the burning diesel fuel spreading across the floor prevented this.

There is a widespread opinion that tanks equipped with petrol engines are much more flammable than tanks with diesel engines. As can be shown from the facts presented above, the fire hazard of combat vehicles to a much greater extent depends on their design and layout, rather than their engine type and fuel type. Therefore it is not appropriate to call, as often happens, all of the Soviet pre-war tanks that had petrol engines fire hazards. We have already looked at a case from the Winter War with Finland, when of the 482 cases of combat damage and mechanical failures of the T-28 tank, only 30 led to a fire that destroyed it. Such an impressive statistic convincingly demonstrates that the sensible positioning of the fuel tanks and the effective fire suppression system that equipped the T-28 successfully resulted in minimizing the number of cases of fatal outbreaks of fire in this tank after the penetration of its armour – despite its use of petrol as fuel.

Interestingly, the fire extinguishers on the Soviet tanks of that time were themselves dangerous for the tankers. The point is that they were filled with tetrachloride, which, under the effect of high temperatures, emits a suffocating gas – phosgene. So when using them inside a closed tank, it was required to don gas masks first.[10]

The question is often discussed: why were the Wehrmacht's tanks equipped with petrol engines? After all, the German engineers had ample experience with successfully designing various diesel engines, intended to equip automobiles, tractors, locomotives, ships and even aircraft. The point is that during the Second World War, there was an acute shortage of diesel fuel in Germany. Unlike petrol, the Germans were unable to synthesize it from coal, and they had plainly insufficient resources of natural oil available. The navy became the primary consumer of diesel fuel in the Third Reich. Many of its combat ships were equipped with diesel engines, including the so–called 'pocket battleships.' The German submarine force used an especially large number of diesel engines. It was in fact the deficit of diesel fuel that became the main reason for the use of petrol engines on the German panzers during the Second World War. There were also other reasons, however. For the ground forces, they filled not only tanks with petrol, but also prime movers, lorries, cars and motorcycles, which significantly simplified the system of the Wehrmacht's supply with fuel. Moreover, a petrol engine has a number of considerable advantages over a diesel engine:

1. The same power is attainable with lower weight and size;
2. A larger operating range of rpms;
3. Superior acceleration;
4. Simplicity and low cost of production;
5. Ease of start at lower temperatures.

Its main shortcoming in comparison with diesel is its lower efficiency. Because of it, tanks equipped with petrol engines, as a rule, have a relatively short range between refills. However, back then, the Germans didn't consider this a significant disadvantage.

Chapter 11

The Tank Battle at Raseiniai, Lithuania, 1941

T he initial phase of the Great Patriotic War went along under German dictates. A characteristic example here was the clash between the Soviet 2nd Tank Division and the German 6th Panzer Division on the Northwestern Front in the first days of Operation Barbarossa (*see* Map 1). At first glance, it isn't difficult to predict the outcome of the battle, because on paper the Soviets had a substantial advantage in armour. It is sufficient to say that the total weight of a salvo from the tank main guns of the Red Army's 2nd Tank Division was almost four times greater than that of the Wehrmacht's 6th Panzer Division. Yet this doesn't even include its 63 BA-10 armoured cars, armed with 45mm cannon, while the German armoured cars were at best equipped with only 20mm cannon. However, life is much more complicated than an utterly simplified scheme, modelled with the help of simple arithmetic, so for a start it is necessary to examine in detail the correlation between the two sides' forces and means, as shown in Table 12.

The table plainly demonstrates that the Wehrmacht's 6th Panzer Division was substantially superior to the Red Army's 2nd Tank Division in a number of key indicators, such as the number of men, firepower and the quantity of transportation. The complete lack of anti-tank guns and armoured personnel carriers in the Soviet division also catches the eye. Moreover, the table, dedicated to the numerical indicators, doesn't reflect such critical qualitative characteristics as staffing levels, the level of combat training, the qualifications of the command staff, combat experience, and so on; in these criteria, the Red Army at the beginning of the war was noticeably inferior to the Wehrmacht. In the Soviet armoured forces this inferiority was aggravated by their recent comprehensive overhaul, which led to the mass replacement of formations that had formed up long ago and were quite cohesive with brand-new formations. Many of them by the beginning of the

Table 12: Correlation of forces and means between the Soviet 2nd Tank and German 6th Panzer Divisions.

Forces and means		Division				Correlation
		Soviet 2nd Tank		German 6th Panzer		
Personnel			9,382		15,600	1:1.66
Machine guns (not counting those in tanks)	Light		174		262	
	Heavy		36		74	
	Four-barrelled		11		None	1:1.48
	Large-calibre		6		None	
	Total		227		336	
Mortars	50mm		27		48	
	Medium	82mm	18	81mm	30	1:1.73
	Total		45		78	
Guns	Anti-tank	None		37mm	30	–
				50mm	18	
				Total	48	
	Field	76mm regimental	4	75mm infantry	20	
		122mm howitzers	8	150mm infantry	4	
		152mm howitzers	12	105mm howitzers	24	1:2.50
		Total	24	150mm howitzers	12	
				Total	60	
	Anti-aircraft	37mm	12	20mm	12	1:1
Tanks	Light	T-26	19	Pz.Kpfw.I	11	
		KhT-26	12	Pz.Kpfw.II	47	
		BT-7	116	Pz.Kpfw.35(t)	155	
		Total	147	Total	213	
	Medium	T-28	27	Pz.Kpfw.IV	30	1:1.11
	Heavy	KV-1	39	None		
		KV-2	18			
		Total	57			
	Command		None		13	
	Total		231		256	

Forces and means		Division				Correlation
		Soviet 2nd Tank		German 6th Panzer		
Armoured cars	Unarmed	None		Sd.Kfz. 260/261	6	1.50:1
	Armed with machine guns	BA-20	27	Sd.Kfz. 221	8	
				Sd.Kfz. 223	8	
				Sd.Kfz. 253/254	18	
	Armed with guns	BA-10	63	Sd.Kfz. 222	8	
				Sd.Kfz. 231/232	6	
				Sd.Kfz. 263	6	
	Total		90	Total	60	
Armoured personnel carriers		None			27	-
Motor vehicles	Cars and trucks up to 1080 kg capacity	26		906		1:1.99
	Lorries and special	1,346		1,818		
	Total	1,372		2,724		
Tractors and prime movers		170		126		1.35:1
Motorcycles		37		1,350		1:36.49

Note: Approximate personnel strength of a German panzer division according to Ellis, J., *The World War II Handbook* (London: Autumn Press Ltd, 1995), p. 205.

Source: N. Askey, *Operation Barbarossa. Volume IIA. The German Forces, Mobilisation and War Economy from June to December 1941* (Raleigh, NC: Lulu Publishing, 2013), pp. 339, 374. T.L. Jentz, *Panzertruppen: The Complete Guide to the Creation & Combat Employment of Germany's Tank Force, 1933–1942* (Atglen, PA: Schiffer Publishing Ltd, 1996), p. 206. M. Kolomiets, *1941: Boi v Pribaltike 22 iunia–10 iulia 1941 goda* [*1941: Fighting in the Baltics 22 June–10 July 1941*] *Frontovaia illiustratsiia*, No. 5 (2002), pp. 10, 12–13. M.V. Kolomiets, Sovetsky tiazhelyi tank KV-1 [Soviet heavy tank KV-1] (Moscow: Lanza/EKSMO, 2017), p. 218.G.F. Nafziger, *The German Order of Battle. Panzers and Artillery in World War II* (London: Greenhill Books, 1999), pp. 23, 61.

war hadn't even finished forming up, and there is no point even talking about their cohesiveness. In addition to all this, the re-equipping with new tanks that had started before the war was far from complete. Even those units that had received them frequently didn't have enough time to master their new combat vehicles.

Against this backdrop, the Soviet 2nd Tank Division didn't look too bad. It had been formed up over a year before the beginning of the war and was the only tank division in the Baltic Special Military District that was armed with heavy KV tanks, which it had started to receive back in August 1940, so had become relatively well familiar with them. This division was rightfully considered one of the best in the Red Army.[1] However, it had to pass a real test of its maturity on the field of battle immediately after the beginning of the Great Patriotic War.

It all began at dawn on 22 June 1941, when the German 6th Panzer Division, operating as part of the XXXXI Motorized Corps of Army Group North's 4th Panzer Group, crossed the Soviet border. The day's task for the division was to break through the Soviet border fortifications south of Tauragė, push on through the small Lithuanian town of Raseiniai, and seize a bridgehead across the Dubysa River. The Red Army's 125th Rifle Division was occupying the 40-kilometre stretch of the border with two regiments in the sector of the 6th Panzer Division's offensive.[2] Although the density of its defence was four times less than regulations, the division fought tenaciously and managed to slow the Germans' advance. Immediately after crossing the Saltuona River, the 6th Panzer Division had to stop for the night. The next morning it headed out with two *kampfgruppen*, named after its commanders, von Seckendorff and Raus.

The Soviet 48th Rifle Division wound up in their path. Since May 1941 six of its rifle battalions had been busy building defensive works in the area of Eržvilkas, 30 kilometres southwest of Raseiniai, and about the same distance from the border. The division's remaining strength, numbering 4,662 men, 26 mortars, 46 anti-tank guns and 58 field guns, set out on the march from Riga at 2200 on 17 June. Moving at night, they were stealthily conducting their march to link up with the forward battalions by 0500 on 23 June.[3] In the vicinity of Raseiniai on the morning of 23 June, the division's columns were subjected to surprise air and artillery strikes, and then attacked by German ground forces. Not expecting such a turn of events, the elements of the 48th Rifle Division were overrun, and, according to the evening report from the 8th Army's chief of staff General-Major G.A. Larionov, 'fled in panic; the attempt to detain them in the vicinity of Lioliai [25 kilometres north of Raseiniai] was unsuccessful.'[4] Taking advantage of the favourable situation, at 1600 (Moscow time) on 23 June *Kampfgruppe* von Seckendorff seized Raseiniai, and two hours later crossed the bridge across the Dubysa River near the village of Kaulakai. Soon thereafter *Kampfgruppe* Raus seized a second bridgehead to the north across the same river, beyond the bridge at the village of Kušeliške.[5] Despite these successes, the German offensive was developing at only half the expected pace, and a new, much more serious adversary was approaching to meet the German 6th Panzer Division.

Its appearance was no coincidence. Stalin, until the very last moment, was hoping to avoid a German invasion and even after its start took some time to realize the real scale of what had happened. Not surprisingly, the first orders he gave were not practical at all. For example, a directive sent to the Western Military Districts at 0715 on 22 June categorically demanded: 'The troops with all their forces and means are to pounce on the enemy forces and destroy them in the areas where they violated the Soviet border.'[6] Having received the corresponding order from his high commander General-Major P.P. Sobennikov, commander of the 8th Army, at 1400 that same day in turn ordered: '3rd Mechanized Corps, having left the 5th Tank Division under the commander of the 11th Army, is to reach the area of Raseiniai on the morning of 23.6.1941 with the 2nd Tank Division and 84th Motorized Division, for an attack in cooperation with the 12th Mechanized Corps and 9th Anti-tank Artillery Brigade against the enemy. By the end of 22.6.41, secure the Dubysa River crossing for yourself.'[7]

However, the 84th Motorized Division was immediately withdrawn from subordination to the commander of the 3rd Mechanized Corps, General-Major A.V. Kurkin, and was instead transferred to the 11th Army. So the 3rd Mechanized Corps had to carry out this order with only one of its three formations – the 2nd Tank Division. At the time it was located in the area of the Gaizunai railway station, approximately 120 kilometres east of Raseiniai. The division set out on the march at 1730, observing complete radio silence, but made very slow progress. The main roads were jammed with refugees and subject to Luftwaffe attacks, so the division had to use winding dirt roads. In the process visibility was restricted not only by the quickly arriving night, but also by the dense clouds of dust. Moreover, the dust was clogging the air filters, but there was little time to clean or replace them. The bridges across the brooks and steams that were encountered en route were not designed to support the weight of the multi-ton KV tanks, and they had to cross them by fording.[8]

According to the plan of the Baltic Special Military District command, the 2nd Tank Division was supposed to attack from out of the Raseiniai area through Skaudviliai into the flank of the Wehrmacht's panzer group advancing towards Riga.[9] However, as it turned out, the German 4th Panzer Group was attacking further south towards Leningrad, and the jumping-off area that was designated for the 2nd Tank Division's attack was already held by the Germans. Instead of a flank attack, it first had to break through the enemy bridgehead, and then engage in an encounter battle with the 6th Panzer Division.

The first attack against the bridgehead occupied by *Kampfgruppe* von Seckendorff by the infantry of the division's 2nd Motorized Rifle Regiment with the support of tanks was organized only by the evening of 23 June. It was poorly staged and driven back, but was followed by a second attack, and the Germans had to evacuate the bridgehead and fall back behind the river. The commander of the 6th Panzer Division, General-Major F. Landgraf, ordered the situation to be restored, and his panzers began to assemble west of Raseiniai for an attack at 0600 on 24 June. However, they were pre-empted by Soviet combat vehicles, which at sunrise with artillery support pushed across the bridge over the Dubysa and kept advancing. The Germans fell into a difficult situation: their panzers' guns and anti-tank guns were impotent against the armour of the Soviet heavy tanks that were completely unknown to them, and there were no 88mm Flak guns at hand. In the 6th Panzer Division's 41st Panzerjäger Battalion, other than the 37mm anti-tank guns, there were 18 much more powerful 50mm anti-tank guns, but even they couldn't deal with the KV tanks. Evidently, by habit they were firing from ranges that were too far. Meanwhile, the Soviet tanks were breaking into the outskirts of Raseiniai. Some of the German soldiers panicked, and one of the officers, bypassing all command levels, reported directly to the field headquarters of Hoeppner, the Commander of 4th Panzer Group: 'Everything was already lost!'[10]

In contrast, there appeared a triumphant entry in the Soviet Northwestern Front's combat diary on this same day: '3rd Mechanized Corps' 2nd Tank Division engaged in a tank battle in the Skaudviliai area, and having destroyed the 100th Motorized Regiment and up to 40 tanks and 40 guns, by the end of the day reached the Raseiniai area without fuel.'[11] Here, reality was replaced by wishful thinking; after all, the 2nd Tank Division didn't in fact succeed in breaking through to Skaudviliai, and the fighting took place east of Raseiniai. Besides, the German 114th Motorized Regiment was engaged there, not the

100th, and its losses were significantly exaggerated. However, the mention of lack of fuel in the fully mechanized and motorized formation presaged the looming catastrophe. Other signs also indicated that everything wasn't going well for the Soviet side. Because of the lack of infantry and artillery in the table of organization of a Soviet tank division, the tanks were fighting on the western bank of the Dubysa River virtually without their support. The medium T-28 and light tanks made no impression on the Germans; in all their descriptions of the fighting near Raseiniai, they emphasized the KV tanks. However, these heavy tanks had their own problems: the KV-1 with the 76mm gun didn't have a single armour-piercing shell, while the KV-2's ammunition load was plainly inadequate for a lengthy combat action – just 36 shells with separate loading. It is no coincidence that there were recorded cases when instead of firing at the German tanks, they tried to ram them. Moreover, the fire of the Soviet tanks was inaccurate, and their command and control proved ineffective. However, the main problem was that the 2nd Tank Division had to fight alone, without any information about the enemy, and with no air cover or support from neighbouring formations. It also lacked reliable communications with higher command and received no help from it.

In contrast the Germans fought collectively, both on the tactical and the operational level. They consistently concentrated fire on the KV tanks, striving to strike their hatches, vision ports and rear, and ultimately achieved successes. In the course of the battle they threw everything available at the KV tanks, including 150mm howitzers. Even a *Nebelwerfer* battery was used against the tanks, though their fire had mostly a psychological effect. Shortly after mid-day, the command of the German XXXXI Motorized Corps sent the division a battery of 88mm Flak guns, which were capable of penetrating the KV's armour even from a distance. However, the Flak gunners quickly exhausted their small supply of armour-piercing shells, so on the night of 24/25 June more were delivered by aircraft to the Raseiniai airfield. The outcome of the battle was finally decided by pivoting the XXXXI Motorized Corps' 1st Panzer Division to the south on the day of 24 June. By evening it had emerged in the rear of the 2nd Tank Division and cut its supply lines. Ultimately the German 269th Infantry Division closed the ring of encirclement from the south.[12]

Having ended up in a trap, the commander of the 2nd Tank Division, General-Major E.N. Soliankin, on the evening of 24 June was forced to withdraw his remaining tanks to the eastern bank of the Dubysa River. Not many of them remained serviceable – only about 30 tanks, including 21 KV.[13] On the evening of that same day the commander of the 3rd Mechanized Corps, General-Major A.V. Kurkin, who was located in the area of operation of his sole division, futilely requested higher command to provide air cover for his forces against relentless bombing attacks.[14] It is interesting that the officers of the German 6th Panzer Division also complained about the absence of aerial support throughout the entire day of 24 June.[15] However, the Luftwaffe at the time was obviously striking not the battlefield but the rear columns of the 2nd Tank Division. As a result, its reserves of fuel and ammunition were dwindling with alarming rapidity. When the noose of encirclement tightened securely around the division's throat, on 25 June Kurkin openly transmitted over the radio a cry of despair: 'Help, I'm encircled.'[16]

It can't be said that the leadership of the Northwestern Front forgot about its division. Its chief of staff, General-Lieutenant P.S. Klenov, on the evening of 24 June assured the General Staff that 'measures are being taken to deliver fuel by aircraft' to the 2nd Tank Division.[17] However, in the conditions of Luftwaffe superiority in the air and the heavy losses of Soviet aircraft, these measures led to nothing. Then the commander of the Northwestern Front, General-Colonel F.I. Kuznetsov, on 26 June issued orders to the commander of the 8th Army and the commanders of its 3rd and 12th Mechanized Corps:

Prepare one strong tank battalion out of your divisions and together with it take fuel and ammunition; thoroughly prepare this battalion; with an attack towards Raseiniai into the enemy rear, to which you are to steal up suddenly, supply the division with fuel and help it break out of encirclement.

Kurkin after refuelling is to organize a breakout from the pocket in the direction of Shavli and make contact with Chernyakhovsky's division [the 28th Tank Division].

The battalion is to begin the operation on the morning of 27.6.41.[18]

This order can only be described as wishful thinking. From the outset there was no hope of carrying it out, because the 8th Army had no tank units in its possession other than the 3rd Mechanized Corps' 2nd Tank Division and the 12th Mechanized Corps. As we know, the 2nd Tank Division had fallen into encirclement, together with the headquarters of the 3rd Mechanized Corps. The situation of the 12th Mechanized Corps at that time was not much better: it was falling back with fighting, striving to avoid encirclement, and suffering heavy losses. On 27 June its headquarters were overrun, and its commander, General-Major N.M. Shestopalov, was badly wounded and captured; on 6 August he died from his wounds.[19] By the end of 1 July there were only 35 tanks remaining in the entire 12th Mechanized Corps.[20]

However, even if a miracle had happened and a tank battalion had somehow managed to break through to Raseiniai, there was nobody left to rescue. On the night of 25/26 June and all through the following morning, remnants of the 2nd Tank Division had vainly attempted to break out of the enemy ring to the north and east. However, all of their attacks were shattered by the German defences on the commanding heights, bolstered by 88mm Flak guns. The division commander, General-Major Soliankin, was killed in action or, according to some testimonies, shot himself dead.[21] The division lost practically all of its materiel, and the overwhelming majority of its men were killed or taken prisoner. Hence, by the evening of 25 June, on the fourth day of the war, out of the 57 Red Army soldiers and officers of the 5th Tank Company of the 2nd Tank Division's 3rd Tank Regiment, only three survived, and all of its heavy KV tanks had been lost irrecoverably.[22] By 11 July only around 400 men and one BT-7 tank had come out of encirclement.[23] Later, a few more lucky souls joined them. For example, the 3rd Mechanized Corps commander, Kurkin, together with a group of officers of his headquarters, managed to reach friendly lines two months later, on 28 August.[24]

Not all of the 2nd Tank Division's KV tanks perished at Raseiniai or when attempting to break out of the pocket. According to German records, in the course of 24 June the 6th Panzer Division destroyed only five KV tanks of the approximately 40–45 that participated in this battle.[25] However, all of the surviving tanks were sooner or later abandoned, immobilized with mechanical failures or because of the lack of fuel. At least a dozen KV tanks never in fact reached the Dubysa River as a result of breakdowns and mishaps in the course of the march. For example, one KV-2 was left behind by the others south of Kėdainiai. The tankers managed to get the tank running again and for some reason headed not to the west, towards Raseiniai, but to the north. Most likely, the crew simply became lost, because after all in the 2nd Tank Division not even the tank company commanders or battalion commanders had any topographical maps; certainly the ordinary tanks had none.[26] On the morning of 24 June, 6 kilometres west of Sheta village, the KV-2 ran into German panzers of the 8th Panzer Division and was totally immobilized in combat with them. The crew abandoned their tank only after it became hopelessly mired in a stream up to its turret, which by that time had been jammed by a shell (*see* Plate 22).[27]

All of the 2nd Tank Division's combat documents were destroyed along with the division, and today it is impossible to trace the fate of all its combat vehicles. However, one of the KV tanks of this division entered history for ever as an example of the courage and military skills of the tankers fighting in it. Moreover, their exploit became known not from Soviet propaganda, which conceived more than a few groundless legends, especially in the war's early days. Participants of the fighting on the German side talked about it, and they can never be accused of the desire to exaggerate the heroism of Soviet soldiers.

The German documents and the accounts of participants in those events describe one and the same thing, with only small discrepancies. Around noon on 24 June, a solitary KV tank had blocked the road from Raseiniai to Šiauliai not far from the village of Dainiai. One can only guess how and why it had wound up there. Probably the tankers had intended to come out of the fighting on the eastern outskirts of Raseiniai and return to the dispositions of their division for repair or refuelling, but had accidentally taken the wrong road. Instead of moving to the northeast, they had taken a northern road and had become immobilized on the way because of some mechanical failure or as a result of running out of fuel. However, the place where the Soviet tank stopped proved to be extremely inconvenient for the Germans: it was obstructing *Kampfgruppe* Raus's sole supply route, and had quickly destroyed 12 totally unsuspecting German lorries. It proved impossible to go around it, since it was swampy on one side of the road, while deep sand lay on the opposite side, which bogged down lorries and cars.

The situation of *Kampfgruppe* Raus became serious. It had not only lost its supply route for fuel, ammunition and food, but it now also had no possibility of evacuating the wounded. It is understandable why it was striving to destroy the uninvited guest, especially since it hadn't been committed to the fighting with the 2nd Tank Division's main forces. Raus didn't immediately assess his adversary properly. At first he sent two 50mm anti-tank guns against it, which from a range of 600 metres achieved eight direct hits, but not a single shell had penetrated the thick armour. Return fire from the tank destroyed both of them. Next a 150mm howitzer placed indirect fire on the KV, but was unable to hit it. Then the Germans decided to call upon their trump card and deployed an 88mm Flak gun against the KV tank, this time from the south, from the direction of Raseiniai. The gunners covertly set it up on the fringe of some woods, 800 metres from the tank, screened by the smoke of the burning lorries. However, the unexpected happened: the Soviet tankers spotted the lethal threat in good time, and coolly waited for the moment when the artillerymen would be preparing to fire, then quickly traversed the turret and with accurate shots knocked out the 88mm gun. There was no luck in calling upon the Luftwaffe, which was operating on more important sectors of the front. So late in the evening, a group of 12 volunteer combat engineers were assembled in order to destroy this terribly stubborn foe. Under the cover of darkness, they managed to steal up to the tank and attached one explosive charge to its track and another to the gun barrel. However, to the deep disappointment of the participants of this sortie, the explosive charges failed to inflict serious damage to the KV. Meanwhile local residents that same night managed to supply its crew with food.

By morning the patience of the Germans had begun to run out, and they took up the job seriously, not least because the crisis in the tank engagement at Raseiniai had passed by this time. After all of the previous attempts to destroy the ill-fated tank had failed, a combined operation was conducted. A group of light Pz.Kpfw.35(t) tanks attacked the KV from the north, from out of the bridgehead. Quickly manoeuvring among the trees in the sparse forest, they opened up a rapid fire and diverted the KV tank crew's attention to themselves. At the same time from the south, out of Raseiniai, another 88mm Flak gun was stealthily moved up, and successfully shot up the KV tank from the rear. It fell silent, although it didn't begin to burn. However, when the triumphant German soldiers climbed up on the KV, its turret suddenly came alive and began to traverse. Everyone scattered in every direction, but two combat engineers coolly pushed hand grenades through a shell hole in the lower part of the tank's turret. Here, the saga ended …

The Germans buried the six dead crew members with military honours. In 1965 their remains were reburied in a fraternal cemetery in Raseiniai. In the process, through personal items and remnants of documents found in the first gravesite, the names of two of the crewmen have been established: Pavel Egorovich Ershov and V.A. Smirnov. A third crew member's initials were preserved, having been scratched into an aluminium spoon: Sh.N.A. Nothing is known about the other three crewmen. However, even those names that have been saved from oblivion didn't allow the clarification of details of the heroes' biographies or the opportunity to locate their family members or kin. Unfortunately, the Red Army's personnel records system during the Great Patriotic War, especially in its initial period, was too far from perfection.

Up to the present day, the debate has continued: what type of tank was this, a KV-1 or a KV-2? Most likely it was the former; the details of its actions that have reached us convincingly show this. In particular, only the KV-1 had a sufficiently large ammunition load for a lengthy battle, and the speed of its turret's traverse, which was almost half as heavy as the KV-2 tank's, allowed it to shift fire quickly. But if it was a KV-1, where did the sixth man in the tank come from, as the KV-1 had only five crew members? There is no definitive answer, but most likely, in the course of the morning combat on 24 June the tank had picked up one of the tank commanders who had lost his own combat vehicle, and the KV-1 was surely roomy enough to accommodate him. The fact that two officers' belts were found among the personal effects of the fallen tankers in particular points to this explanation.[28]

The unknown tankers carried out their military oath to the end. They had an opportunity to run away, but preferred to remain and sell their lives as expensively as possible. At the same time they once again confirmed the wisdom of the old Russian saying: 'One on the field is not a warrior'. The solitary KV tank for almost 24 hours kept its capability to resist in large part thanks to the fact that the outcome of the tank clash at Raseiniai was decided to the south. There, hundreds of Soviet tanks, including dozens of heavy KV tanks, suffered a crushing defeat at the hands of an adversary who was formally inferior to them in combat strength, but who was far better organized, experienced and skilful. This example plainly demonstrates that, irrespective of its combat qualities, no tank, even the most superb design, can become a wonder weapon, capable of defeating any foe.

Chapter 12

The Results of the Initial Fighting

At the beginning of the Great Patriotic War, events which were to a greater or lesser degree similar to the ones described in the preceding chapter unfolded along the entire Soviet-German front. By this time the Wehrmacht had enough successful experience of combat with British and French tanks, protected by anti-projectile armour, so the Soviet tanks didn't become a large surprise for it also. Primarily it was the German anti-tank artillery that was responsible for countering the Red Army's tanks, although frequently it was necessary to bring up Flak guns and heavy artillery against the T-34 and KV tanks. The Luftwaffe made its own weighty contribution to this struggle. The infantry also didn't lag behind, even though its small-calibre anti-tank weapons were much less than effective against the thick armour of the T-34 and KV tanks. In order to offset this weakness, specially selected and trained teams of tank hunters, consisting of two to six men each, were formed in the Wehrmacht's infantry and combat engineer companies. A special badge was created to honour any soldier who knocked out a Soviet tank in close combat, but for knocking out a T-34 or KV tank they received correspondingly a leave for 8 or 14 days and a trip back to Germany.[1]

As a rule, the Germans used simple and available means against the enemy combat vehicles: hand grenades, mines (including anti-tank magnetic mines), demolition packs, bottles filled with a flammable liquid, and canisters filled with petrol. First of all they sought to immobilize the tank by firing at its running gear. After this was accomplished, they would steal up to the tank, taking advantage of its poor visibility, or by blinding the tankers with smoke grenades or smoke candles. Once they got to it, they would blow it up or set it ablaze, or sometimes they would simply work open the closed hatches with pry bars and sledgehammers, in order to kill or capture the crew. Here, the Germans were often undoubtedly helped by the Soviet tanks' lack of support from their own infantry and artillery in the early phase of the Great Patriotic War and their lack of practised cooperation, not to mention by the 'blindness' and 'deafness' of the tanks themselves.

Of all the Soviet tanks in the initial period of the war, the KV tank stood out as the best. It was these tanks that were most often mentioned by Wehrmacht personnel in their letters, diaries and memoirs. However, the reason for this was not simply the KV tank's superb armour protection. Prior to the war, only regular Red Army officers were appointed as commanders of the Red Army's heavy tanks, and such men fought as a rule much more effectively than the conscripted sergeants who commanded the medium and light tanks. Only in the autumn of 1941 did the T-34 tanks get the Germans' proper attention, once they began to be used more sensibly on the defensive, using the tactic of mobile ambushes, with frequent switching between previously prepared dominating positions and conducting accurate fire from the halt. The ambushes were skilfully combined with sudden, sharp counterattacks. Prior to this point, the main type of combat for the tanks of the RKKA had been offensive. But they attacked without appropriate preparation, reconnaissance, support, supply and cooperation, and moreover they attacked not only when on the offensive. No one bothered with digging in the tanks or setting up defensive positions for them, because after all, even in defence, the tanks were first of all supposed to counterattack.

During the attacks, in the majority of cases the Soviet tanks fired while on the move. However, for the tanks of that time, which were not equipped with effective gun stabilizers, the probability of hitting a target while moving decreased by 3 to 3.5 times. At the same time, the rate of fire fell by 1.5 to 2 times.[2] Thus the overall effectiveness of fire when moving thereby fell by 4.5 to 7 times. It is no coincidence that for the German tanks, the main type of gunnery was fire from a halt or after short stops.

Soviet tankers at the beginning of the war were substantially inferior to the German tankers in training, particularly tactical training. The Wehrmacht's tactics were described in Directive No. 0127 from the Commander of the Northwestern Front on 5 August 1941 entitled 'On the shortcomings in the employment and operations of tanks together with combined-arms formations and measures to eliminate them':

It has been noted that the enemy, prior to each of his attacks, as a rule, thoroughly organizes the coordination of all branches of forces.

A short, powerful artillery and mortar barrage on the positions of our forces precedes each offensive, reinforced by the supporting actions of aircraft.

Typically the enemy tanks before the start of the general attack are used to strengthen the fire barrage by means of fire from their guns from static dug-in positions. Under the cover of artillery and infantry fire, the tanks attack the defensive fortifications together with infantry usually only after the fire of our anti-tank artillery has been suppressed.

The advance of the combat formation is going methodically from objective to objective. Having reached a specified objective with the help of the tanks, the infantry quickly secure it.

Meanwhile, the tanks are dug in and with their fire cover the infantry's organization of the defence of the seized line. At the same time, artillery is brought up, primarily anti-tank guns and mortars. After this, the bounding advance to the next objective is organized.

Several cases have been observed that while the infantry is seizing the next objective, some of the tanks and supporting weapons are held back on the already achieved line, as if making up a second echelon. These means were used for holding the line, in the event of a lack of success by the first echelon, and for launching outflanking manoeuvres from behind the combat formation of the troops operating out in front.

On the defensive, and even when preparing for an offensive, the tanks are dug into the ground.[3]

The inadequacies of the use of Soviet tanks, which are criticized in the aforementioned NKO Order No. 325 from 16 October 1942, 'On the combat use of tank and mechanized units and formations', look particularly sad against this backdrop:

The practical experience of the war against the German fascists has shown that in the matter of using tank units we have, up to now, great shortcomings. The main shortcomings can be summarized as follows:

1. During an attack on the enemy defence our tanks become separated from the infantry and relinquish their coordination with it. The infantry, being cut off from the tanks by enemy fire, does not support our tanks with its artillery fire. The tanks, after separating from the infantry, find themselves alone in battle against enemy artillery, tanks and infantry, and suffer heavy losses.

2. Tanks are thrown against an enemy defence without the necessary artillery support. Before the commencement of the tank attack the artillery has not suppressed the anti-tank weapons on the forward edge of the enemy defence, and tank support guns are not always used. With the approach to the enemy's forward edge, tanks encounter enemy anti-tank artillery fire and suffer heavy losses.

    Tank and artillery commanders do not coordinate their actions on the terrain with respect to local objects and lines, and do not establish signals for calling up and ceasing artillery fire.

    Artillery commanders supporting the tank attack control artillery fire from distant observation posts and do not use radio-equipped tanks as mobile forward artillery observation posts.

3. Tanks are pressed into battle hastily, without reconnoitring the terrain adjacent to the forward edge of the enemy defence, without studying the terrain in the depth of the enemy deployment, and without the tankers' carefully studying the enemy's system of fire.

    Tank commanders, not having the time to organize the tank attack, do not deliver the mission to the tank crews; as a result of not knowing the enemy and the terrain, the tanks attack slowly and without confidence. Firing from the march is not conducted, and tanks fire from the halt only, and only with cannons.

    As a rule, tanks do not manoeuvre on the battlefield, do not use the terrain for a covert approach and surprise strike on the flank and in the rear, and most often attack head-on.

    Combined-arms commanders do not allot the time necessary for the technical preparation of tanks for battle, and do not prepare the terrain in an engineer respect on the direction of tank action. Mine fields are poorly reconnoitred and are not cleared. Passages are not made in anti-tank obstacles and the assistance necessary to overcome terrain sectors which are difficult to negotiate is not rendered. Sappers are not always designated to accompany tanks.

This leads to tanks being blown up on mines, getting stuck in bogs and on anti-tank obstacles, and not participating in the battle.

4. Tanks do not carry out their primary mission of destroying enemy infantry and are diverted to fighting against enemy tanks and artillery. The established practice of using our tanks to counter enemy tank attacks and engaging them in tank battles is incorrect and harmful.

5. Tank combat actions are not provided with sufficient aviation cover, aerial reconnaissance, or air guidance. As a rule, aviation does not accompany tank formations in the depth of the enemy defence, and aviation combat actions are not coordinated with tank attacks.

6. Control of tanks on the battlefield is poorly organized. Radio is insufficiently used as a control means. Commanders of tank units and formations located at command posts become separated from the battle formations, do not observe tank actions in battle, and do not influence the course of the tank battle.

Commanders of companies and battalions moving in front of the battle formations are not able to monitor tanks or control the battle of their subunits, and turn into ordinary tank commanders, while the units, not having control, lose their orientation and roam around the battlefield, suffering pointless losses.[4]

It is even more frustrating that such mistakes continued to occur even after the accumulation of a year's experience of intensive combat operations, acquired at the cost of the heaviest losses. After all, many of these failings had been mentioned as early as 21 August 1941 in his order to the troops of the Reserve Front No. 005 'On the shortcomings of using tanks and measures to eliminate them' from its commander, General of the Army G.K. Zhukov:

On the basis of the experience of the fighting in the Yelnya area, I've established the unacceptable ignorance of using tanks and tank units in combat, which as a result of their incorrect employment suffered heavy losses in personnel and materiel.

The formation commanders didn't allow enough time for conducting tank reconnaissance and for the organization of the coordination between the tanks, infantry, artillery and aircraft.

Coordination was being organized not on the terrain, but distant from the battlefield, on maps.

Tanks were thrown into the attack without having any information about the dispositions of the enemy's system of fire and the nature of the terrain.

Commanders of the units and combined-arms formations gave unclear and dubious tasks to the tanks, and failed to arrange air, infantry and artillery support for the tanks. Mutual recognition, calling for fire and target indication, was not being organized. There were cases of shooting up our own tanks by friendly artillery because of the lack of coordination of artillery fire.

With the forward advance of the tanks, the infantry as a rule didn't follow the tanks and didn't secure objectives seized by the tanks. The tanks, operating alone, suffered needless losses and returned back to the jump–off position.

The tank commanders didn't show the necessary firmness in front of the combined-arms commanders regarding the proper use of tanks; casually released from their grasp the command of the tank groups assigned for infantry support; didn't organize the evacuation of disabled and bogged down tanks from the battlefield; have not been taking steps for the immediate dispatch of the tanks to the collection points for broken down vehicles for their repair and rapid return to service.[5]

These, and many other documents similar to them, more than eloquently disclose the real reasons for the superiority of the German panzer forces over the Soviet armoured forces in the initial period of the war. It is particularly indicative that no sort of technical superiorities or shortcomings of the tanks themselves are even mentioned in them. This is in fact natural, because the tanks themselves weren't a big part of the problems. The tanks of one generation, which were developed in various countries but designated for resolving similar tasks, are as a rule similar to each other according to an array of performance indicators. In some respect or another, some of them were somewhat superior to the others, but in other respects were inferior to them. Actually, each country developed and produced tanks that to the greatest extent corresponded to the capabilities of its industry and the requirements of its army. Thus the best tanks for the Soviet Union were combat vehicles of Soviet production, for Germany of German production, for the USA of American production, and so forth. Therefore, endless debates on the subject of which was the 'best' tank of the Second World War make no practical sense. In fact, no tank was head and shoulders above all the others – their peers in the same weight class – in terms of performance qualities, which enabled them beforehand to determine the outcome of a battle with their participation.

The human factor has an incomparably greater influence on the results of battles. Even the best tank can't compensate for the poor training of the crew and ignorant use of it by the command staff. It isn't the tanks themselves that are fighting, but the tankers, and those who emerge victorious are the ones who are able to better use both the advantages of their own tank and the shortcomings of the enemy's tank. To no less degree, the success of employing tank elements, units and formations depends on their strategy, tactics, training, organization, command and control, combat and rear support, cooperation with other troop branches, and so on. Finally, of course, the military leadership is obliged to strive to plan the combat operations in such a manner as to make the best possible conditions for their own forces and the worst possible conditions for the enemy. However, this is a subject for a different work.

The German General F. von Mellenthin made the following comment about the Red Army's unsuccessful experience with forming up and using their first tank armies in 1942: 'We thought the Russians had created a tool which they would never be able to handle expertly.'[6] However, by the end of the following year, he – together with the entire Wehrmacht – would be convinced that this opinion no longer applied. The Soviet tank armies, together with the tank and mechanized corps of the new organization, became a powerful tool, under the attacks of which the Wehrmacht's defences collapsed. Indeed, not even the latest Tigers, Panthers and Elefants were able to prevent this, despite all their menacing power and wild animal names. Wars are won and lost not by tanks, but by people.

Report on Long-Range Test March of Three T-34 Tanks

24 December 1940

According to the Directive of the Deputy People's Commissar of Defence No. 76791 from 25.10.1940, testing of T-34 tanks was conducted using long-range march off-base combined with gunnery missions.

Due to the lack of the approved tactical and technical requirements for the T-34 tank, the conclusions and assessments were made based on the actual performance characteristics. ...

Test objectives:

1. To determine the tactical and technical characteristics of the tank as a whole and establish its compliance with the tactical and technical requirements set by the General Staff.
2. To determine the reliability and dependability of the tank components during a long-range march.
3. To determine compliance of armament, ammunition load, observation and communication equipment with the tactical tasks facing tanks of this class.
4. To determine if the tank is fully provided with on-board spare parts and tools, and finalize the set. To determine the scope and frequency of maintenance of the tank in the field. To determine the repair capabilities of the tank in the field. ...

The whole route took 14 running days. Technical inspections and repairs during the march took 11 days, while 8 days were spent on special tests. Preparation and turnover of the vehicles took 2 more days. In total: 38 days [the remaining days were holidays].

The results of firing for accuracy, obtained after all the gunnery exercises and expressed via mean deviations in width and height, are greater than the tabular data for the 76 mm gun M1927.

The results of firing accuracy from the march should be considered low due to the hindrance of the aiming with significant backlashes in the traversing and lifting mechanisms.

The results of firing from machine guns show that the bullet spread for the machine gun coaxial with the main gun do not exceed the normal data for a DT machine gun.

When firing the radio-operator's machine gun, the amount of bullet spread increases significantly and exceeds normal data, and the number of bullet-holes [on target] is reduced.

As a result of the combat gunnery that included execution of fire missions, shortcomings were revealed:

1) The lack of space for the crew in the fighting compartment caused by the small size of the turret based on the turret ring.
2) The inconvenience of using the ammunition load, which is stowed on the floor of the fighting compartment.
3) Delay in shifting fire as a result of the inconvenient position of the turret's traversing mechanism (both manual and electric drive).
4) The absence of visual contact between the tanks while executing a fire mission because the sole device that permits all-round vision – the PT-6 sight – is used only for aiming.
5) The impossibility of using the TOD-6 sight as a result of the obstruction of its angles of sight's scale with the PT-6 sight.
6) The significant and slowly subsiding rocking of the tank when moving negatively affects the accuracy of fire from the cannon and machine guns.

The noted shortcomings lower the rate of fire and cause a large waste of time when executing a fire mission.

Determination of the 76mm cannon's rapidity of fire ...

The maximum rate of fire – 5–6 rounds a minute. Fire from the halt. The shells were stored in the most conveniently located cases. The rubber mat and lid of the cases had been removed.

The obtained average practical rate of fire – two rounds a minute. The rapidity of fire is insufficient. ...

THE FIRE DIRECTION FROM THE TANK AND THE CONVENIENCE OF USING SIGHTS, OBSERVATION DEVICES AND THE AMMUNITION LOAD

Traversing mechanism of the turret (manual)

The traversing of the turret is done with the right hand. The position of the handwheel and handle of the traversing mechanism doesn't allow for a rapid turret rotation and causes heavy arm fatigue.

When simultaneously working the traversing mechanism and observing through the PT-6 device, the handwheel and the control handle butts up against the chest, hindering rapid turret rotation. The force required to turn the handwheel of the traversing mechanism increases rapidly with increasing of the angle of the turret's tilting and makes traversing significantly harder. ...

The turret's electrical traversing mechanism

Access to the starting handwheel is obstructed from below by the electrical motor's body, from the left by the vision device and turret wall, and from the right by the forehead rest of the PT-6 sight. The traversing of the turret any direction is possible only after moving the head away from the forehead rest of the PT-6 sight, which means the traversing of the turret is essentially done blindly. ...

The TOD-6 telescopic sight

The lever of the PT-6 sight's angles of sight obstructs view of the telescopic sight's window of the angles of sight's scale. ... The setting of the aiming data is possible only at angles of elevation of 4.5–5 degrees and 9–12 degrees, which essentially eliminates the possibility of conducting fire using the TOD-6 telescopic sight. The knob of the angles of sight's scale is positioned in the middle of the sight and is extremely difficult to access.

The PT-6 periscopic sight

At an angle of elevation of 7° and lower, down to the maximum angle of depression, access to the handle of the panoramic view mechanism is possible only with three fingers because the sector gear of the main gun's elevation mechanism doesn't permit the grasping of the handle with the entire hand. In such condition a rapid scanning of the terrain is impossible.

All-round observation device

Access to the device is extremely difficult and observation is possible only in a restricted sector of up to 120° to the right. … The limited sector of view, the complete impossibility of viewing the rest of the perimeter and … the awkward position of the head when observing makes the observation device unsuitable in practice.

Turret vision devices (side)

The position of the vision devices relative to the viewer is inconvenient. The significant dead space (15.5 metres), the small angle of vision, the impossibility of cleaning the protecting glass without getting out of the tank and their low position relative to the seats are their shortcomings.

Driver's vision devices …

In practical work, driving the tank with the hatch closed revealed substantial shortcomings with the driver's vision devices. When moving along a muddy dirt road or fallow fields, after 5–10 minutes the vision devices became obstructed with mud to the point of complete loss of vision. The wiper of the central port doesn't clear the protective glass of mud. Driving the tank with the hatch closed is extremely difficult. During gunnery, the protective glass of the vision devices shatters. …

The vision devices for the driver on the whole are unfit.

All of the sights equipping the tank, the PT-6 and TOD-6, as well as the vision devices in the fighting compartment and driver's compartment, have no protection from atmospheric precipitate, road dust and mud. In each individual case of loss of vision, the devices can only be cleaned from outside the tank. In conditions of reduced visibility (fog), the PT-6's sight head fogs up within 3–5 minutes up to the complete loss of vision.

CONVENIENCE OF USING ON-BOARD AMMUNITION

The ammunition load of the 76mm cannon

The stowage of the shells in cases doesn't allow a sufficient rate of fire for the following reasons:

1) The inconvenience of fetching the shells out of their cases.
2) The extremely difficult access to the cases, which are positioned on the left side of the tank.
3) The stowage of the shells in the cases is made harder by the large number of covers (24) and rubber mats between the shells. The time required to pack a full ammunition load is determined to be 2 to 2.5 hours.
4) The shells in the cases are not packed tightly enough, which leads to loosening of the time fuses and primers.
5) The sharp edges of the cases resulted in wounds to the loaders' arms.
6) After a run of 200–300 kilometres in the autumn time, the ammunition load becomes quite dirty. The full ammunition load can be used only after first being cleaned.

Ammunition load for the DT machine guns

Firing from the machine guns revealed the following shortcomings:

1) The severe filthiness of the magazines in the driver's compartment.
2) The dustiness of the protruding parts of the magazines, which are stowed in the turret bustle.
3) The impossibility of using the ammunition without first cleaning the dirt from it.

4) Extraction of an individual magazine from the turret bustle is difficult because of the jamming of them in the stowage.

Comfort of the working places and illumination of the fighting compartment

1) The seats of the commander and loader in the turret are of large size. The backrests of the seats don't ensure a comfortable position for the body, take up too much space, and don't guard against the catching of articles of uniform clothing on the turret race (loader's seat). When conducting combat fire, the loader's position makes it hard to extract shells, constrains movement and interferes with the side ammunition stowage. This situation is made worse by the significant overcrowding of the crew in the driver's compartment. ...

The general shortcomings of the L-11 artillery system, installed in the tanks, are:

1) Failure of the trigger mechanism. ...
2) The loader's lack of protection from being struck by the breech–opening lever during semi–automatic operation.
3) The unreliability of the foot pedal's action, which allows the jamming of the trigger mechanism's slide and failure to return to battery if the foot isn't completely removed from the pedal in time. ...

Conclusion

The mounting of the gun, optics and ammunition stowage in the T–34 tank do not satisfy the requirements for contemporary combat vehicles.

The main shortcomings are:

a) The cramped fighting compartment.
b) The tank's blindness.
c) The unsuccessfully resolved stowage of on–board ammunition.

In order to provide a normal positioning of the armament, fire control and observation devices, and the crew, the following is necessary:

Expand the overall dimensions of the turret.

Regarding the 76mm gun:

Replace the shield of the triggering mechanism with a better design, which ensures dependability in operation.

Enclose the handle of the breechblock with a shield or make it collapsible.

Remove the foot-actuated trigger, replacing it with triggers on the handles of the aiming mechanisms.

Regarding the DT machine gun:

Provide the co-axial machine gun with the possibility of separate firing.

Equip the radio operator's machine gun with an optical sight in order to increase its field of vision and firing accuracy. ...

Regarding the aiming mechanisms and sights

The traversing mechanism (manual) is unsuitable. Replace it with a new design that requires less effort and greater ease of operation. ...

Position the control knob for the electrical traversing mechanism of the turret so that it allows the turret to be turned while maintaining simultaneous observation of the terrain.

Replace the TOD-6 telescopic sight with a sight of the TMF type with a scale of sighting angles in the sight's field of vision.

Regarding the vision devices

Replace the driver's vision device, which is plainly unsuitable, with a more advanced design.

Mount a device on the roof of the turret which provides all-round field of vision.

Regarding on-board ammunition stowage

Stowing the 76mm gun's ammunition in cases is unsuitable. The stowage of the shells should be such that an entire row of shells is simultaneously accessible. ...

THE ARMOURED HULL

Conclusions

The tank's hull and turret in the given version are unsatisfactory. It is necessary to increase the size of the turret by increasing the turret ring and changing the angle of slope of the armoured plates.

The hull's usable space can be increased by changing the suspension system and by the abandonment of the on-board columns [for suspension springs].

MEANS OF COMMUNICATION

Conclusions

The mounting of the radio has been done unsatisfactorily for the following reasons:

The antenna when it is lowered has no protection against damage. ... The design and location of the handle of the mechanism to raise the antenna do not provide reliable action. The receiver's rotary converter is mounted under the radio operator's feet, so the wire terminal gets damaged and the rotary converter becomes dirty.

The receiver is mounted too low and too far from the radio operator, making tuning difficult.

The radio's battery terminals (of the new type) are unsuitable in use – they have many projections that catch clothing and cut hands. ...

The mounting of the radio on the whole doesn't ensure stable operation of the radio at maximum range.

PERFORMANCE INDICATORS AND RELIABILITY OF THE TANK'S COMPONENTS

Tank dynamics

In difficult road conditions, when shifting the drive from 2nd gear to 3rd gear, during the shifting the tank loses so much momentum that it results in a stop or extended slippage of the engine clutch. This fact makes the use of 3rd gear difficult in road conditions that should fully allow for its use.

In the conditions of a rainy autumn or spring and a snowy winter, this shortcoming of the tank leads to a sharp decrease in its speed along country roads and cross-country. ...

The sharp difference between cruising speed and average marching speed is a result of frequent breakdowns of the engine clutch and tracks (track links' breakages, connecting pins' disengagement, etc.)

Conclusions

In view of the fact that the 3rd gear, which is needed the most in field use, cannot be fully used – the tank's performance on the whole must be considered unsatisfactory.

Operational speeds are low, which is caused by the unreliability of the engine clutch and running gear.

Off-road performance

The T-34's off-road performance in autumnal conditions is unsatisfactory for the following reasons:

The track surface in contact with the ground is too smooth, as a result of which the tracks slip when climbing slopes even given slightly damp ground. The effectiveness of the add-on side grousers which are included with tracks is low.

The guiding of the track by the road wheels is unreliable. ...

The small number of road wheels negatively affects the off-road performance across boggy areas, despite the overall low ground pressure.

The fording of water obstacles by the T-34 tank should be considered fully satisfactory.

The maximum day's march along a main road, achieved in the run, was 255 kilometres; along dirt roads 225 kilometres.

These distances are the utmost achievable, since in the majority of cases the failure of components significantly shortened the daily marches.

Conclusion

The length of a day's march is limited by failure in the work of components, mainly the tracks and engine clutch.

Aforementioned lengths of a day's march are fully provided by tank's fuel and engine oil capacity.

RELIABILITY OF THE TANK'S COMPONENTS

Engine, fuel, oil and cooling systems and control instruments

Conclusions

The reliability of the engine within its warranty period (100 hours) is satisfactory. The guaranteed operating time of the engine, especially for this heavily armoured vehicle, is low. It is necessary to bring it up to not less than 250 hours.

The continuous leakage of oil and the breakdown of control instruments characterize the work of the oil system and the connections of the control instruments as unsatisfactory.

Engine clutch

The work of the engine clutch and the fan on the whole is unsatisfactory.

Note: The unreliability of the engine clutch and the fan was also noted in the conclusions of the army commission.

Gearbox

During the test run, the 'loss of neutral gear' (the gear lever was in the neutral position, but the engine was still in gear) and the difficulty in shifting gears were repeatedly noted in all the vehicles. ...

The incorrect choice of gear ratios in the gearbox is the reason for the tank's unsatisfactory performance and reduces its tactical value.

The taxing gear shifting and the 'loss of neutral gear' makes handling the tank difficult and leads to compulsory stops.

The gearbox and its selector mechanism require fundamental changes.

Steering clutches

During the test run, the steering clutches, the brake bands with Ferodo linings and the cast-iron brake pads worked satisfactorily.

Note: the operation of the gearbox, steering clutches and final drives couldn't be fully checked from the point of view of their reliability because of the fact that the engine clutch would break down first, serving like a quasi-safety device for the tank's entire transmission system.

Running gear

The limited service time and the poor traction performance of the track links, the impediment of the tank components' arrangement due to the columns for suspension springs, the large consumption of rubber for the road wheels' rims and the [outdated] type of engagement between tracks and drive wheels with horned links and rollers characterize the design and durability of the running gear as unsatisfactory.

Electrical equipment

The ST-200 starter and the RS-371 relay switch, given the existing assembly and production defects, are unsuitable for installation in the T-34 tanks.

Stowage of spare parts, tools, personal gear, food supply and special equipment

The stowage of spare parts, tools, personal gear, food supply, engineer and chemical equipment in the T-34 hasn't been worked out.

Repair

The correlation between the net movement time, repair time, and stops due to mechanical breakdowns is shown in the table below:

Type of Activity	Time		Notes
	Hours	%	
Total time	922 hours, 56 minutes	100	
Net movement time	350 hours, 47 minutes	38	
Time spent on repair	414 hours	45	Done by a two-man repair team
Minor fixes en route	158 hours, 9 minutes	17	Done by crews

Conclusion

The correlation between the net movement time and the time spent doing repair work (38 per cent and 62 per cent) testifies to the low quality of the tank's production.

The volume and complexity of basic repair jobs exclude the possibility that the tank can be made operational again through the crew's efforts, and requires the means of a Repair & Maintenance Battalion.

The fact that so many repairs were required within the warranty period indicated that the tanks cannot be used independently of repair means, which in the conditions of field use is unacceptable.

Service

The large volume and time spent servicing the tanks, caused by the unreliable performance of some components, are unacceptable for field use.

In the form presented for testing, the T-34 tank doesn't satisfy the contemporary requirements for the given class of tanks for the following reasons:

a) The tank's firepower cannot be fully used as a consequence of the unsuitability of the observation devices, defects in the mounting of the gun and optics, the cramped conditions of the fighting compartment, and the awkward use of the stowed ammunition.

b) Given the engine's sufficient reserve of power and maximum speed, the dynamic characteristics of the tank have been selected unsuccessfully, and reduce the tank's speed and off-road performance.

c) The tactical use of the tank separate from the repair bases is impossible because of the unreliability of the main components – the engine clutch and running gear.

d) The range and reliability of the communication means, obtained in the trials, is insufficient for a tank of the given class, which results from both the performance of the 71 TK-3 radio, and the poor quality of its mounting in the T-34 tank.[1]

Appendix II

Tactical and Technical Specifications of Soviet and German Tanks in the Initial Period of the Great Patriotic War

Model	Combat weight (kg)	Crew (men)	Armour thickness (mm) / slope of armour (degrees)				Maximum engine power (hp)	Maximum speed (km/h)r	Range	
			Turret		Hull				On road	Cross country
			Front	Side	Front	Side			(km)	
Soviet Tanks										
T-27	2,700	2	None	None	10	10	40	42	110	60
T-37A	3,200	2	9/0	9/0	9/20	9/0	40	40	230	120
T-38	3,300	2	9/0	9/0	9/20	9/0	40	40	250	120
T-40	5,500	2	10/25	10/25	9/30 9/10	9/25 9/0	85	45	300	220
T-26 M1932	8,200	3	15/0	15/0	15/18 15/10	15/0 15/23	90	31	140	80
T-26 M1939	10,250	3	15/18	15/18	15/18 15/10	15/0 15/23	95	30	225	170
BT-2 M1932	11,000	3	13/0	13/0	13/61 20/18	13/0	400	52/72	160/200*	160
BT-5 M1935	11,500	3	15/0	15/0	13/61 20/18	13/0	400	52/72*	150/200*	160
BT-7 M1937	13,800	3	15/15	15/15	15/60 22/18	13/0	500	52/72*	375/500*	360
BT-7M	14,650	3	15/15	15/15	15/60 22/18	13/0	500	62/86*	630/1250*	520
T-28 M1936	25,400	6	20/0	20/0	30/22 15/65	20/0	500	42	190	140
T-34 M1941	28,120	4	45** 52***	45/30** 52/30***	45/60 45/53	40/40 45/0	500	55	300	250
KV-1 M1941	47,000	5	75/20	75/15	75/30 40/65	75/0	600	34	225	180
KV-2 M1941	52,000	6	75/0	75/0	75/30 40/65	75/0	600	34	225	180

Model	Combat weight (kg)	Crew (men)	Armour thickness (mm)/slope of armour (degrees)				Maximum engine power (hp)	Maximum speed (km/h)r	Range On road (km)	Range Cross country (km)
			Turret Front	Turret Side	Hull Front	Hull Side				
German Tanks										
Pz.Kpfw.I Ausf. A	5,400	2	14/8	13/21	13/25 13/21	13/21 13/0	60	37	140	93
Pz.Kpfw.I Ausf. B	5,800	2	14/8	13/21	13/25 13/21	13/21 13/0	100	40	170	115
Pz.Kpfw.II Ausf. c; A, B, C	8,900	3	14.5/0-16	14.5/0-22	14.5/0-73	14.5/0	140	40	190	126
Pz.Kpfw.II Ausf. F	9.500	3	30/0-16	14.5/22	35/13 30/9	14.5/0	140	40	190	125
Pz.Kpfw.35(t)	10,500	4	25/10	16/14	25/30 25/17	16/0	120	34	190	115
Pz.Kpfw.38(t) Ausf. A, B, C, D	9,725	4	25/10	15/9	25/19 25/14	15/0	125	42	265	165
Pz.Kpfw.38(t) Ausf. E, F	9,850	4	25+25/10	30/9	25+25/19 25+25/14	30/0 15/0	125	42	250	160
Pz.Kpfw.III Ausf. E, F, G	19,500	5	30/15	30/25	30/21 30/9	30/0	300	67	165	95
Pz.Kpfw.III Ausf. H	21,500	5	30/15	30/25	30+30/21 30+30/9	30/0	300	40	165	95
Pz.Kpfw.III Ausf. J	21,600	5	50/15	30/25	50/21 50/9	30/0	300	40	155	95

Pz.Kpfw.IV Ausf. D	20,000	5	30/10	20/25	30/14 30/9	20/0	300	42	210	130
Pz.Kpfw.IV Ausf. E	22,000	5	30/10	20/25	50/14 30+30/9	20+20/0	300	42	210	130
Pz.Kpfw.IV Ausf. F	22,300	5	50/10	30/25	50/14 50/9	30/0	300	42	210	130

Notes:
* on tracks/on wheels
** welded turret
*** cast turret

Appendix III

Dimensions and Cross-country Performance Specifications of Soviet and German Tanks in the Initial Period of the Great Patriotic War

Model	Dimensions (mm)				Track width	Ground Pressure (g/cm2)	Grade (degrees)	Negotiated obstacles (mm)		
	Length	Width	Height	Ground clearance				Trench crossing	Vertical step	Fording depth
Soviet Tanks										
T-27	2,600	1,825	1,443	240	150	0.75	30	1,200	500	500
T-37A	3,730	1,940	1,840	285	200	0.45	35	1,400	500	amphibious
T-38	3,780	2,334	1,630	300	200	0.44	33	1,600	500	amphibious
T-40	4,110	2,230	1,905	300	260	0.46	34	1,700	600	amphibious
T-26 M1932	4,620	2,440	2,190	380	260	0.57	32	2,000	750	800
T-26 M1939	4,620	2,445	2,330	380	260	0.71	40	2,650	750	800
BT-2 M1932	5,500	2,230	2,174	350	263	0.59	32/15*	2,250	850	850
BT-5 M1935	5,580	2,230	2,250	350	260	0.65	37/20*	2,000	800	900
BT-7 M1937	5,660	2,230	2,417	390	260	0.85	37/15*	2,400	800	1,200
BT-7M	5,660	2,290	2,447	390	260	0.90	36/15*	2,500	750	1,200
T-28 M1936	7,370	2,870	2,625	500	380	0.62	45	3,500	1,000	1,000
T-34 M1941	5,920	3,000	2,400	400	550	0.69	30	2,500	730	1,300
KV-1 M1941	6,675	3,320	2,710	450	700	0.77	36	2,700	1,200	1,600
KV-2 M1941	6,675	3,320	3,240	430	700	0.85	36	2,700	1,200	1,600

Model	Dimensions (mm)					Ground Pressure (kg/cm2)	Grade (degrees)	Negotiated obstacles (mm)		
	Length	Width	Height	Ground clearance	Track width			Trench crossing	Vertical step	Fording depth
German Tanks										
Pz.Kpfw.I Ausf.A	4,020	2,060	1,720	295	280	0.39	30	1,400	370	600
Pz.Kpfw.I Ausf.B	4,420	2,060	1,720	295	280	0.52	30	1,400	370	600
Pz.Kpfw.II Ausf.c, A, B, C	4,810	2,223	1,990	345	300	0.62	30	1,700	420	925
Pz.Kpfw.II Ausf.F	4,810	2,280	2,150	345	300	0.66	30	1,700	420	925
Pz.Kpfw.35(t)	4,900	2,055	2,370	350	320	0.51	41	2,000	800	800
Pz.Kpfw.38(t) Ausf.A,B,C, D	4,610	2,135	2,252	400	293	0.57	35	1,900	850	900
Pz.Kpfw.38(t) Ausf.E,F	4,610	2,135	2,252	400	293	0.58	35	1,900	850	900
Pz.Kpfw.III Ausf.E, F, G	5,380	2,910	2,500	385	380	0.90	30	2,300	600	800
Pz.Kpfw.III Ausf.H	5,380	2,950	2,500	385	400	0.94	30	2,300	600	800
Pz.Kpfw.III Ausf.J	5,495	2,950	2,500	385	400	0.94	30	2,300	600	800
Pz.Kpfw.IV Ausf.C	5,920	2,830	2,680	400	380	0.77	30	2,300	600	800
Pz.Kpfw.IV Ausf.D	5,920	2,840	2,680	400	380	0.83	30	2,300	600	800
Pz.Kpfw.IV Ausf.E	5,920	2,840	2,680	400	380	0.91	30	2,300	600	800
Pz.Kpfw.IV Ausf.F	5,920	2,880	2,680	400	400	0.88	30	2,300	600	800

Notes:
* on tracks/on wheels

Appendix IV

Armaments of Soviet and German Tanks in the Initial Period of the Great Patriotic War

	Cannon								Machine guns		
	Calibre (mm) and barrel length (calibres)	Ammunition load (shells)	Armour-piercing shell		Armour penetration (mm) at an angle of 30° to normal Range (m)				Calibre (mm)	Number	Ammunition load (rounds)
Model			Weight (kg)	Muzzle velocity (m/s)	100	500	1,000	1,500			
Soviet Tanks											
T-27	None	—	—	—	—	—	—	—	7.62	1	2,520
T-37A									7.62	1	2,142
T-38										1	1,512
T-40									12.7	1	500
									7.62	1	2,016
T-26 M1932										2	6,615
T-26 M1939	45 L/46	165/186*	1.425	757	43	31	28	**		3	3,087/3,528*
BT-2 M1932	37 L/45	92	0.660	820	34	28	23	**		1	2,709
BT-5 M1935	45 L/46	72/115*							7.62	1	2,709
BT-7 M1937		146/188*	1.425	757	43	31	28	**		2	2,394
BT-7M		146/188*								2	1,827/2,331*
T-28 M1936	76.2 L/16.5	69	6.300	370	28	25	23	21		4	7,938
T-34 M1941	76.2 L/41.6	77		662	69	59	50	43		2	2,394/2,646*
KV-1 M1941	76.2 L/30.5	111		612	55	49	43	38		3	3,024
KV-2 M1941	152.4 L/23.1	36	51.000	436	***	***	85	***		3	3,087

Model	Cannon Calibre (mm) and barrel length (calibres)	Ammunition load (shells)	Armour-piercing shell Weight (kg)	Muzzle velocity (m/s)	Armour penetration (mm) at an angle of 30° to normal, Range (m) 100	500	1,000	1,500	Machine guns Calibre (mm)	Number	Ammunition load (rounds)
German Tanks											
Pz.Kpfw.I Ausf.A	None	–	–	–	–	–	–	–	7.92	2	2,250
Pz.Kpfw.I Ausf.B										2	2,250
Pz.Kpfw.II Ausf.c A, B, C	20 L/55	180	0.148	780	20	14	9	**		1	1,425
Pz.Kpfw.II Ausf.F			0.100	1,050	40	20	**	**		1	2,100
Pz.Kpfw.35(t)	37 L/39.4	78	0.815	690	37	31	26	22		2	2,700
Pz.Kpfw.38(t) Ausf.A, B, C, D	37 L/47.8	90	0.815	750	41	35	29	24		2	2,700
Pz.Kpfw.38(t) Ausf.E, F			0.368	1,040	64	34	**	**		2	2,700
Pz.Kpfw.III Ausf. E. F, G	37 L/45	125	0.685	745	35	29	22	20		3	4,500
			0.368	1,020	64	31	**	**			
Pz.Kpfw.III Ausf.H	50 L/42	99	2.060	685	53	43	32	24		2	3,750
Pz.Kpfw.III Ausf.J			0.925	1,050	94	55	21	**		2	3,750
Pz.Kpfw.IV Ausf.C	75 L/24	80	6.800	385	41	38	35	32		1	2,400
Pz.Kpfw.IV Ausf.D										2	2,700
Pz.Kpfw.IV Ausf.E										2	3,150
Pz.Kpfw.IV Ausf.F										2	3,150

Notes:
* with radio/without radio
** beyond the range of effective fire
*** no data available

Notes

Introduction

1. I. Stalin, *O Velikoi Otechestvennoi voine Sovetskogo Soiuza* [*On the Great Patriotic War of the Soviet Union*] (Moscow: Gosudarstvennoe izdatel'stvo politicheskoi literatury, 1947), pp. 25–6.

Chapter 2

1. Khlystov, F.L., *Tanki i mekhanicheskaia tiaga v artillerii* [*Tanks and mechanical traction in the artillery*] (Leningrad: Voenno-Tekhnicheskaia Akademiia RKKA im. Dzerzhinskogo, 1929), p. 27.
2. Kuznetsov, T.P., *Taktika tankovykh voisk* [*Tactics of armoured forces*, hereafter cited as Kuznetsov, *Tactics of Armoured Forces*] (Moscow: Voenizdat NKO SSSR, 1940), p. 14.
3. Svirin, M., Legky tank T-26. Chast' 1 [Light tank T-26. Part I]. *Armada*, No. 20 (2000), p. 7.
4. Kuznetsov, *Tactics of Armoured Forces*, p. 77.
5. TsAMO, F. 221, op. 10633ss, d. 6, ll. 55–8; as cited by *Sbornik boevykh dokumentov Velikoi Otechestvennoi voiny* [*Collection of combat documents of the Great Patriotic War* – hereafter cited as SBD] Issue 21 (Moscow: Voenizdat, 1954), p. 7.
6. TsAMO, F. 208, op. 33783ss, d. 1, ll. 51–60; as cited by SBD, Issue 21, p. 13.
7. Biryukov, N.I., *Tanki – frontu! Zapiski sovetskogo generala* [*Tanks – to the front! Notes of a Soviet general*, hereafter cited as Biryukov, *Tanks – to the front!*] (Smolensk: Rusich, 2005), pp. 275–6.
8. RGVA, F. 4, op. 12, d. 106, ll. 112–22; as cited by *Russky arkhiv: Velikaia Otechestvennaia* [*Russian archive: Great Patriotic War*] T. 13 (2–2) *Prikazy Narodnogo komissara oborony SSSR* [*Orders of the People's Commissar of Defence SSSR*, hereafter cited as *Russian archive*, T. 13 (2–2)] 22 June 1941 – 1942 (Moscow: TERRA, 1997), pp. 335–6.

Chapter 3

1. *Polevye ustavy inostrannykh armii* [*Field Service Regulations of Foreign Armies*] (Moscow: Voenizdat, 1936), p. 114.
2. Jentz, T.L., *Panzertruppen: The Complete Guide to the Creation & Combat Employment of Germany's Tank Force, 1933–1942* [hereafter cited as Jentz, *Panzertruppen*] (Atglen, PA: Schiffer Publishing Ltd, 1996), pp. 11, 14, 20.
3. Edwards, R. *Panzer. A Revolution in Warfare, 1939–1945* (London: Brockhampton Press, 1939–1945), p. 81.
4. *Germany and the Second World War, Volume IV: The Attack on the Soviet Union* [hereafter cited as *Germany and the Second World War, Volume IV*] (New York: Oxford University Press, 1999), p. 364.
5. Ibid., pp. 202, 204.

Chapter 4

1. Jentz, T. L., *Panzer Tracts No. 1–2: Panzerkampfwagen I Kl.Pz.Bef.Wg. to VK 18.01* [hereafter cited as Jentz, *Panzer Tracts No. 1–2*] (Boyds, MD: Panzer Tracts, 2002), p. 171.

2. RGFA, F. 31811, op. 2, d. 916; as cited by *Dokumental'no-istorichesky sbornik No. 2* [*Documentary-historical collection No. 2,* hereafter cited as *Documentary-historical collection No. 2*] (Moscow: Muzeino-memorial'nyi kompleks 'Istoriia Tanka T-34', 2015), p. 80.

3. Jentz, T.L. and Doyle H.L., *Panzer Tracts No. 3–1: Panzerkampfwagen III Ausf. A, B, C und D* [hereafter cited as Jentz and Doyle, *Panzer Tracts No. 3–1*] (Boyd, MD: Panzer Tracts, 2006), pp. 17–18.

4. Ibid., pp. 22–3.

5. Jentz, T. L., *Panzer Tracts 1–1: Panzerkampfwagen I. Kleintraktor to Ausf. B* [hereafter cited as Jentz, *Panzer Tracts No. 1–1*] (Boyd, MD: Panzer Tracts, 2002), pp. 2–23.

6. Jentz, *Panzer Tracts No. 1–2*, pp. 121, 125.

7. Jentz, *Panzer Tracts No. 1–1*, pp. 25–34.

8. Ibid., pp. 60–1.

9. Jentz, *Panzertruppen*, pp. 19–20.

10. Jentz, *Panzer Tracts No. 1–1*, pp. 78, 87.

11. Jentz T.L. and Doyle H.L., *Panzer Tracts No. 2–1. Panzerkampfwagen II. Ausf.a/1, a/2, a/3, b,c, A, B, and C* [hereafter cited as Jentz and Doyle, *Panzer Tracts No. 2–1*] (Boyds, MD: Panzer Tracts, 2008), pp. 2–5, 26–7.

12. Spielberger, W.J., *Panzers I and II & their Variants* (Atglen, PA: Schiffer Publishing Ltd, 2007), p. 74.

13. Jentz and Doyle, *Panzer Tracts No. 2–1*, pp. 26–8.

14. Jentz, T.L. and Doyle, H.L., *Panzer Tracts No. 2–3: Panzerkampfwagen II Ausf.D, E, and F* [hereafter cited as Jentz and Doyle, *Panzer Tracts No. 2–3*] (Boyds, MD: Panzer Tracts, 2010), pp. 7, 12, 14, 28.

15. Jentz and Doyle, *Panzer Tracts No. 3–1*, pp. 25–6, 28, 30, 39, 44–5, 61–4.

16. Jentz, T.L. and Doyle, H.L., *Panzer Tracts No. 3–2. Panzerkampfwagen III Ausf. E, F, G and H* [hereafter cited as Jentz and Doyle, *Panzer Tracts No. 3–2*] (Boyd, MD: Panzer Tracts, 2007), pp. 12–15, 40, 46, 55, 68, 84.

17. Jentz and Doyle, *Panzer Tracts* No. 3–1, pp. 62–4; Jentz and Doyle, *Panzer Tracts No. 3–2*, pp. 4, 11, 12, 16, 45, 46, 79; T.L. Jentz and H.L. Doyle, *Panzer Tracts No. 3–3. Panzerkampfwagen III Ausf.J, L, M and N* [hereafter cited as Jentz and Doyle, *Panzer Tracts No. 3–3*] (Boyd, MD: Panzer Tracts, 2009), pp. 22, 23.

18. Svirin, M.N., *Tankovaia moshch' SSSR* [*Tank power of the USSR,* hereafter cited as Svirin, *Tank power of the USSR*] (Moscow: Iauza/Eksmo, 2008), pp. 288, 290–1.

19. Jentz, T.L., *Panzer Tracts No. 4. Panzerkampfwagen IV, Grosstraktor to Panzerbefehlswagen IV* [hereafter cited as Jentz, *Panzer Tracts No. 4*] (Darlington, MD: Darlington Productions, Inc., 1997), p. 6.

20. Jentz, *Panzertruppen*, pp. 113, 115.

21. TsAMO, F. 23, op. 7237, d. 2, ll. 21–50 as cited by *Voennaia razvedka informiruet: Dokumenty Razvedupravleniia Krasnoi Armii, Ianvar'1939–Iun' 1941* [*Military intelligence informs: Documents of the Red Army's Intelligence Directorate, January 1939 to June 1941*] (Moscow: MFD, 2008), p. 555; TM 30–450. *Handbook on German Military Forces* (Washington, DC: War Department, December 17 1941), pp. 142, 146, 155–6, 158, 166–9.

22. Jentz, *Panzer Tracts No. 4*, p. 10.

23. Spielberger, W.J., *Panzer IV & its Variants* [hereafter cited as Spielberger, *Panzer IV & its Variants*] (Atglen, PA: Schiffer Publishing Ltd, 1993), p. 10.

24. Jentz, *Panzer Tracts No. 4*, pp. 10, 12.

25. Ibid., p. 24.

26. Jentz, *Panzertruppen*, p. 266; Spielberger, W.J., *Panzer I and II & their Variants* (Atglen, PA: Schiffer Publishing Ltd, 2007), p. 106; Spielberger, *Panzer IV & its Variants*, pp. 39, 44; Spielberger, W.J., Doyle, H.L. and Jentz, T. L., *Panzer IV & its Variants 1935–1945. Book 2* [hereafter cited as Spielberger, Doyle and Jentz. *Panzer IV & its Variants. Book 2*] (Atglen, PA: Schiffer Publishing Ltd, 2011), pp. 73, 101, 116, 128, 151, 162.

27. Jentz, *Panzer Tracts No. 1–2*, pp. 102, 109.

28. Jentz, T. L. and Doyle, H.L., *Panzer Tracts No. 3–4. Panzerbefehlswagen Ausf.D1, E, H, J and K; development and production from 1935 to 1943* (Boyds, MD: Panzer Tracts, 2010), p. 54.

29. Spielberger, W.J., *Sturmgeschütz & its Variants* [hereafter cited as Spielberger, *Sturmgeschütz & its Variants*] (Atglen, PA: Schiffer Publishing Ltd, 1993), pp. 11, 12.

30. Jentz, T. L., *Panzer Tracts No. 8. Sturmgeschuetz, s. Pak to Sturmmoerser* [hereafter cited as Jentz, *Panzer Tracts No. 8*] (Darlington, MD: Darlington Productions, Inc., 1999), pp. 1, 2, 4.

31. Spielberger, *Sturmgeschuetz & its Variants*, pp. 37–8, 40, 45, 48, 179.

32. Regenberg, W., *Captured American & British Tanks Under the German Flag* [hereafter cited as Regenberg, *Captured American & British Tanks Under the German Flag*] (Atglen, PA: Schiffer Publishing Ltd, 1993), p. 3.

33. Jentz, T.L. and Regenberg, W., *Panzer Tracts No. 19–1. Beute-Panzerkampfwagen; Czech, Polish and French Tanks Captured from 1939 to 1940* [hereafter cited as Jentz and Regenberg, *Panzer Tracts No. 19–1*] (Boyds, MD: Panzer Tracts, 2007), pp. 11–12.

34. Regenberg W. and Scheibert, H., *Captured French Tanks Under the German Flag* [hereafter cited as Regenberg and Scheibert, *Captured French Tanks Under the German Flag*] (Atglen, PA: Schiffers Publishing Ltd, 1993), p. 3.

35. Jentz and Regenberg, *Panzer Tracts No. 19–1*, pp. 16–17, 20.

36. Jentz, T.L. and Doyle, H.L., *Panzer Tracts No. 7–1. Panzerjaeger* (Boyds, MD: Panzer Tracts, 2004), p. 62.

37. Halder, F., *Voennyi dnevnik, 1940–1941* [*War Diary, 1940–1941*] (Moscow: AST, 2003), p. 130.

38. Sawodny, W., *German Armored Trains 1904–1945* (Atglen, PA: Schiffer Publishing Ltd, 2010), pp. 118–119, 320–2.

39. Regenberg and Scheibert, *Captured French Tanks under the German Flag*, pp. 11, 31.

40. Matev, K., *Equipment and Armour in the Bulgarian Army* (Sofia: Angela Publishers, 2000), pp. 20, 26–7.

41. Regenberg and Scheibert, *Captured French Tanks under the German Flag*, pp. 19, 31.

42. Axworthy M, Scafes, C., and Craciunoiu, C., *Third Axis Fourth Ally: Romanian Armed Forces in the European War, 1941–1945* (London: Arms and Armour Press, 1995), p. 37.

43. Jentz and Regenberg, *Panzer Tracts No. 19–1*, pp. 17, 24, 30, 32. Regenberg and Scheibert, *Captured French Tanks under the German Flag*, pp. 6–7.

44. Jentz and Regenberg, *Panzer Tracts No. 19–1*, pp. 20, 30, 48–9.

45. Jentz, *Panzertruppen*, p. 193.

46. Regenberg. *Captured American & British Tanks under the German Flag*, p. 3.

47. Jentz T.L.and Regenberg, W. *Panzer Tracts No. 19–2. Beute-Panzerkampfwagen. British, American, Russian and Italian Tanks Captured from 1940 to 1945* (Boyds, MD: Panzer Tracts, 2008), p. 62.

48. Kliment, C.K. and Francev, V., *Czechoslovak Armoured Fighting Vehicles, 1918–1948* [hereafter cited as Kliment and Francev, *Czechoslovak Armoured Fighting Vehicles*] (Atglen, PA: Schiffer Publishing Ltd, 1997), pp. 38, 44, 48–50, 54–6, 58–9.
49. Kniazev, M., Legky tank LT vz.35 [Light tank LT vz.35], *Bronekollektsiia*, No. 4 (2003), p. 8.
50. Svirin, *Tank power of the USSR*, p. 225.
51. Kolomiets, M.V., *KV 'Klim Voroshilov' – tank proryva* [*KV 'Klim Voroshilov' – breakthrough tank*, hereafter cited as Kolomiets, *'Klim Voroshilov'*] (Moscow: Kollektsiia, Iauza/EKSMO, 2006), p. 7.
52. Kolomiets, M.V., *T-26: Tiazhelaia sud'ba legkogo tanka* [*T-26: The heavy fate of a light tank*, hereafter cited as Kolomiets, *T-26: The heavy fate of a light tank*] (Moscow: Iauza, Strategiia KM, EKSMO, 2007), p. 54.
53. Kliment and Francev, *Czechoslovak Armoured Fighting Vehicles*, pp. 60, 65–7.
54. Jentz and Regenberg, *Panzer Tracts No. 19–1*, p. 2.
55. Ibid.; Kliment and Francev, *Czechoslovak Armoured Fighting Vehicles*, pp. 66, 175.
56. Ibid., pp. 74–5, 77–8, 203.
57. Jentz, T. L. and Doyle, H.L., *Panzer Tracts No. 18. Panzerkampfwagen 38(t) Ausf.A to G and S* (Boyds, MD: Panzer Tracts, 2007), pp. 10–14, 17.
58. Ibid., p. 7.

Chapter 5
1. Jentz, *Panzer Tracts No. 1–2*, pp. 174–6.
2. Jentz, *Panzertruppen*, p. 46.
3. Ibid., pp. 88, 92.
4. Zaloga, S. and Madej, V., *The Polish Campaign 1939* (New York, NY: Hippocrene Books, Inc., 1985), pp. 64–5, 88–9, 91, 107.
5. Kennedy, R.M., *The German Campaign in Poland (1939)* (Washington, DC: Department of the Army, 1956), pp. 132–3.
6. Tessin, G., *Verbände und Truppen der deutschen Wehrmacht und Waffen-SS im Zweiten Weltkrieg 1939–1945. Zweiter Band: Die Landstreitkräfte 1–5* [Formations and Troops of the German Wehrmacht and Waffen-SS in the Second World War 1939–1945. Volume Two: The Land Forces 1–5] (Frankfurt/Main:Verlag E.S. Mittler & Sohn GmbH, 1973), pp. 31, 107, 175, 244, 294–5.
7. Jentz, *Panzertruppen*, p. 104; Jentz, *Panzer Tracts No. 1–2*, p. 180.
8. Jentz, *Panzertruppen*, pp. 256, 260, 262, 266, 270.
9. Jentz and Doyle, *Panzer Tract No. 2–1, p. 61*.
10. Ritgen, H., *The 6th Panzer Division 1937–1945* (Oxford, UK: Osprey Publishing Ltd, 2002), p. 13.
11. Jentz, *Panzertruppen*, p. 117.
12. Frieser, K.-H., *The Blitzkrieg Legend: The 1940 Campaign in the West* [hereafter cited as Frieser, *The Blitzkrieg Legend*] (Annapolis, MD: Naval Institute Press, 2005), pp. 37–8.
13. Sharp, L., *The French Army 1939–1940: Organization, Order of Battle, Operational History*, Volume 2 (London: Military Press, 2001), pp. 136–7, 145–8, 152; Sharp, L., *The French Army 1939–1940: Organization, Order of Battle, Operational History*, Volume 5 (London: Military Press, 2006), pp. 90, 97, 101, 104, 106–7.
14. Sharp, L., *The French Army 1939–1940: Organization, Order of Battle, Operational History*, Volume 3 (London: Military Press, 2003), pp. 172–3, 175, 178, 181, 183–5.
15. Frieser, *The Blitzkrieg Legend*, p. 29.

16. Ellis, J., *The World War II Handbook* [hereafter cited as Ellis, *The World War II Handbook*] (London: Autumn Press Ltd, 1995), p. 217.
17. Legrand, N., 'De l'or noir pour les braves' ['The black gold for the braves'], *Batailles & Blindes*, No. 18 (2007), p. 37.
18. Frieser, *The Blitzkrieg Legend*, pp. 102, 110.
19. Corum, J.S., *The Roots of Blitzkrieg* (Lawrence, KS: University Press of Kansas, 1992), p. 205.
20. Jentz, *Panzertruppen*, pp. 110, 115, 141.
21. Jentz and Doyle, *Panzer Tracts No. 2–3*, p. 39.
22. Jentz and Doyle, *Panzer Tracts No. 3–2*, pp. 60, 64.
23. Jentz and Doyle, *Panzer Tracts No. 3–3*, pp. 2, 3.
24. Spielberger, Doyle and Jentz, *Panzer IV & its Variants Book 2*, pp. 100, 115, 127, 144, 147, 149, 157, 163.
25. Jentz, *Panzer Tracts No. 8*, p. 8.
26. Jentz, *Panzertruppen*, pp. 154–7.
27. Blau, G.E., *Invasion Balkans! The German Campaign in the Balkans, Spring 1941* (Shippensburg, PA: Burd Street Press, 1997), p. 146.
28. Jentz, *Panzertruppen*, p. 186.
29. Jentz, T. L., *Panzer Tracts No. 14: Gepanzerte Pionier-Fahrzeuge [Armoured Combat Engineer Vehicles]* (Darlington, MD: Darlington Productions, Inc., 1998), pp. 2–3.
30. Englemann, J., *German Artillery in World War II 1939–1945* (Atglen, PA: Schiffer Publishing Ltd, 1995), p. 110.
31. Spielberger, *Sturmgeschütz & its Variants*, pp. 235–6, 247, 250–1.

Chapter 6

1. RGVA, F. 31811, op. 2, d. 143, ll. 2–3, 15, 19, 24–5, 34; as cited by *Glavnoe avtobronetankovoe upravlenie: Liudi, sobytiia, fakty v dokumentakh 1929–1941 [Main Automotive-Armoured-Tank Directorate: Men, events, facts in documents 1929–1941*, hereafter cited as *GABTU. 1929–1941]* (Moscow: GABTU, 2004), p. 338.
2. Sheptura, V.N., 'Vliianie teorii glubokoi operatsii i glubokogo boia na razrabotku osnov organizatsii sviazi nakanune Velikoi Otechestvennoi voiny 1941–1945' ['Influence of the theory of the deep operation and deep battle on working out the foundations of organizing communications on the eve of the Great Patriotic War 1941–1945'], *Voenno-istorichesky zhurnal*, No. 7 (2006), p. 26.
3. Gorlov, S.A., *Sovershenno sekretno: al'ians Moskva-Berlin, 1920–1933 [Top secret: the Moscow-Berlin alliance, 1920–1933]* (Moscow: OLMA-PRESS, 2001), p. 223.
4. Drig, E., *Mekhanizirovannye korpusa RKKA v boiu [Mechanized Corps of the RKKA (Workers' and Peasants' Red Army) in combat*, hereafter cited as Drig, *Mechanized Corps]* (Moscow: AST, 2005), p. 9.
5. *Voennyi sovet pri narodnom kommisare oborony SSSR. Dekabr' 1934: dokumenty i materialy [Military Council under the USSR People's Commissar of Defence. December 1934: documents and materials*, hereafter cited as *Military Council under the USSR People's Commissar of Defence. December 1934]* (Moscow: ROSSPEN, 2007), p. 492.
6. Drig, *Mechanized Corps*, p. 11.
7. *Military Council under the USSR People's Commissar of Defence. December 1934*, p. 492.
8. TsAMO, F. 15, op. 2154, d. 4, ll. 1–30; as cited in *1941 god, v 2-x kn. Kn. 2 [The year 1941, in two books. Book 2*, hereafter cited as *1941. Book 2]* (Moscow: MFD, 1998), pp. 537–8; Drig, *Mechanized Corps*, p. 13.

9. Svirin, *Tank power of the USSR*, p. 204.

10. RGFA, F. 40442, op. 2, d. 128, ll. 120–39; as cited by *Glavnyi voennyi sovet RKKA, 13 marta 1939 – 20 iunia 1941: dokumenty i materialy* [*Main Military Council of the RKKA, 13 March 1939 – 20 June 1941: documents and materials*, hereafter cited as *Main Military Council of the RKKA*] (Moscow: ROSSPEN, 2004), pp. 443–4.

11. RGVA, F. 4, op. 18, d. 49, ll. 1–26; as cited by *Main Military Council of the RKKA*, p. 272.

12. Mel'tiukhov, M.I., *Upushchennyi shans Stalina* [*Stalin's missed opportunity*, hereafter cited as Mel'tiukhov, *Stalin's missed opportunity*] (Moscow: Veche, 2008), p. 481.

13. RGVA, F. 4, op. 18, d. 49, ll. 1–26; as cited by *Main Military Council of the RKKA*, pp. 272–3, 284; TsKhSD, F. 89, per. 74, d. 6, as cited by *Voenno-istorichesky zhurnal*, No. 3 (1996), p. 24.

14. RGVA, F. 4, op. 18, d. 49, 11.1–26; as cited by *Main Military Council of the RKKA*, pp. 269–70.

15. Dessberg, F. and Ken, O.N., '1937–1938: Krasnaia armiia v doneseniiakh frantsuzskikh voennykh attashe' ['1937–1938: Red Army in the reports of French military attachés' *Voprosy istorii*, No. 10 (2004), p. 41.

16. RGVA, F. 4, op. 14, d. 2737, ll. 124–9; as cited from *Zimniaia voina: Rabota nad oshibkami (aprel'-mai 1940)* [*Winter War: Correction of mistakes (April-May 1940)*] (Moscow: Letny sad, 2004), p. 78.

17. Zakharov, M.V., *General'nyi shtab v predvoennye gody* [*General Staff in the pre-war years*] (Moscow: AST, 2005), pp. 323–4; *Na prieme u Stalina: Tetrady zapisei lits, priniatykh I.V. Stalinym (1924–1953)* [*At the reception of Stalin: The appointment book of individuals who were received by Stalin (1924–1953)*] (Moscow: 2008), p. 299.

18. RGFA, F. 40442, op. 2a, d. 169, ll. 145–54; as cited by *Nakanune: Zapadnyi Osobyi voennyi okrug (konets 1939–1941)* [*On the eve: The Western Special Military District (end of 1939 to 1941)*, hereafter cited as *On the eve*] (Minsk: NARB, 2007), pp. 80–2.

19. RGVA, F. 40442, op. 2a, d. 169, ll. 165–75, 181–8, as cited by *On the eve*, pp. 90–4; Drig, *Mechanized Corps*, p. 20.

20. *1941 god, v 2-kh knigakh; Kniga 1* [*The year 1941, in two books; Book 1*, hereafter cited as *1941. Book 1*] (Moscow: MFD, 1998), p. 296.

21. RGFA, F. 40442, op. 2a, d. 169, ll. 312–18; as cited by *On the eve*, pp. 230–2.

22. RGASPI, F. 17, op. 162, d. 29, l. 135; as cited by *On the eve*, p. 11.

23. TsAMO, F. 16, op. 2154, d. 4, ll. 199–250; as cited by *1941: Book 1*, p. 608.

24. Gor'kov, Iu.A., *Kreml', Stavka, Genshtab* [*Kremlin, the Stavka, the General Staff*] (Tver': RIF LTD, 1995), p. 34.

25. *1941: Book 2*, p. 105; Drig, *Mechanized Corps*, p. 592.

26. Zhukov, G.K. *Vospominaniia i razmyshleniia, v 3 tomakh; Tom 1* [*Reminiscences and reflections, in 3 volumes; Volume 1*, hereafter cited as Zhukov, *Reminiscences and reflections*] (Moscow: APN, 1985), p. 254.

27. Kazakov, M.I., *Nad kartoi bylykh srazheny* [*Over the map of past battles*] (Moscow: Voenizdat, 1971), pp. 60–1.

28. TsAMO, F. 16, op. 2951, d. 239, ll. 197–277; as cited by *1941: Book 1*, pp. 237, 484.

29. RGVA, F. 40442, op. 2a, d. 169, ll. 145–54; as cited by *On the eve*, p. 80.

30. Drig, *Mechanized Corps*, pp. 54–5.

31. TsAMO, F. 38, op. 11373, d. 67, ll. 97–116; as cited by *Glavnoe avtobronetankovoe upravlenie: Liudi, sobytiia, fakty v dokumentakh, 1940–1942* [*Main Automotive-Armoured-Tank Directorate: Men, events, facts in documents, 1940–1942*, hereafter cited as *GABTU. 1940–1942*] (Moscow: GABTU, 2005), p. 49.

32. TsAMO, F. 16, op. 2951, d. 242, ll. 226–8; as cited by *1941: Book 1*, pp. 676–7.

33. TsAMO, F. 38, op. 11373, d. 67, ll. 97–116; as cited by *GABTU, 1940–1942*, p. 50.

34. Zhukov, *Reminiscences and reflections*, p. 255.

35. RGVA, F. 41107, op. 1, d. 48, ll. 1–58; as cited by *1941: Book 2*, p. 506.

36. Ibid., p. 505.

37. Novobranets, V.A., '*Ia preduprezhdal o voine Stalina.*' *Zapiski voennogo razvedchika* ['*I warned Stalin about the war.*' *Notes of a military intelligence officer*] (Moscow: Iauza, EKSMO, 2009), pp. 73–6.

38. *1941 god – uroki i vyvody* [*The year 1941 – lessons and conclusions*, hereafter cited as *1941 – lessons and conclusions*] (Moscow: Voenizdat, 1992), p. 29.

39. Drig, *Mechanized Corps*, pp. 85, 136, 343, 603.

40. Kolomiets, M. and Makarov M., *Preliudia k 'Barbarosse'* [*Prelude to 'Barbarossa'*, hereafter cited as Kolomiets and Makarov, *Prelude to 'Barbarossa'*] *Frontovaia illiustratsiia*, No. 4 (2001), p. 48.

41. *On the eve*, p. 12.

42. Mel'tiukhov, *Stalin's missed opportunity*, pp. 263–4.

43. *On the eve*, pp. 12–13.

44. Ibid., pp. 12, 561.

45. TsAMO, F. 127, op. 12915, d. 75, ll. 74–8; as cited by *1941: Dokumenty i materialy k 70-letiiu nachala Velikoi Otechestvennoi voiny, Tom 1* [*1941: Documents and materials for the 70th anniversary of the beginning of the Great Patriotic War*, hereafter cited as *1941. Documents and materials*] (Saint Petersburg: FGBU 'Prezidentskaia biblioteka imeni B.N. Yel'tsin', 2011), p. 377.

46. TsAMO, F. 81, op. 12094, d. 56, l. 272.

47. *1941 – lessons and conclusions*, p. 28.

48. TsAMO, F. 16, op. 2154, d. 4, ll. 251–2; as cited by *1941: Book 1*, p. 631.

49. TsAMO, F. 208, op. 2526, d. 28, ll. 65–72; as cited by *Voenno-istorichesky zhurnal*, No. 9 (1989), p. 17.

50. TsAMO, F. 131, op. 12980, d. 2, l. 311.

51. AP RF, F. 45, op. 1, d. 478, ll. 3–6; as cited by *1941: Book 2*, p. 471.

52. TsAMO, F. 38, op. 11373, d. 67, ll. 97–116; as cited by GABTU, 1940–1942, p. 49.

Chapter 7

1. Kolomiets, M. and Fedoseev, S., Legky tank Renault FT-17 [Light tank Renault FT-17] *Frontovaia illiustratsiia*, No. 1 (2004), pp. 7, 9, 51, 54, 59, 61–4; Svirin, *Tank power of the USSR*, p. 33.

2. Sokolov, A.K., *Ot voenproma k VPK: Sovetskaia voennaia promyshlennost' 1917 – iun' 1941* [*From military industry to the military-industrial complex: Soviet military industry from 1917 to June 1941*, hereafter cited as Sokolov, *From military industry to the military-industrial complex*] (Moscow: Novyi khronograf, 2012), pp. 15, 32, 44.

3. Svirin, *Tank power of the USSR*, p. 41.

4. Sokolov, *From military industry to the military-industrial complex*, p. 254.

5. RGVA, F. 4, op. 19, d. 55, ll. 24–7; as cited by *Main Military Council of the RKKA*, p. 336.

6. Svirin, M. and Beskurnikov, A., Pervye sovetskie tanki [First Soviet tanks, hereafter cited as First Soviet tanks] *Armada, No. 1* (1995), pp. 7, 9, 43, 50–2, 56–7.

7. RGVA, f. 4, op. 18, d. 15, ll. 189–204; as cited by *GABTU, 1929–1941*, pp. 129–30.

8. Mukhin, M.Iu., 'Amtorg: Amerikanskie tanki dlia RKKA' ['Amtorg: American tanks for the RKKA', hereafter cited as 'Amtorg'] *Otechestvennaia istoriia*, No. 3 (2001), pp. 57, 58.

9. RGVA, f. 31811, op. 1, d. 7, ll. 35–47; as cited by *GABTU, 1929–1941*, pp. 201–3.

10. Fletcher, D., *Mechanized Force: British tanks between the wars*, hereafter cited as Fletcher, *Mechanized Force* (London: HMSO, 1991), p. 82.

11. Svirin, *Tank power of the USSR*, pp. 83, 85.

12. Foss, S.F. and McKenzie, P., *Vickers Tanks: From Landships to Challenger II*, hereafter cited as Foss and McKenzie, *Vickers Tanks* (Newcastle upon Tyne, UK: Keepdate Publishing Ltd, 1995), p. 78.

13. Svirin, *Tank power of the USSR*, pp. 92–4; Kolomiets, *T-26: The heavy fate of a light tank*, pp. 6–7.

14. Kolomiets, *T-26: The heavy fate of a light tank*, pp. 9, 11, 21, 33, 50, 54, 66, 75, 125.

15. Fletcher, *Mechanized Force*, pp. 15, 18.

16. Svirin, *Tank power of the USSR*, pp. 126–30.

17. Kolomiets, M.V., *Sredny tank T-28: Trexgolovyi monstr Stalina* [*Medium tank T-28: Stalin's three-headed monster*, hereafter cited as Kolomiets, *Medium tank T-28*] (Moscow: Strategiia KM, Iauza/EKSMO, 2007), p. 23.

18. Kolomiets, M.V., *Zimniaia voina: 'Lomiat tanki shirokie proseki'* [*Winter War: 'The tanks are breaking through wide clearings'*] (Moscow: Strategiia KM, Iauza/EKSMO, 2014), pp. 135–7, 150–2.

19. Kolomiets, *Medium tank T-28*, pp. 39–40, 80–1, 88.

20. Kolomiets, M.V., *Manevrennye tanki SSSR: T-12, T-24, TG, D-4 i dr.* [*Manoeuvring tanks of the USSR: T-12, T-24, TG, D-4 and others*, hereafter cited as Kolomiets, *Manoeuvring tanks of the USSR*] (Moscow: Strategiia KM, Iauza/EKSMO, 2014), pp. 55, 56, 69.

21. Kolomiets, M.V. and Svirin, M.N., *Tiazhelyi tank T-35: Sukhoputnyi drednout Krasnoi Armii* [*Heavy tank T-35: Red Army's land dreadnought*, hereafter cited as Kolomiets and Svirin, *Heavy tank T-35*] (Moscow: Strategiia KM, Iauza/EKSMO, 2007), pp. 15, 16, 18, 47.

22. Veretennikov, A.I., Rasskazov, I.I., Pivnev, A.I., Sidorov, K.V. and Reshetilo, E.I., *Khar'kovskoe konstruktorskoe biuro po mashinostroeniiu imeni A.A. Morozov* [*A.A. Morozov Kharkov design bureau for machine building*] (Kharkov: TO 'SINTEZ', 2002), p. 26.

23. Kolomiets, M.V., *T-35: sukhoputnye linkory Stalina* [*T-35: Stalin's land battleships*, hereafter cited as Kolomiets, *T-35*] (Moscow: Strategiia KM, Iauza/EKSMO, 2014), pp. 11, 19, 36, 57.

24. Kolomiets and Svirin, *Heavy tank T-35*, p. 59.

25. Terry, T.W., Jackson, S.R., Ryley, C.E.S., Jones, B.E., and Wormell, P.J.H., *Fighting Vehicles* (London, UK: Brassley's, 1991), p. 111.

26. Ogorkiewicz, R.M., *Armoured Forces* (New York, NY: Arco Publishing Inc., 1970), p. 191.

27. Hoffman, G.F., 'A Yankee Inventor and the Military Establishment: The Christie Tank Controversy', *Military Affairs*, Vol. 39, No. 1 (February 1975), pp. 12, 14.

28. Mukhin, 'Amtorg', pp. 52, 59; Kolomiets, M.V., *Legkie tanki BT: 'Letaiushchii' tank 1930-kh* [*Light BT tanks: 'Flying' tank of the 1930s*, hereafter cited as Kolomiets, *Light BT tanks*] (Moscow: Strategiia KM, Iauza/EKSMO, 2007), pp. 12–14.

29. Ibragimov, D.S., *Bronia Sovetov*, [*Armour of the Soviets*, hereafter cited as Ibragimov, *Armour of the Soviets*] (Moscow: ANO IITs 'INSAN', 2008), pp. 200–1, 209.

30. Pavlov, M.V., Zheltov, I.G. and Pavlov, I.V., *Tanki BT* [*BT tanks*, hereafter cited as Pavlov, Zheltov and Pavlov, *BT tanks*] (Moscow: Eksprint, 2001), pp. 10–13, 53–5, 115–16, 118, 122, 132; Kolomiets, *Light BT tanks*, p. 73.

31. RGVA, F. 4, op. 14, d. 2021, ll. 259–260obr; as cited by *Main Military Council of the RKKA*, p. 506.

32. Svirin, *Tank power of the USSR*, p. 233.
33. Kolomiets, M.V., *'Chudo-oruzhie' Stalina: Plavaiushchie tanki Velikoi Otechestvennoi T-37, T-38, T-40* [*Stalin's 'wonder weapon': Amphibious tanks of the Great Patriotic War T-37, T-38, T-40*, hereafter cited as Kolomiets, *Amphibious tanks of the Great Patriotic War*] (Moscow: Strategiia KM, Iauza/EKSMO, 2011), pp. 7, 14–15, 22.
34. GARF, F. R-8418, op. 28, d. 2, ll. 72–9; as cited by *Stanovlenie oboronno-promyshlennogo kompleksa SSSR (1933–1937)* [*Establishment of the defence-industrial complex of the USSR (1933–1937]* (Moscow: TERRA, 2011), p. 146.
35. Kolomiets, *Amphibious tanks of the Great Patriotic War*, pp. 43–4, 49; Svirin, M., *Mnogostradal'nyi tank T-38* [*Troubled tank T-38*] *M-Khobbi*, No. 9 (1997), p. 34.

Chapter 8

1. TsAMO, F. 38, op. 11569, d. 300, ll. 16–24; as cited by *GABTU 1940–1942*, p. 21.
2. Kolomiets, *Amphibious tanks of the Great Patriotic War*, pp. 62, 64, 65.
3. Tikhonov, S.G., *Oboronnye predpriiatiia SSSR i Rossii, Tom 1* [*Defence industry plants of the USSR and Russia, Volume 1*] (Moscow: TOM, 2010), p. 559.
4. Vasil'eva, L., Zheltov, I., and Chikova G., *Pravda o tanke T-34* [*Truth about the T-34 tank*, hereafter cited as Vasil'eva, Zheltov and Chikova, *Truth about the T-34 tank*] (Moscow: RKPOO 'Atlantida-XXI vek'), pp. 43, 48.
5. Kolomiets, *Manoeuvring tanks of the USSR*, pp. 15, 16, 22, 28–9, 36.
6. Kul'chitsky, E.A., 'Na dal'nykh podstupakh' ['On distant approaches'] in *T-34: put' k Pobede – vospominaniia tankostroitelei i tankistov* [*T-34: the path to Victory – recollections of tank builders and tankers*] (Kiev: Politizdat Ukrainy, 1989), p. 12.
7. Kolomiets, *Manoeuvring tanks of the USSR*, pp. 40, 45.
8. RGVA, f. 4, op. 19, d. 55, ll. 24–7; as cited by *Main Military Council of the RKKA*, pp. 335–6.
9. Ibragimov, *Armour of the Soviets*, p. 209.
10. Sokolov, *From military industry to the military-industrial complex*, pp. 133, 145–6.
11. Ibragimov, *Armour of the Soviets*, pp. 188, 192, 195–6, 199, 296, 350.
12. Sokolov, *From military industry to the military-industrial complex*, pp. 115, 135–6, 138–9.
13. Ibragimov, *Armour of the Soviets*, pp. 188–90, 210.
14. Pavlov, Zheltov and Pavlov, *BT tanks*, p. 68.
15. *Tank BT-5. Nastavlenie avtobronetankovykh voisk RKKA* [*BT-5 tank. Service manual of the Automotive-Armoured Forces of the RKKA*, hereafter cited as *BT-5 tank. Service manual*] (Moscow: Otdel izdatel'stva NKO SSSR, 1935), p. 78; *Tank BT-7. Nastavlenie avtobronetankovykh voisk RKKA* [*BT-7 tank. Service manual of the Automotive-Armoured Forces of the RKKA*, hereafter cited as *BT-7 tank. Service manual*] (Moscow: Voenizdat, 1938), p. 61.
16. Vasil'eva, Zheltov and Chikova, *Truth about the T-34 tank*, pp. 34–5.
17. Ibragimov, *Armour of the Soviets*, pp. 349–50, 352, 355, 506.
18. Soliankin, A.G., Pavlov, M.V., Pavlov, I.V. and Zheltov, I.G., *Otechestvennye bronirovannye mashiny, Tom 1: 1905–1941* [*Domestic armoured vehicles, Volume 1: 1905–1941*, hereafter cited as Soliankin et. al., *Domestic armoured vehicles*] (Moscow: Eksprint, 2002), p. 17.
19. Kolomiets, M.V., *T-34. Pervaia polnaia entsiklopediia* [*T-34. First complete encyclopedia*, hereafter cited as Kolomiets, *T-34*] (Moscow: Strategiia KM, Iauza/EKSMO, 2009), pp. 12, 13, 15–16.
20. RGVA, f. 31811, op. 2, d. 551, l. 412; as cited by *GABTU, 1929–1941*, p. 472.
21. Kolomiets, *T-34*, p. 13.

22. Zheltov, I., Pavlov, M., Pavlov, I., Sergeev, A. and Soliankin, A., *Neizvestnyi T-34* [*Unknown T-34*, hereafter cited as Zheltov et. al., *Unknown T-34*] (Moscow: Eksprint, 2001), p. 8.

23. Kolomiets, *T-34*, pp. 15–16.

24. Zheltov et. al., *Unknown T-34*, pp. 10–11.

25. Kolomiets, *T-34*, pp. 18–19.

26. Ibragimov, *Armour of the Soviets*, pp. 451, 506; Kolomiets, *T-34*, pp. 19, 21.

27. Sobol', N.A., *Vospominaniia direktora zavoda* [*Memoirs of a factory director*] (Kharkov: Prapor, 1995), p. 58; Okhotin N and Roginsky, A., 'Iz istorii 'nemetskoi operatsii' NKVD 1937–1938' ['From the history of the NKVD's 'German operation' 1937–1938'] in *Repressii protiv sovetskikh nemtsev: Nakazannyi narod* [*Repressions against the Soviet Germans: Punished nationality*] (Moscow: Zven'ia, 1999), pp. 63–4.

28. Zheltov et. al., *Unknown T-34*, p. 11.

29. Bystrichenko, A.V., Dobrovol'sky, E.I., Drobotenko, A.P. et. al., *KhPZ – Malyshev Factory, 1895–1995: Kratkaia istoriia razvitia* [*Kharkov Locomotive Factory – Malyshev Factory, 1895–1995: A short history of the development*] (Kharkov: Prapor, 1995), pp. 220, 222, 223, 226, 229, 235, 236, 243; Ibragimov, *Armour of the Soviets*, p. 369.

30. Rybalkin, Iu., *Operatsiia 'X': Sovetskaia voennaia pomoshch' respublikanskoi Ispanii (1936–1939)* [*Operation 'X': Soviet military assistance to the Republican Spain (1936–1939)*] (Moscow: AIRO-XX, 2000), pp. 45, 64.

31. Svirin, *Tank power of the USSR*, p. 204.

32. Ibid., p. 208.

33. Zheltov et. al, *Unknown T-34*, p. 12.

34. Kolomiets, *T-34*, p. 26.

35. RGVA, f. 4, op. 19, d. 55, ll. 1–9; as cited by *Main Military Council of the RKKA*, p. 340.

36. Vasil'eva, Zheltov and Chikova, *Truth about the T-34 tank*, p. 52.

37. Kolomiets, *T-34*, p. 26.

38. Svirin, *Tank power of the USSR*, p. 280.

39. Kolomiets, *T-34*, p. 29.

40. Zheltov I. and Makarov, A., *A-34: Rozhdenie T-34* [*A-34: Birth of the T-34*, hereafter cited as Zheltov and Makarov, *A-34*] (Moscow: Taktikal Press, 2014), pp. 8, 12.

41. Svirin, *Tank power of the USSR*, p. 235.

42. Zheltov and Makarov, *A-34*, p. 198.

43. Ibid., pp. 199–206, 208.

44. Svirin, *Tank power of the USSR*, p. 273.

45. TsAMO, f. 38, op. 11355, d. 41, l. 16.

46. Zheltov et. al., *Unknown T-34*, pp. 37–8; Kolomiets, *T-34*, p. 137.

47. TsAMO, f. 38, op. 11355, d. 633, l. 9; as cited by *Glavnoe avtobronetankovoe upravlenie: Liudi, sobytiia, fakty v dokumentakh, 1943–1944* [*Main Automotive-Armoured-Tank Directorate: People, events, facts in documents, 1943–1944*, hereafter cited as *GABTU, 1943–1944*] (Moscow: GABTU, 2006), p. 545.

48. Kolomiets, M., *Leningradskie KV-1* [*Leningrad KV-1*, hereafter cited as Kolomiets, *Leningrad KV-1*] (Moscow: Taktikal Press, 2012), pp. 3–9.

49. Kolomiets, *'Klim Voroshilov'*, pp. 5, 7.

50. Popov, N.S., Petrov, V.I., Popov, A.N. and Ashik, M.V., *Bez tain i sekretov* [*Without mysteries and secrets*] (Saint Petersburg: ITTs 'Prana', 1997), p. 30.

51. Kolomiets, *Leningrad KV-1*, pp. 15, 16, 20–2.

52. Ibid., pp. 155–6; Kolomiets, *'Klim Voroshilov'* pp. 52, 100.

53. Kolomiets, M.V., *Tiazhelyi tank KV-2* [*Heavy tank KV-2*, hereafter cited as Kolomiets, *Heavy tank KV-2*] (Moscow: Strategiia KM, Iauza/EKSMO, 2013), pp. 7–9, 15; Svirin, *Tank power of the USSR*, p. 254.

54. TsAMO, f. 38, op. 11569, d. 300, ll. 16–24; as cited by *GABTU, 1940–1942*, p. 20.

55. Svirin, *Tank power of the USSR*, p. 284.

56. Kolomiets, *Heavy tank KV-2*, p. 11.

57. TsAMO, op. 24119, d. 4, ll. 160–1; Ibid., op. 7237, d. 2, ll. 21–50; as cited by *1941: Book 1*, pp. 704, 747, 752.

58. Kolomiets, '*Klim Voroshilov*', p. 31; Kolomiets, *Leningrad KV-1*, pp. 117, 121, 129.

59. Kolomiets, *Heavy tank KV-2*, pp. 16–17.

60. Kolomiets, '*Klim Voroshilov*', pp. 31–4, 42–3.

61. Soliankin et. al., *Domestic armoured vehicles*, p. 17.

62. *Boevoi i chislennyi sostav Vooruzhennykh sil SSSR v period Velikoi Otechestvennoi voiny. Statistichesky sbornik No. 1. 22 iunia 1941 goda* [*The order of battle and numerical strength of the USSR armed forces during the Great Patriotic War. Statistical collection No. 1. 22 June 1941*] (Moscow: IVI MO RF, 1994), pp. 4–5.

63. Ibid., pp. 21–2, 234; Mel'tiukhov, *Stalin's missed opportunity*, p. 526.

Chapter 9

1. Kolomiets, *T-34*, pp. 91, 92.

2. Kolomiets, '*Klim Voroshilov*', pp. 46, 53.

3. Kolomiets, *Heavy tank KV-2*, p. 22.

4. Ermolov, A.Iu., *Gosudarstvennoe upravlenie voennoi promyshlennost'iu v 1940-e gody: tankovaia promyshlennost'* [*State control of the military industry in the 1940s: tank industry*, hereafter cited as Ermolov, *Tank industry*] (Saint Petersburg, Aleteia, 2015), p. 172; Ust'iantsev, S.V. and Kolmakov, D.G., *Boevye mashiny Uralvagonzavoda. Tank T-34* [*Combat vehicles of the Ural Railcar Factory: T-34 tank*, hereafter cited as Ust'iantsev and Kolmakov, *T-34 tank*] (Nizhny Tagil: Media-Print, 2005), p. 184.

5. TsAMO, f. 38, op. 11355, d. 634, ll. 30–1; as cited by *GABTU, 1940–1942*, p. 171.

6. Mitchell, B.R., *International Historical Statistics: Europe, 1750–1993* (London: Macmillan Reference Ltd, 1998), p. 736; Lensky, A.G., *Sukhoputnye sily RKKA v predvoennye gody. Spravochnik.* [*Ground forces of the RKKA in the pre-war years. Handbook*] (Saint Petersburg: B&K, 2000), p. 18.

7. Ermolov, *Tank industry*, p. 127.

8. Ust'iantsev and Kolmakov, *T-34 tank*, p. 52.

9. Ermolov, *Tank industry*, pp. 228, 229, 305.

10. Jentz, *Panzertruppen*, p. 208.

11. German Tank Maintenance In World War II (Washington, DC: U.S. Government Printing Office, 1987), pp. 5–14, 17–19.

12. Muller-Hillerbrandt, B. *Sukhoputnaia armiia Germanii 1933–1945* [*German Ground Forces 1933–1945*] (Moscow: Izografius, 2002), p. 719.

13. TsAMO, f. 38, op. 11373, d. 67, ll. 97–116; as cited by *GABTU, 1940–1942*, pp. 49, 52, 54, 55.

14. TsAMO, f. 38, op. 11355, d. 231, ll. 3–10; as cited by *GABTU, 1940–1942*, p. 96.

15. *Tank T-34: Rukovodstvo sluzhby* [*T-34 tank: Service manual*, hereafter cited as *T-34 tank: Service manual*] (Moscow: Voenizdat, 1941), pp. 79, 270–2.

16. Svirin, *Tank power of the USSR*, p. 342.

17. TsAMO, f. 38, op. 11355, d. 958, ll. 58–61; as cited by *GABTU, 1940–1942*, p. 278.

18. Ust'iantsev and Kolmakov, *T-34 tank*, p. 163.

19. Svirin, *Tank power of the USSR*, p. 566.
20. For more detail, see B. Kavalerchik, 'Once Again About the T-34', *Journal of Slavic Military Studies*, 28 (1), 2015, pp. 186–214.
21. TsAMO, f. 38, op. 11355, d. 235, l. 23; as cited by Ulanov, A. and Shein, D., *Pervye T-34 [First T-34s*, hereafter cited as Ulanov and Shein, *First T-34s]* (Moscow: Taktikal Press, 2013), p. 190; TsAMO, f.38, op. 11355, d. 785, l. 2.
22. Biryukov, *Tanks – to the front!*, p. 150.
23. Svirin, *Tank power of the USSR*, p. 565.
24. TsAMO, f. 38, op. 11355, d. 785, ll. 16, 18.
25. TsAMO, f. 229, op. 3780ss, d. 6, ll. 150–7; as cited by *SBD, Issue 33* [hereafter cited as *SBD, Issue 33]* (Moscow: Voenizdat, 1957), p. 186.
26. TsAMO, f. 38, op. 11355, d. 817, l. 37.
27. Zolotov, N.P. and Isaev, S.I., 'Boegotovy byli. Istoriko-statisticheskoe issledovanie kolichestvenno-kachestvennogo sostoianiia tankovogo parka Krasnoi Armii nakanune Velikoi Otechestvennoi voiny' ['They were combat-ready: Historical-statistical research into the quantitative and qualitative condition of the Red Army's tank park on the eve of the Great Patriotic War'] *Voenno-istorichesky zhurnal*, No. 11 (1993) p. 76.
28. RGVA, f. 4, op. 15a, d. 352, l. 75; as cited by *Military Council under the USSR People's Commissar of Defence. December 1934*, p. 493.
29. RGVA, f. 34891, op. 1, d. 3, ll. 143–54; as cited by *Main Military Council of the RKKA*, p. 390.
30. RGVA, f. 4, op. 3, d. 3314, ll. 283–6; as cited by *GABTU, 1929–1941*, pp. 672–4.
31. Kolomiets and Makarov, *Prelude to 'Barbarossa'*, p. 66.
32. Ulanov and Shein, *First T-34s*, p. 88.
33. TsAMO, f. 229, op. 213, d. 12, ll. 73–8; as cited by *Voenno-istorichesky zhurnal*, No. 9 (1989), p. 18.
34. Halder, F., *Voennyi dnevnik 1941–1942 [War diary 1941–1942]* (Moscow: AST, 2003), p. 131.
35. TsAMO, f. 229, op. 161, d. 89, l. 86.
36. RGVA, f. 4, op. 3, d. 3314, l. 508; as cited by *GABTU, 1929–1941*, pp. 678–9.
37. Svirin, *Tank power of the USSR*, p. 333.
38. *T-34 tank: Service manual*, p. 258.
39. TsAMO, f. 38, op. 11355, d. 138, l. 115; as cited by Ulanov and Shein, *First T-34s*, p. 194.
40. RGVA, f. 31811, op. 3, d. 2165, ll. 1–85; as cited by *Dokumental'no-istorichesky sbornik No. 4 [Documentary-historical collection No. 4*, hereafter cited as *Documentary-historical collection No. 4]* (Moscow: Muzeino-memorial'nyi kompleks 'Istoriia Tanka T-34', 2015), p. 88.
41. Isaev, A.V., *Dubno 1941: Velichaishee tankovoe srazhenie Vtoroi mirovoi [Dubno 1941: The greatest tank battle of the Second World War]* (Moscow: Iauza/EKSMO, 2009), p. 171.
42. TsAMO, f. 229, op. 161, d. 89, l. 78.
43. *Handbook on German Military Forces* (Baton Rouge: Louisiana State University Press, 1990), p. 426.
44. *Preliminary Report No. 20: Russian T-34* [hereafter cited as *Preliminary Report No. 20]* (Chobham Lane, Chertsey: Military College of Science, School of Tank Technology), February 1944, pp. 11, 12.
45. TsAMO, f. 38, op. 11355, d. 832, ll. 78–9.
46. Svirin, *Tank power of the USSR*, pp. 288–290, 374; *Osnovaniia ustroistva i konstruktsiia orudy i boepripasov nazemnoi artillerii [Basics of the design and operation of guns and ammunition of ground artillery]* (Moscow: Voenizdat, 1976), p. 103.
47. TsAMO, f. 38, Op. 11355, d. 832, ll. 77–8.

48. Balysh, A.N., *Voenno-promyshlennyi kompleks SSSR v 30-40-e gg. XX veka: promyshlennost'
    boepripasov* [*Military-industrial complex of the USSR in the 1930s and 1940s of the XX
    century: munitions industry*, hereafter cited as Balysh, *Munitions industry*] (Moscow: MAI-
    PRINT, 2009), pp. 176, 177, 178.
49. TsAMO, f. 38, op. 11355, d. 776, ll. 5, 6.
50. *1941. Documents and materials*, p. 139.
51. Svirin, *Tank power of the USSR*, p. 428.
52. TsAMO, f. 38, op. 11377, d. 12, ll. 23, 29.
53. TsAMO, f. 38, op. 11369, d. 709, ll. 3–4; as cited by *Glavnoe avtobronetankovoe upravlenie:
    Liudi, sobytiia, fakty v dokumentakh, 1944–1945* [*Main Automotive-Armoured-Tank Directorate:
    Men, events, facts in documents, 1944–1945, hereafter cited as GABTU, 1944–1945*] *(Moscow:
    GABTU, 2007), p. 323.*
54. TsAMO, f. 38, op. 11369, d. 698, ll. 36–41; as cited by *GABTU, 1944–1945*, p. 620.
55. TsAMO, f. 81, op. 12104, d. 789, ll. 89–91; as cited by *1941 god: Strana v ogne, Kniga 2,
    dokumenty i materialy* [*Year 1941: Country on fire, Book 2, documents and materials*] (Moscow:
    OLMA Media Grupp, 2011), p. 23.
56. *Izvestiia TsK KPSS*, No. 5 (1990) (Moscow: Pravda), p. 204.
57. *Artilleriiskoe snabzhenie v Velikoi Otechestvennoi voine 1941–1945 gg., T. 1* [*Artillery supply
    in the Great Patriotic War 1941–1945*, Vol. 1, hereafter cited as *Artillery Supply*] (Moscow-
    Tula: GRAU, 1977), p. 261.
58. Balysh, *Munitions industry*, p. 179.
59. TsAMO, f. 38, op. 11353, d. 5, ll. 51–4; as cited by *Voenno-istorichesky zhurnal*, No. 11
    (1988), p. 33.
60. Balysh, *Munitions industry*, pp. 179–81; *Artillery Supply*, p. 420.
61. TsAMO, f. 208, op. 10169ss, d. 4, ll. 186–9; as cited by *SBD, Issue 35* (Moscow: Voenizdat,
    1958), p. 123.
62. TsAMO, f. 251, op. 646, d. 808, ll. 94–9; as cited by *SBD, Issue 39* (Moscow: Voenizdat,
    1959), p. 104.
63. Svirin, *Tank power of the USSR*, p. 374.
64. Kolomiets and Makarov, *Prelude to 'Barbarossa'*, p. 51.
65. TsAMO, f. 38, op. 11355a, d. 360t, ll. 1–6, 23–9; as cited by *GABTU, 1943–1944*, p. 425.
66. TsAMO, f. 38, op. 11351, d. 169, ll. 51–3; as cited by *GABTU, 1943–1944*, p. 246.
67. Svirin, *Tank power of the USSR*, p. 351.
68. TsAMO, f. 38, op. 11355, d. 785, l. 3.
69. TsAMO, f. 38, op. 11355, d. 279, ll. 7–8; as cited by Ulanov and Shein, *First T-34s*, p. 187.
70. Ust'iantsev and Kolmakov, *T-34 tank*, pp. 66–7.
71. Kolomiets, M., *KV-1 TankoMaster*, No. 4–6 (1998), p. 11.
72. TsAMO, f. 38, op. 11355, d. 776, l. 17.
73. Kolomiets, *T-34*, p. 470.
74. Hahn, F., *Waffen und Geheimwaffen des Deutschen Heeres 1933–1945. Band 2* [*Weapons and
    Secret Weapons of the German Ground Forces, 1933–1945. Vol. 2*] (Eggolsheim: Dörfler
    Verlag, 2003), p. 212.
75. Kolomiets, *T-34*, p. 470.
76. Ust'iantsev and Kolmakov, *T-34 tank*, p. 67.
77. Kliment and Francev, *Czechoslovak Armoured Fighting Vehicles*, pp. 60, 81.
78. TsAMO, f. 38, op. 11355, d. 832, l. 77.
79. Svirin, *Tank power of the USSR*, p. 282.
80. Ust'iantsev and Kolmakov, *T-34 tank*, p. 49.

81. TsAMO, f. 38, op. 11355, d. 634, ll. 174–5; as cited by *GABTU, 1940–1942*, p. 247.

82. TsAMO, f. 38, op. 11355, d. 958, ll. 58–61; as cited by *GABTU, 1940–1942*, p. 278.

83. Jentz, *Panzer Tracts No. 4*, p. 1.

84. RGVA, f. 31811, op. 3, d. 2165, ll. 1–85; as cited by *Documentary-historical collection No. 4*, p. 79.

85. Chobitok, V., 'Khodovaia chast' tankov: Podveska' ['Running gear of tanks: Suspension'] *Tekhnika i Vooruzheniie*, No. 8 (2005), p. 48; Ibid., No. 11 (2005), p. 33.

86. Kolomiets, *Heavy tank KV-2*, p. 10.

87. TsAMO, f. 38, op. 11360, d. 7, ll. 307–313; as cited by *GABTU, 1940–1942*, p. 167.

88. TsAMO, f. 38, op. 11355, d. 817, ll. 6, 7, 28, 33, 34.

89. RGVA, f. 31811, op. 3, d. 2165, ll. 1–85; as cited by *Documentary-historical collection No. 4*, p. 85.

90. Svirin, M., "Lapti" dlia T-34' ['Bast shoes for the T-34'], *Poligon*, No. 2 (2000), pp. 36–9.

91. TsAMO, f. 38, op. 11355, d. 634, ll. 174–5; as cited by *GABTU, 1940–1942*, p. 248.

92. Svirin, *Tank power of the USSR*, p. 156.

93. Foss and McKenzie, *Vickers Tanks*, p. 78.

94. Kliment and Francev, *Czechoslovak Armoured Fighting Vehicles*, p. 65.

95. Kolomiets, *T-35*, p. 18.

96. RGVA, f. 4, op. 19, d. 55, ll. 1–9; as cited by *Main Military Council of the RKKA*, p. 340.

97. Ulanov, A.A. and Shein, D.V., *Poriadok v tankovykh voiskakh [Order in the tank forces*, hereafter cited as Ulanov and Shein, *Order in the tank forces*] (Moscow: Veche, 2011), pp. 124, 125.

98. TsAMO, f. 38, op. 11355a, d. 361d, l. 204; as cited by *GABTU, 1944–1945*, p. 234.

99. Jentz, *Panzertruppen*, p. 272.

100. *Material'naia chast' tanka MS-1: Nastavlenie bronesil RKKA [Service manual of the MS-1 tank: Handbook of the RKKA's armoured forces]* (Moscow, UMM RKKA, 1931), pp. 3–6.

101. Svirin and Beskurnikov, *First Soviet tanks*, pp. 13, 41.

102. Soliankin et. al., *Domestic armoured vehicles*, p. 39.

103. RGVA, f. 31811, op. 3, d. 2165, ll. 1–85; as cited by *Documentary-historical collection No. 4*, p. 85.

104. *T-34 tank: Service manual*, p. 14.

105. Ulanov and Shein, *Order in the tank forces*, pp. 83–4.

106. Ibid., p. 200.

107. Drabkin, A., *Ia dralsia na T-34 [I fought in a T-34,* hereafter cited as Drabkin, *I fought in a T-34]* (Moscow: Iauza/EKSMO, 2009), pp. 77, 90.

108. Svirin, *Tank power of the USSR*, pp. 274, 276.

109. Drabkin, *I fought in a T-34*, p. 90.

110. *Preliminary Report No. 20*, p. 17.

111. RGVA, f. 31811, op. 2, d. 1181, l. 87–98; as cited by *Documentary-historical collection No. 4*, pp. 70–2.

112. Kolomiets, *T-34*, p. 334.

113. TsAMO, f. 38, op. 11355, d. 1377, l. 193; as cited by *GABTU, 1943–1944*, p. 272.

114. Carell, P., *Vostochnyi front, Kniga 1: Gitler idet na Vostok [Eastern Front, Book 1: Hitler moves East]* (Moscow: EKSMO, 2008), pp. 39–40.

115. TsAMO, f. 38, op. 11355, d. 895, ll. 347–8.

116. TsAMO, f. 38, op. 11353, d. 425, ll. 23–5; as cited by *GABTU, 1943–1944*, p. 83.

117. Zheltov et al., *Unknown T-34*, p. 28.

118. RGVA, f. 31811, op. 3, d. 2165, ll. 1–85; as cited by *Documentary-historical collection No. 4*, pp. 90–1.
119. Kolomiets, *T-34*, pp. 40, 51, 56.
120. TsAMO, f. 38, op. 11369, d. 483, ll. 82–4; as cited by *GABTU, 1943–1944*, p. 758.
121. Spielberger, *Panzer III & Its Variants* (Atglen, PA: Schiffer Publishing Ltd, 1993), p. 132.
122. Ermolov, *Tank industry*, p. 267.
123. Ulanov and Shein, *Order in the tank forces*, p. 135; Makarov, A., 'Khroniki pervykh 'tridtsat'chetverok' ['Chronicles of the first T-34s'] *Tekhnika i vooruzheniie*, No. 1 (2011), p. 10.
124. Kolomiets, *T-34*, p. 242.
125. TsAMO, f. 38, op. 11355, d. 41, l. 15; Kolomiets, *T-34*, pp. 118, 484.
126. Svirin, M., *Artilleriiskoe vooruzhenie sovetskikh tankov, 1940–1945* [*Artillery armament of Soviet tanks, 1940–1945*] (Moscow: Eksprint, 1999), p. 23.
127. Kolomiets, 'Klim Voroshilov', pp. 20, 23.
128. TsAMO, f. 38, op. 11389, d. 18, ll. 15–25; Ibid., op. 11355, d. 2282, ll. 2–3; as cited by *GABTU, 1943–1944*, pp. 596, 702.
129. Ulanov and Shein, *Order in the tank forces*, p. 135.
130. Spielberger, Doyle and Jentz, *Panzer IV & Its Variants, Book 2*, pp. 91, 186.
131. RGVA, f. 31811, op. 2, d. 1181, ll. 32–5; as cited by *GABTU, 1929–1941*, p. 635.
132. Kolomiets, *T-34*, p. 436.
133. TsAMO, f. 38, op. 11355, d. 958, ll. 58–61; as cited by *GABTU, 1940–1942*, p. 278.
134. *T-34 tank: Service manual*, p. 8.
135. Makarov, A., Lagutin, A., and Sergeev, A., *Opytnye obraztsy tanka T-34* [*Prototypes of the T-34 tank*] (Moscow: MEGALION, 2010), pp. 56, 82, 113, 145, 146.
136. Ulanov and Shein, *First T-34s*, p. 24.
137. Drabkin, *I fought in a T-34*, pp. 24, 155.
138. Arkhipov, V.S., *Vremia tankovykh atak* [*Time of tank attacks*] (Moscow: Iauza/EKSMO, 2009), p. 196.
139. *Boevoi ustav bronetankovykh i mekhanizirovannykh voisk Krasnoi Armii: Chast' 1 (tank, tankovyi vzvod, tankovaia rota)* [*Field Manual of the armoured and mechanized forces of the Red Army: Part 1 (tank, tank platoon, tank company)*] (Moscow: Voenizdat, 1944), p. 190.
140. *Tank BT-5, Service manual*, p. 13; *Tank BT-5, Service manual*, p. 5; *Tank BT-7: Rukovodstvo sluzhby* [*Tank BT-7: Service manual*] (Moscow: Voenizdat, 1941), p. 7; *Al'bom fotografii i kharakteristika tanka BT-7* [*Album of photographs and performance of the BT-7 tank*] (Kharkov: 'Komintern' Factory No. 183, 1940), p. 3; *Nastavlenie avtobronetankovykh sil RKKA, Kniga pervaia, Chast' 1: Material'naia chast', vozhdenie, ukhod i regulirovanie tanka T-28* [*Service manual of the RKKA's automotive-armoured forces, Book one, Part 1: Equipment, driving, care and tuning of the T-28 tank*] (Moscow: Voenizdat, 1935), p. 12; *T-34 tank: Service manual*, p. 6; *Tank KV: Rukovodstvo sluzhby* [*KV tank: Service manual*, hereafter cited as *KV tank: Service manual*] (Moscow: Voenizdat, 1941), p. 5; *Tank T-26: Rukovodstvo sluzhby* [*T-26 tank: Service manual*] (Moscow: Voenizdat, 1940), p. 57.

Chapter 10

1. Jentz and Doyle, *Panzer Tracts No. 3–2*, p. 6.
2. Spielberger, Jentz and Doyle, *Panzer IV & Its Variants. Book 2*, p. 62.
3. Zheltov and Makarov, *A-34*, p. 89.
4. *KV tank: Service manual*, pp. 7, 13.

5. *Otchet spetslaboratorii NKV No. 101–1 'Izuchenie osobennostei porazheniia toplivnykh bakov tanka T-34 broneboino-fugasnymi i kumuliativnymi (broneprozhigaiushchimi) boepripasami germanskoi fashistskoi armii ot 11.09.1944 [Report of the NKV No. 101–1 special laboratory 'Study of the details of a hit against the T-34's fuel tanks by armour-piercing high explosive and high explosive hollow-charge ammunition of the German fascist army from 11 September 1944]*, a document from the collection of M.N. Svirin.

6. Balagansky, I.A. and Merzhievsky, L.A., *Deistvie sredstv porazheniia i boepripasov: Uchebnik [Effect of munitions and ammunition: Textbook]* (Novosibirsk: Izdatel'stvo NGTU, 2004), p. 204.

7. *Otchet spetslaboratorii 123 'Izuchenie pozharoopasnosti tankov ot 14.09.1942' [Report of Special Laboratory 123 'Study of the fire hazards of tanks' from 14 September 1942]*. Document from the collection of M.N. Svirin.

8. *T-34 tank: Service manual*, p. 17.

9. Zheltov and Makarov, *A-34*, p. 183.

10. *Dokumental'no-istorichesky sbornik No. 1. Muzeino-memorial'nyi complex 'Istoriia tanka T-34' [Documentary-history digest, No. 1. Memorial museum complex 'History of the T-34 tank']*, p. 39; *KV tank: Service manual*, p. 188.

Chapter 11

1. Kolomiets, M., 1941: *Boi v Pribaltike 22 iunia–10 iulia 1941 goda [1941: Fighting in the Baltics 22 June–10 July 1941*, hereafter cited as Kolomiets, *Fighting in the Baltics]*, p. 9.

2. Abaturov, B.B., and Morozov, M.E., *Neizvestnye tragedii Velikoi Otechestvennoi Voiny. Srazheniia bez pobed [The unknown tragedies of the great Patriotic war. Battles without victories*, hereafter cited as Abaturov and Morozov, *Battles without victories]* (Moscow: Iauza/EKSMO, 2008), p. 49.

3. TsAMO, f. 344, op. 5554, d. 34, l. 1, 3; Ibid., d. 54, ll. 31–2; Ibid., f. 395, op. 9136, d. 500, l. 282.

4. TsAMO, f. 221, op. 1351, d. 64, l. 14.

5. *The Initial Period of the War on the Eastern Front: 22 June–August 1941* [hereafter cited as *The Initial Period of the War on the Eastern Front]* (London, UK: Frank Cass & Co., 1993), p. 113.

6. TsAMO, f. 132a, Op. 2642, d. 41, ll. 1–2; as cited by *1941: Book 2*, p. 431.

7. TsAMO, f. 221, op. 1351, d. 23, ll. 5–6.

8. Osadchy, D.I., 'S marsha v boi' ['From the march into battle', hereafter cited as Osadchy, *From the march into battle] Voenni-istorichsky zhurnal*, No. 6 (1988), pp. 52–3.

9. TsAMO, f. 221, op. 1351, d. 57, l. 38.

10. *The Initial Period of War on the Eastern Front*, pp. 113–14.

11. TsAMO, f. 221, op. 1351, d. 200, l. 8.

12. Zhardinskas, A., 'Legenda ob odinokom tanke' ['The legend of the lone tank'], in *1941: Zabytye pobedy Krasnoi Armii [Forgotten Victories of the Red Army*, hereafter cited as Zhardinskas, *The legend of the lone tank]* (Moscow: Iauza/EKSMO, 2009), p. 41; *Initial Period of War on the Eastern Front*, pp. 114, 116, 142, 148.

13. Osadchy, *From the march into battle*, p. 56.

14. TsAMO, f. 344, op. 5564, d. 1, l. 77; as cited in *Voenno-istorichesky zhurnal*, No. 7 (1989), p. 25.

15. *Initial Period of War on the Eastern Front*, p. 114.

16. TsAMO, f. 221, op. 2467ss, d. 39, ll. 346–8; as cited by *SBD, Issue 34* [hereafter cited as *SBD, Issue 34]* (Moscow: Voenizdat, 1958), p. 67.

17. TsAMO, f. 221, op. 2467ss, d. 39, ll. 325–7; as cited by *SBD, Issue 34*, p. 67.

18. TsAMO, f. 221, op. 2467ss, d. 39, ll. 352–3; as cited by *SBD, Issue 34*, p. 69.

19. *Velikaia Otechestvennaia. Komkory: Voennyi biografichesky slovar', T. 2 [Great Patriotic War. Corps commanders: Military biographical dictionary, Vol. 2]* (Moscow: Kuchkovo pole, 2006), pp. 261–2.

20. TsAMO, f. 221, op. 2467ss, d. 40, ll. 205–206; as cited by *SBD, Issue 34*, p. 107.

21. Abaturov and Morozov, *Battles without victories*, p. 81.

22. Osadchy, *From the march into battle*, p. 57.

23. TsAMO, f. 38–9, op. 80058ss, d. 1, ll. 44–7; as cited by *SBD, Issue 33*, p. 14.

24. *Velikaia Otechestvennaia. Komandarmy: voennyi biografichesky slovar' [Great Patriotic War. Army commanders: Military biographical dictionary]* (Moscow: Kuchkovo pole, 2005), p. 124.

25. Kolomiets, *Fighting in the Baltics*, pp. 42, 50.

26. Osadchy, *From the march into battle*, p. 52.

27. Kolomiets, *Heavy tank KV-2*, pp. 69–70.

28. Zhardinskas, *The legend of the lone tank*, pp. 32–48; *Small Unit Actions During the German Campaign in Russia* (Washington, D.C.: Department of the Army, 1953), pp. 76–84; *Panzers on the Eastern Front* (London, UK: Greenhill Books, 2002), pp. 38–45.

Chapter 12

1. *Dokumental'no-istorichesky sbornik*, No. 2, pp. 56–7.

2. Moshchansky, I., *1941. Taktika tankovoi voiny [1941. Tactics of tank warfare]* (Moscow: PKV, 2001), p. 31.

3. TsAMO, f. 221, op. 10633ss, d. 6, ll. 55–8; as cited by *SBD, Issue 21*, p. 7.

4. RGVA, f. 4, op. 12, d. 106, ll. 112–122; as cited by *Russky arkhiv*, Vol. 13 (2–2), pp. 334–5.

5. TsAMO, f. 38–9, op. 30425ss, d. 45, ll. 24–6; as cited by *SBD, Issue 33*, p. 78.

6. Mellenthin, F. von, *Bronirovannyi kulak vermakhta [Armoured fist of the Wehrmacht]* (Smolensk: Rusich, 1999), p. 439; this is the Russian translation of Mellenthin's memoirs, which have been translated into English under the title *Panzer Battles: A Study of the Employment of Armour in the Second World War*, first published by the University of Oklahoma Press in 1956. The cited passage can be found on page 302 of the later Konecky&Konecky English language translation.

Appendices

1. RGVA, f. 31811, op. 3, d. 2116; as cited by Ulanov and Shein, *Order in the tank forces*, pp. 85–95; Ulanor and Shein, *First T-34s*, pp. 19–25.

Index